Innovation Project Management Handbook

Innovation Project Management Handbook

Dr. Gregory C. McLaughlin
Dr. William R. Kennedy

CRC Press
Taylor & Francis Group
Boca Raton London New York

CRC Press is an imprint of the
Taylor & Francis Group, an **informa** business

A PRODUCTIVITY PRESS BOOK

CRC Press
Taylor & Francis Group
6000 Broken Sound Parkway NW, Suite 300
Boca Raton, FL 33487-2742

© 2016 by Taylor & Francis Group, LLC
CRC Press is an imprint of Taylor & Francis Group, an Informa business

No claim to original U.S. Government works

Printed on acid-free paper
Version Date: 20160104
Printed at CPI on sustainably sourced paper

International Standard Book Number-13: 978-1-4987-2571-2 (Paperback)

Visit the Taylor & Francis Web site at
http://www.taylorandfrancis.com

and the CRC Press Web site at
http://www.crcpress.com

Contents

List of Figures

List of Tables

Preface

This book represents a maturing of our knowledge, experience, and practice in innovation, and focuses on innovation opportunity project success. There are numerous texts on innovation management—what it is and why it is important. That said, there are few on how to implement innovation at the macrolevel, and more specifically, at the microlevel within an organization. This handbook is a compendium of our own and previously developed and widely known innovation process support tools. The new tools and processes we have developed in this book are a result of the decades of work in the field of innovation. In tandem with established tools created by other pioneers, we have also tested them successfully in actual field conditions. Each tool and process is described in detail in an "easy to follow" format and complemented with actual application scenarios and exercises. We feel this format best serves innovation leaders, teams, and professionals in implementing or commercializing an innovation opportunity within their organization.

In a world of constant change, we continue to build upon the knowledge shared in our prior books. The seminal difference from this book and our previous writings is that we have included many new innovation tools, such as the innovation opportunity profile (Chapter 3), and revisions to a few of the first-, second-, and third-generation tools. We also provide a more detailed process for innovation project success. We introduced the term "innovation opportunity," which broadly acknowledges the reality that innovation success is truly a favorable combination of key performance parameters associated with an unfulfilled need, time, actionable information (data), and the human element. By design, this is truly an *Innovation Project Manager and Practitioner Handbook*, a "how to" guide on identifying, selecting, and managing a successful innovation opportunity project resulting in sustained success.

We acknowledge there is a wide spectrum of innovation tools, approaches, and methodologies already in use today, both in the private and public sectors. Some of the tools from legacy methodologies such as Six Sigma, Lean, Agile, continuous process improvement, project, and change management methodologies, incorporate and share some of the same or very similar processes and tools. We also acknowledge this handbook is not intended as a stand-alone resource or tool bag for the N²OVATE™ methodology and sustained innovation success. Subsequently, we suggest the reader to first examine *A Guide to Innovation Processes and Solutions for Government* as a prequel to this book. The government book was designed to introduce a new alternative methodology (N²OVATE™) to what many perceive is a very bureaucratic, complex, and industrial age requirements definition and acquisition process that literally hamstrings the timely pursuit of any type of innovation in the government. Although the book introduced a tailorable, flexible, and timely approach for government agencies and private sector entities working with the government, it is certainly applicable to any type of organization seeking a roadmap to sustained innovation opportunity success.

As a precursor to embarking on any innovation opportunity project, it is critical to first develop an enterprise innovation strategy that will set the tone across the organization and ensure a receptive culture and environment conducive to innovation. Organizations that repeatedly succeed in identifying and capitalizing on innovation opportunities embrace innovation as a core value or part of the culture and organizational DNA. These organizations support innovation not only in spirit, but they repeatedly pass the litmus test by investing the necessary resources (financial and human) with tenacity, commitment, and determination.

Fundamentally, we believe innovations come from human needs that remain unsatisfied. Over time, these unfulfilled needs are either met by the organization or competitor, remain undiscovered, or eventually usurped by another more compelling need. Individuals performing the work or those receiving the product or service can best identify, define, and articulate these needs. Appropriately, we use the information generated by individuals to define the innovation opportunity projects and develop the potential outcomes. Numerous examples provide a platform for describing tools and demonstrating principles and practices associated with the N²OVATE™ process. We identify seven unique processes, based on innovative outcomes. We recognize that each outcome has its own unique circumstances. Subsequently, the reader can tailor the processes and associated tool sets offered in this handbook to the needs of their organization and situation. After selecting one of the seven processes that fit your desired innovation outcome, follow the detailed process maps provided in the applicable chapter to achieve a desired outcome. Worthy of note, the processes and example scenarios in each chapter cover the common types of innovation projects. Our approach is to innovate incrementally rather than to rely on discovery or chance.

Innovation will continue to evolve in organizations and new tools, better facilitation, and more controls will emerge to maintain and strengthen existing innovation processes and methodologies. Economic conditions will change and the slide rule of time will continue to move, opening windows of innovation opportunity and eventually closing others. New tools and processes will surface and legacy approaches will be replaced. The human resource and organizational culture will also evolve, adding to the number of unique innovation opportunities. We encourage you to use, adapt, and improve on the tools and techniques offered in this handbook to achieve a positive innovation outcome and add value to your organization, customers, stakeholders, and shareholders. As we continually employ these tools in our own consulting practice, we remain committed to evolve not only our methodology and tools, but also the innovation body of knowledge. Finally, we hope you find value in our book and encourage those interested in innovation to use these processes and tools with an eye on continuously improving and modifying them for universal application and adoption. We also enjoy feedback, so please share your experiences and outcomes (good or bad). We are always willing to help and invite you to follow our progress at our web site, www.ipsinnovate.com.

Authors

Greg McLaughlin is a managing partner at Innovation Processes and Solutions (IPS), LLC. Greg brings a broad set of technical and practical expertise in quality improvement, innovation, and data analysis. Beginning as an analyst, he progressed quickly to the director of research at a Fortune 200 company. Refining his skills in continuous quality improvement, he worked for Dr. W. Edwards Deming as an instructor/consultant. Greg authored a book for research and development in organizations (*Total Quality in Research and Development*, 1995) committed to quality improvement. He was an early adopter of Six Sigma and worked for many years as a Six Sigma Senior Master Black Belt, saving organizations over $300 million. Many projects resulted in innovative products and services. His most accomplished skill is in interpreting data, finding a practical application. He can look beyond the numbers to find a solution to complex problems. His skill set organically transitioned into developing innovation strategies, deployment, and sustained success as evidenced by the creation of the ENOVALE™ and N²OVATE™ methodologies. He maintains a leadership role in developing training, tools, books, and publications for both practitioners and scholars. His latest publications are *Chance or Choice: Unlocking Innovation Success* (2013); and *Enovale: Unlocking Innovation Project Success* (October 2013); *Leading Latino Talent to Champion Innovation* (2014); *Unlocking Sustained Innovation Success in Healthcare* (2014); *A Guide to Innovation Processes and Solutions in Government* (2015); *Innovation Project Management Handbook* (2015); *Innovation Processes and Solutions for Innovation Project Success: A Workbook* (2015); and *Dubai: The Epicenter of Modern Innovation* (2016).

His educational achievements include a doctorate in business administration (DBA) from Nova Southeastern University, a master of science degree in statistics from the Florida State University, and an undergraduate degree in meteorology from the Florida State University. Greg was the director of doctoral research at Nova Southeastern University and was instrumental in creating an innovative dissertation process for the DBA degree at Capella University. Since its creation, the DBA program is the largest and most profitable doctoral program in Capella University history.

William R. "Buzz" Kennedy is currently an independent consultant and primary managing partner at IPS Consulting. He is an internationally renowned award-winning organizational leader and author with over 30 years' experience in the public and private sector. Buzz has an extensive background in leadership and management with a proven track record of success leading world-class business strategy development, organizational culture, and change management efforts across multiple industries. He is considered a subject matter expert in executive and organizational leadership, government and aerospace program and project management, information technology and aircraft platform management, acquisition, and international procurement. He has led several pioneering strategy and innovation development initiatives in the aircraft, manufacturing and production, and maintenance management disciplines (using Six Sigma, Agile, Lean manufacturing, and Lean supply chain management methodologies) and has designed, developed, and published a series of research studies, reliability-centered maintenance, professional sales, and business development training courses and programs. His latest publications are *A Guide to Innovation Processes and Solutions for Government* (2015), *Innovation Project Management Handbook* (2015), and *Dubai: The Epicenter of Modern Innovation* (2016).

A highly decorated United States Air Force combat veteran with a global perspective, he has lived abroad for over 20 years garnering firsthand international business experience across Asia, the Middle East, and Europe. This diverse experience coupled with his natural ability in developing tailored innovative solutions to difficult situations. In tandem with his exceptional communications and human relations skills, his lengthy history of establishing high-performance, result-oriented teams have led multiple organizations to achieve world-class performance. His educational achievements include a doctorate in business administration (DBA) from Capella University, a masters degree in secondary education from Grand Canyon University, and a bachelors degree in business management from the University of Maryland.

Chapter 1

Using the Handbook

Introduction

This book, or more appropriately handbook, is a complete revision of the book, *ENOVALE™: How to Unlock Sustained Innovation Project Success* (McLaughlin and Caraballo, 2013a). This book revises the original process including new tools and a distinctly improved, better-defined process for successful innovation opportunity projects. This does not negate the original material rather "evolving" it to a better and more adaptive state.

Designed as a handbook, this book provides a systematic and validated approach for conducting innovation projects. The intention is not to teach innovation per se, but to provide a detailed approach and process for creating innovative products, service, or technologies. In any case, effectively capitalizing on the innovation opportunity requires a disciplined project management approach if that innovation is to reach and deliver value to the consumers. In this handbook, we present seven unique, process-derived approaches (we will explain how we achieved this number) for the innovation team and organizational leadership to consider, each of which has a very different objective.

Unlike other techniques that have a common purpose, for instance: audits (for compliance), quality (to reduce defects), or accounting (for debits/credits); the innovation opportunity processes offered in this discussion are agile but predictive and disciplined in approach. The business or organization can accomplish multiple objectives by innovating, depending on the type of innovation desired. Improvement is one objective, discovery another, and competitive advantage a typical third goal or objective. Given that innovation can accomplish multiple objectives, it is easy to comprehend the outcome of following just one implementation method for every innovation opportunity can greatly diminish the chance of success. If the leadership of an organization needs an agile or flexible approach to innovation then following one method seems unrealistic and wasteful. That is not to say that a single methodology or approach can accomplish great success, as it is certainly possible. However, the caveat to the last statement is we feel there is not a single "catch all" method sufficient to achieve an organization's complete complement of desired innovation objectives.

The handbook begins (Chapter 1) with an innovation primer, for those who need a refresher on innovation. Next, we discuss how we evolved the original model (ENOVALE) to N²OVATE™. Chapter 2 provides an overview on how to select a project for each type of innovation opportunity. Chapters 3 through 9 describe in greater detail an appropriate implementation process depending upon the identified innovation type (described in this chapter).

Innovation Primer

Introduction

For many, innovation remains a misunderstood or poorly understood concept. Innovation as a concept conjures up a litany of personal experiences that frame each individual's understanding of innovation. Many people consider only discoveries and inventions as pure innovations, while others see innovation through a different lens. Of the 60+ accepted definitions of innovation, there appears to be no one definition that captures the essence of what innovation means. Therefore, we encourage every reader of this discussion to try this simple exercise to help them gain better insight on their personal understanding and perspective of what innovation is.

1. What do the differences say about and to the group?
2. Are there similarities—what does this indicate?
3. Is it possible to develop (agree) on a single definition?

> **EXERCISE 1.1**
>
> Gather a group of people within your organization into a room. This may be a diverse or specialized group. Ask them to write down their own definition of innovation. Keep the definitions in the context of the individual (i.e., what does innovation mean to me?). Provide the group 10 minutes to think about the proposition and then another 10 minutes to capture their thoughts in writing. Allow each individual to read their definitions aloud, capturing the key words on a flip chart or white board. This exercise works well electronically as well so it can also be useful with geographically separated innovation teams. As a group, examine the key words with an eye on defining the intended meaning of each term or word—the deeper meaning of the definitions. Use the following questions to synchronize the team's understanding:

Our experience tells us that it will be difficult to agree on a single definition of innovation that captures everyone's input but this is a normal and expected result of this exercise. It is natural to find that some participants will try to convince others that their definition or their understanding (recognition) of innovation is the most appropriate (again, a normal response to this exercise). Herein lies the Holy Grail when it comes to arriving at a common agreement on a definitive understanding and judgment of innovation. How do you convince others (such as customers, employees, stakeholders, etc.) that your product, technology, or service is truly innovative, if everyone recognizes innovation differently?

It is prudent to acknowledge at this juncture that innovation, as a concept, has many different definitions, each with its own meaning. The *Merriam-Webster Dictionary* defines innovation in terms of the words "new" or "novel." The more compelling question is whether an innovation can be something more than something new or novel.

> Baregheh, Rowley, and Sambrook, (2009) reported 60 individual definitions of the word "innovation." Obviously, innovation means many things to different people. Some see innovation as a novel idea, a new and unique product, or new technology. Innovation occurs when humans employ a creative process to meet a particular need; innovation begins at a very human level. You could even call this the "organic" level. Therefore, a correct definition should include how individuals view and judge innovation. Humans address a need and how that need becomes a reality is the process of Innovation (McLaughlin and Caraballo, 2013b, p. 8).

Therefore, the essence of the term "innovation" requires a broader definition; one that transcends (defines) what the innovation opportunity will accomplish. Baregheh et al. (2009) decided to examine the "means of innovation" (p. 1334), to understand how innovation "transforms ideas into new, improved or changed" (p. 1334) outcomes, and how this impacts products, services, or people. The resulting definition would not restrict innovations to only "new" outcomes but includes innovation opportunities that improve or change products, services, and technology. We support the notion that focusing on innovation outcomes facilitates a better definition of how innovation opportunities can transform products, services, processes, and technology. Subsequently, this frame of reference will better serve to clarify how individuals perceive (understand) innovation opportunities. At the fundamental level, we use our knowledge and experience of a product, service, or technology (which we refer to as an "item") and its performance to judge whether it is innovative.

> The three main descriptors are new, improved, and change that describes how the product, technology, or service is transformed. In other words, how the product, service, or technology is "transformed" into something we define as innovative, as it better meets (satisfies) our needs. There is a distinctive and different strategy for each of the three descriptors. When customers or users experience a product, service or

technology that exceeds their expectations, it is innovative (McLaughlin and Caraballo, 2013b, p. 9).

Although ideas can initiate innovation, it must be in tandem with a need. This is why we continually question the process of collecting only ideas from employees for future innovation opportunities. There is a possibility of finding a "gem" of an innovation opportunity (over the long haul the odds are about 10%) but that leaves a 90% chance of finding nothing worthwhile (Dahl et al., 2011). Selecting and pursuing innovation opportunities becomes a numbers game—creating a large number of ideas and then following a disciplined process of identifying the "winner" that we expect will add value to the shareholder, stakeholder, and/or customer. While we welcome ideas, innovation typically begins when a need persists. For those organizations with an innovation opportunity or "idea" entry process, we suggest that the process be modified to capture both the need and the idea. If the need is not compelling or possible, the idea is shelved, cataloged, or forgotten until such time both the idea and need (often referred to as a "requirement") align.

Innovation is both real and imagined. Innovation can begin with an idea that leads to a discovery, invention, or breakthrough product, service, or process. As a concept, innovation involves both tangible and intangible elements. The tangible elements are simple to define as they fall in the categories of new features, improved performance, and a substitute for an existing item. Innovation offers an intangible perspective as well which manifests itself in feelings of satisfaction and general perceptions. Innovation also consists of both experience and knowledge. However, we all experience innovation from a different perspective, so we tend to know innovation when we experience it (McLaughlin and Kennedy, 2015).

This underlies the message that innovation opportunities begin and end with an individual—a topic found in all the books in our series on innovation. Without humans, innovation would exist only at some base level. People create the idea (innovation opportunity), based on a specific unsatisfied need. This philosophy guides us throughout the book. If you, the reader, have read any of our books, you can easily skip this chapter. For those unfamiliar with our philosophy, this chapter should orient you well to our philosophy and unique methodologies.

Defining the "Means" of Innovation

The process of transformation is what a producer, manufacturer, or designer seeks to achieve and the user (customer) then judges as either innovative or not. Given that the innovation opportunity can manifest itself in many forms, the "means" of innovation describes how it differentiates itself from the product, service, or technology it replaces. We used available research (Zhuang, 1995; Zhuang et al., 1999; Baragreh et al., 2009; Caraballo and McLaughlin, 2012) to decide on three transformations ("means") that can occur as new, improved, and changed. Innovation can be "new" (unique) or improved (better than its predecessor) or changed (replaced). Think of these as three distinctive transformations of accomplishing the same goal, innovation. For example, consider that stocks, bonds, or commodities are methods (means) to invest money. All accomplish the same intended goal and are classified by the type or category of investment. Each investment type requires a unique (and often unrelated) strategy, even though the end goal is the same. Innovation opportunities follow the same pattern satisfying new or existing needs by offering something better than its predecessor offered.

There are three means (or ways of) innovating. We often refer to these "means" as themes or (descriptors):

Theme 1: *New* (something new, novel, or unique)—normally we think of an invention or discovery.

Theme 2: *Improvement* (improving the performance)—this relates to products, processes, or services. Performance measures the amount of value added or improvement. For those products, processes, or services that are under-performing or those where increasing performance would yield additional competitive advantage.

Theme 3: *Change* (replacing what currently exists with something different)—this greatly affects people both physically and emotionally. Innovative change is positive change benefitting the individual and the organization (McLaughlin, 2012).

An innovation opportunity reveals itself in the performance delivered. "New" items have innovation characteristics that provide an enhancement or add value to an existing item. Thus, improved innovation increases the performance or value of an existing item; and change replaces the existing item with an item that has additional or better characteristics than its predecessor.

Individuals are the best judge of whether something is innovative or not. Where we differ from most authors, scholars, and/or researchers, is that innovation is more than a new product, service, or technology. It is a means to satisfy a need (or requirement) with something better than what presently exists. Each innovation opportunity type is distinctive, yet interrelated, as all innovation types need the individual to initiate the innovation. What is markedly different is how the individual perceives the innovation opportunity.

Innovation Comprehension Survey

To determine how an individual perceives innovation, have prospective innovation team members complete a simple set of nine questions (Table 1.1). Have each team member check the response in Table 1.1 that best agrees with the statements that best define how each individual team member understands innovation. The definitions relate to how innovation transforms a product, service, or technology. The objective of the survey is to identify which of the three classifications best describes how each individual perceives innovation.

Table 1.1 Innovation Comprehension Survey

Statement Number	Instructions: Check the Box That Best Matches Your Understanding of How Innovation Is Defined by Each Statement	Undefined	Poorly Defined	Marginally Defined	Defined	Well Defined	My Choice
1	A new discovery	1	2	3	4	5	
2	New or novel (unique) products and services	1	2	3	4	5	
3	Making something better	1	2	3	4	5	
4	Replacing what does not seem to work	1	2	3	4	5	
5	Improving products and services over time	1	2	3	4	5	
6	Improving something to make it better	1	2	3	4	5	
7	Changing what does not work	1	2	3	4	5	
8	A new invention or patent	1	2	3	4	5	
9	Improving on something that already exists	1	2	3	4	5	
10	Changing for the better	1	2	3	4	5	
Totals	Scores	New	#DIV/0!	Improved	#DIV/0!	Change	#DIV/0!
Totals	Scores	New	0	Improved	0	Change	0

Interpretation

Enter a number in the "My Choice" column that represents your perception. Use the following formula to construct an average and range value.

New: Average: (Statements 1 + 2 + 8)/3; Range = Max–Min
Improve: Average (Statements 3 + 5 + 6 + 9)/4; Range = Max–Min
Change: Average (Statements 4 + 7 + 10)/3; Range = Max–Min

The largest average value (with a range less than 1.5), indicates the innovation type the individual. Large ranges indicate inconsistency.

The three dimensions (concepts) are:

■ New types of innovation: Statements 1, 2, 8
■ Improved innovation: Statements 3, 5, 6, 9
■ Change innovation: Statements 4, 7, 10

Calculate the average and range for each concept. The larger the average, the more that person will perceive (and purchase) that type of innovation. Large range differences indicate inconsistent or changing perceptions. Although an individual may favor one type, there is ample evidence that some individuals (approximately 20%) understand different types of innovation and can respond favorably to all types.

Scoring

Assign a numerical score to each response—1: strongly disagree; 2: disagree; 3: neither disagree nor agree; 4: agree; or 5: strongly agree. Calculate an average and range of the following descriptions:

New average: (statements 1 + 2 + 8)/3; range = Max–Min
Improve average: (statements 3 + 5 + 6 + 9)/4; range = Max–Min
Change average: (statements 4 + 7 + 10)/3; range = Max–Min

Interpretation

Whichever of the three components of the innovation comprehension score, the highest average is the preferred method of recognizing innovation. In other words, you are looking for a range value that is less than 1.5. A higher range value indicates mixed feelings or opinions. Responses from this small survey are not conclusive but will provide an initial understanding of what the respondent perceives (understands) about innovation. Low average scores suggest little or no interest in innovation. Individuals with like scores (those that share similar sentiments regarding innovation) will work best on an innovation team. Excel Spreadsheet available from Innovation Process and Solutions, LLC by request.

> **EXERCISE 1.2: INNOVATION COMPREHENSION SURVEY**
>
> Conduct a survey with a minimum of 20 people to determine their innovation comprehension score. Calculate the scores and interpret the data. What does the diversity of responses say about people's perception of innovation?

Transformation can take many forms. It could be a very new technology, a vastly improved product, or a significant change to personnel. The process of transforming an outcome is required for an understanding of its requirements (both functional and user), the objective it will accomplish, and what the item will become. It is not enough to "make something better," it often requires the product, technology, process, or service meets more than existing needs. Customers typically respond (by purchasing) when producers satisfy their needs.

The Evolution of ENOVALE

As with aspects of innovation, even the basic process must evolve as learning and experiences increase. This is true with the innovation process called ENOVALE, which was introduced in the book titled, *Chance or Choice: Unlocking Sustained Innovation Success* (McLaughlin and Caraballo, 2013b). ENOVALE is the first letter of a seven-step process.

1. E— Envision the need
2. N—Nominate the best people
3. O—Objectify
4. V—Validate
5. A—Align
6. L— Link to performance
7. E— Execute

These seven steps (Figure 1.1) help identify if an innovation opportunity project is capable of producing sustained innovation success.

The evolution from the ENOVALE flowchart to the N²OVATE™ flowchart (Figure 1.1) represents a strategic and phenomenal leap in innovation knowledge and experience. Clients require detail that is more specific and this handbook provides that level of detail. Previously, there were seven steps for each type of innovation (new, improved, and changed). For innovation opportunity projects classified as "new," there are three distinctive characteristics (outcomes):

1. Products, services, or technology that are unique (truly a new item)
2. Products, services, or technology that are a new application (new uses)
3. Products, services, or technology that take a new approach (new markets, reformulation)

For example, there are three steps for all "new" types of innovations, which include the three distinctive outcomes (new/unique, new application/use, and new approach). Except for some modifications, each of the three outcomes employs the same process. Upon further analysis, each innovation type truly requires its own specific process. It is simpler to keep each new type of innovation opportunity distinctly separate. Three chapters of this book are dedicated to new types of innovation opportunity outcomes.

For improvement, we developed two processes (sharing some common steps). Improvement is either associated with increasing performance (which exceeds

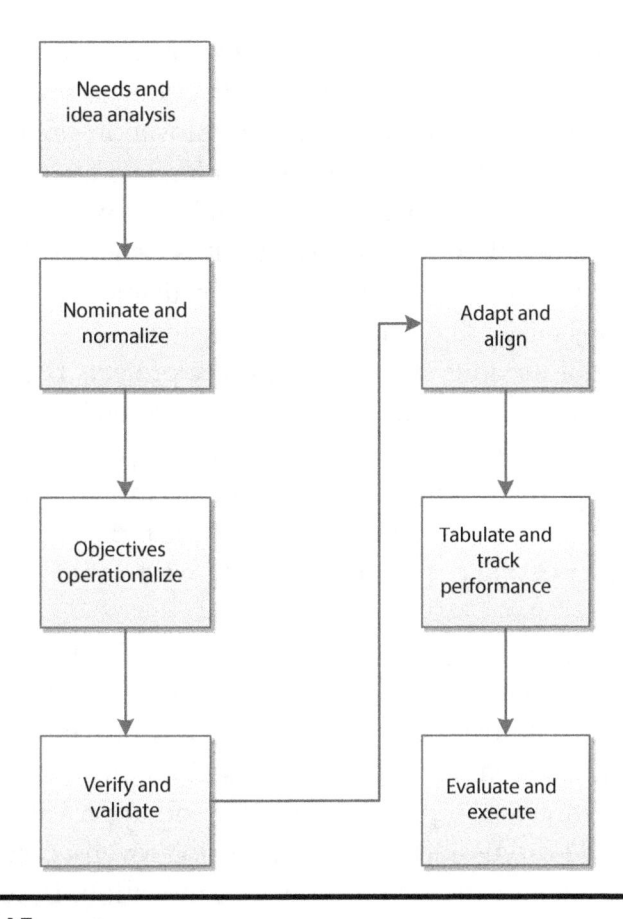

Figure 1.1 ENOVALE process.

performance standards to meet expectations) or bringing performance back in-line to meet its original set of expectations. Finally, the change innovation opportunity type recognizes that replacement is a viable option. Each of the seven processes build on the N²OVATE™ methodology platform. We expect and encourage our clients to develop their own proprietary processes, as not every substep within the N²OVATE™ methodology may apply to their particular industry, business, or organizational culture. We maintain that our methodology will foster a change in mindset that will ultimately lead to the creation of an innovation-supportive culture.

Innovation is not just about meeting or exceeding needs, it is also about meeting or exceeding performance standards and expectations. At times, we will find that people will identify innovation which is purely "performance-driven" as the objective is to meet all critical needs. We also know that individuals identify with improvement when needs are met in a realistic timeframe. It is best to understand that people perceive something as innovative because it exceeds the performance of something with which they have firsthand experience or knowledge about. Again, for the businessperson, it is not important to try to make everyone recognize that what you offer or sell is innovative. What is more important is to understand that the organization should be addressing what a customer or user needs, and how the product, service, or technology that they produce can deliver value and better performance.

In the next chapter, we will review the process of selecting a project using the N²OVATE™ methodology. The tools used reflect our philosophy that innovation emanates from the individual. Selecting an innovation opportunity project involves more than process tools, it requires an adequate assessment of needs, wants, and desires of the customer and user. Combined with the process and tools is the need for evaluation and assessment. It is critical to know your business, core competencies (what you are good at), available resources, and organization's strategic objectives that support your business strategy and plan. Therefore, screening of the innovation opportunity projects before implementation is tantamount. Innovation projects that fail the screening process will not produce benefit or sustained success. The N²OVATE™ processes provide a level of screening excellence that justifies its use. Once an innovation opportunity project has passed the screening criteria, a 30%–50% reduction of implementation time is a distinct possibility that reduces risk, waste, and resource allocation requirements.

Chapter 2 describes the project selection process prior to implementing an innovation opportunity project. Chapter 3 introduces our innovation opportunity profile (IOP) template used to collect relevant information necessary for providing timely and actionable empirically based data to the organization's key decision makers for innovation project selection and approval. In Chapters 4 through 9, we provide discussion and examples for seven complete implementation processes for each of the seven types of innovation, based on a desired outcome.

Summary

Innovation begins and ends with the individual. Needs drive innovation; and a growing population will require additional needs, thereby requiring more innovation. Of course, meeting all needs is impossible. Innovation brings about opportunity to businesses and organizations. Those who meet needs (those of today and in the future) with innovation will have sustained success and competitive advantage. Those who innovate infrequently will achieve some success, but they remain at the mercy of their competition. The path is open to those who innovate and those who do not. Innovators will continue to add value to society and reap the benefits of their labors.

References

Baregheh, A., Rowley, J., and Sambrook, S. 2009. Towards a multidisciplinary definition of innovation. *Management Decision*, 47(8), 1323–1339.

Caraballo, E. and McLaughlin, G. 2012. Perceptions of innovation: A multi-dimensional construct. *Journal of Business & Economics Research*, 10(10), 1–16.

Dahl, A., Lawrence, J., and Pierce, J. 2011. Building an innovation community. *Research—Technology Management*, September–October, 19–27.

McLaughlin, G. and Caraballo, E. 2013a. *ENOVALE: How to Unlock Sustained Innovation Project Success*. Productivity Press, Boca Raton, FL.

McLaughlin, G. and Caraballo, E. 2013b. *Chance or Choice: Unlocking Innovation Process*. Productivity Press, Boca Raton, FL. ISBN: 9781466581869.

McLaughlin, G. and Kennedy, W.R. 2015. *A Guide to Innovation Processes and Solutions for Government*. Productivity Press, Boca Raton, FL. ISBN: 978-1-4987-2157-8.

Zhuang, L. 1995. Bridging the Gap Between Technology and Business Strategy: A Pilot Study on the Innovation Process. *Management Decision*, 33(8), 13–19.

Zhuang, L., Williamson, D., and Carter, M. 1999. Innovate or liquidate—Are all organizations convinced? A two-phased study into the innovation process. *Management Decisions*, 37(1), 57–71. doi: 10.1108/00251749910252030.

Chapter 2

Selecting an Innovation Project

Introduction

There has been little uniformity in how to select an idea or need for a possible innovation project or opportunity. Some organizational leaders and decision makers repeatedly rely and seek the suggestions on innovation opportunities from their research and design (R&D) or engineering departments, while others rely on their marketing department, and others remain wedded or enamored with their own personal knowledge and experience as a method of choosing an innovation project or opportunity. This process incorporates the best of intentions, but it is often hit or miss, very random, and wide open to chance and a negative outcome. Choosing an innovation opportunity project first requires a true understanding of the need, and balancing that need with the company's core competency requirements, validating its strategic objectives, and considering its assumptions and limitations.

The N^2OVATE^{TM} methodology and baseline process provide the template from which to judge innovation project and opportunity success. N^2OVATE^{TM} acronym stands for:

Step 1. N: Needs and new ideas
Step 2. N: Normalize and nominate
Step 3. O: Objectives and operationalize
Step 4. V: Verify and validate
Step 5. A: Adapt and align
Step 6. T: Tabulate and track performance
Step 7. E: Evaluate and execute

In order to help the reader to better understand this methodology, we offer a hypothetical case study as an example using all seven steps in the N^2OVATE^{TM} methodology. The case study will follow an innovation project or opportunity from idea generation to acceptance or rejection. This initial phase develops and validates an innovation opportunity project that can produce true value (profit) and performance improvements. A discussion of the actual implementation phase and the associated steps begins in Chapter 3. However, the first step in any innovation opportunity is ensuring you have a clear and concise understanding of the needs or requirements that are driving the innovation opportunity.

Step 1: Needs and New Ideas

The first step begins with identifying and focusing on the needs that drive the innovation opportunity. Figure 2.1 details the subprocesses associated in identifying and characterizing the need assessment. To help illustrate this selection process, we will use the case study described in the next paragraph.

The case study begins with a need and at least one objective that has quantifiable value. Assume the need is critical but unsatisfied. For this example, the need is for a more effective (efficient) aircraft parts procurement system to replace an existing legacy system initialized in the early 2000s.

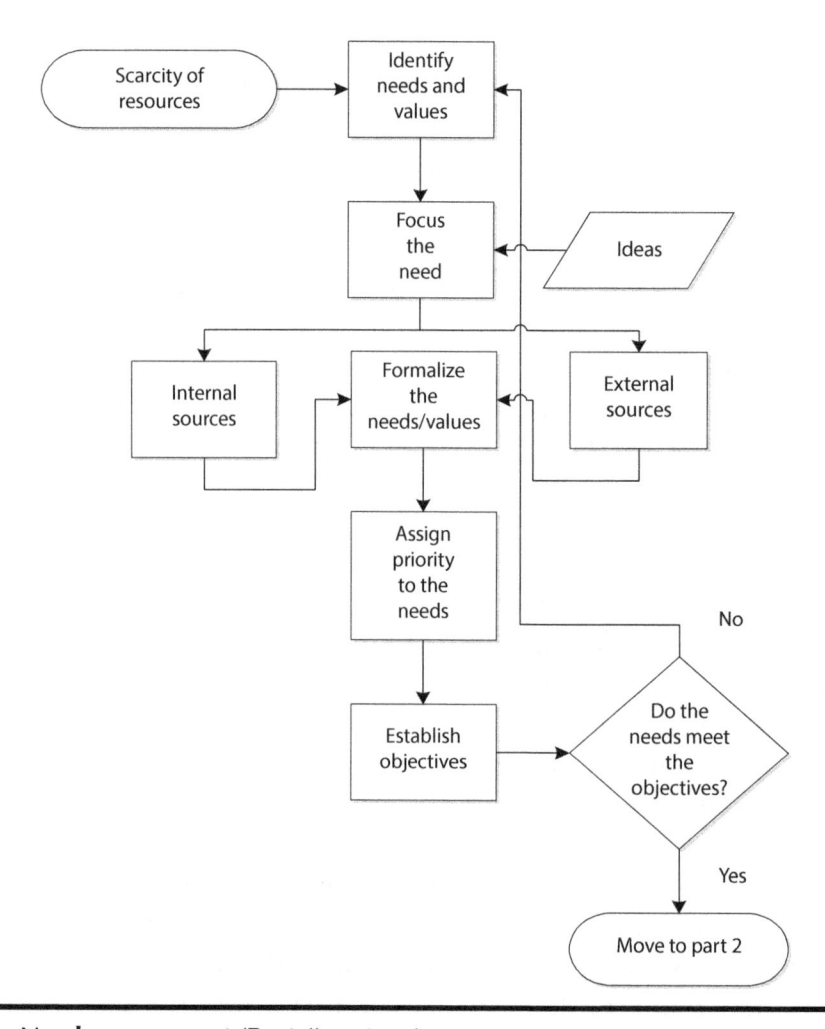

Figure 2.1   Needs assessment (Part 1)—step 1.

The logistics and life cycle management requirements are for the associated hardware and software specifically for the Boeing 737 aircraft platform. The 737, which first hit the drawing boards of Boeing engineers in 1964, did not reach full production and the commercial airline industry (passenger and cargo transportation) service until 1968. For this scenario, we have excluded airborne avionics instrumentation, navigational and meteorological aides, and crew and passenger communication systems. Thus, the parts associated with this case study are not high risk and limited to those material items used for general maintenance and sustainment of Federal Aviation Authority (FAA) airworthiness requirements and standards. Key performance objectives for this scenario are that the platform replacement parts:

1. Arrive on time
2. Meet FAA airworthiness standards
3. Meet form, function, and fit standards
4. Meet planned and programmed sustainability costs

The objectives are the innovation success measures, which meet the requirements of the Needs Assessment—Part 1.

Part 2 (Figure 2.2) provides the process step to evaluate the identified needs. For the case study scenario, data analysis has shown that simple high-wear parts replaced during the recurring safety and quality checks required every 500-flight hours of service reduce the percentage of overall unscheduled maintenance activities. Historical evidence provides that unscheduled maintenance activities reduce platform availability and utilization rates. Parts often take a lead time of 60–90 days to acquire from supply chain sources. Based on the part order lead time, this requires additional inventory be stored at forward supply points, which are often at a sunk cost and added expense for storage and acquisition. Coupled with high-failure-rate parts, the cost of maintaining acceptable availability and utilization rates complicates the sustainability picture. In sum, the need exists for a more agile, responsive, efficient, and effective procurement/inventory management system.

Needs must meet three criteria—viability, capability, and sustainability. *Viability* refers to usability of the item, *capability* refers to the meeting of objectives consistently, and *sustainability* refers to the overall life cycle management of the item (McLaughlin and Kennedy, 2015). For this particular procurement management system case study example, the three criteria (needs) are defined as:

▪ Viability: Changes would improve performance and reliability
▪ Capability: System must be cost effective and function within stated parameters
▪ Sustainability: Procurement system must be valid and timely, and add more value than the previous process (McLaughlin and Kennedy, 2015)

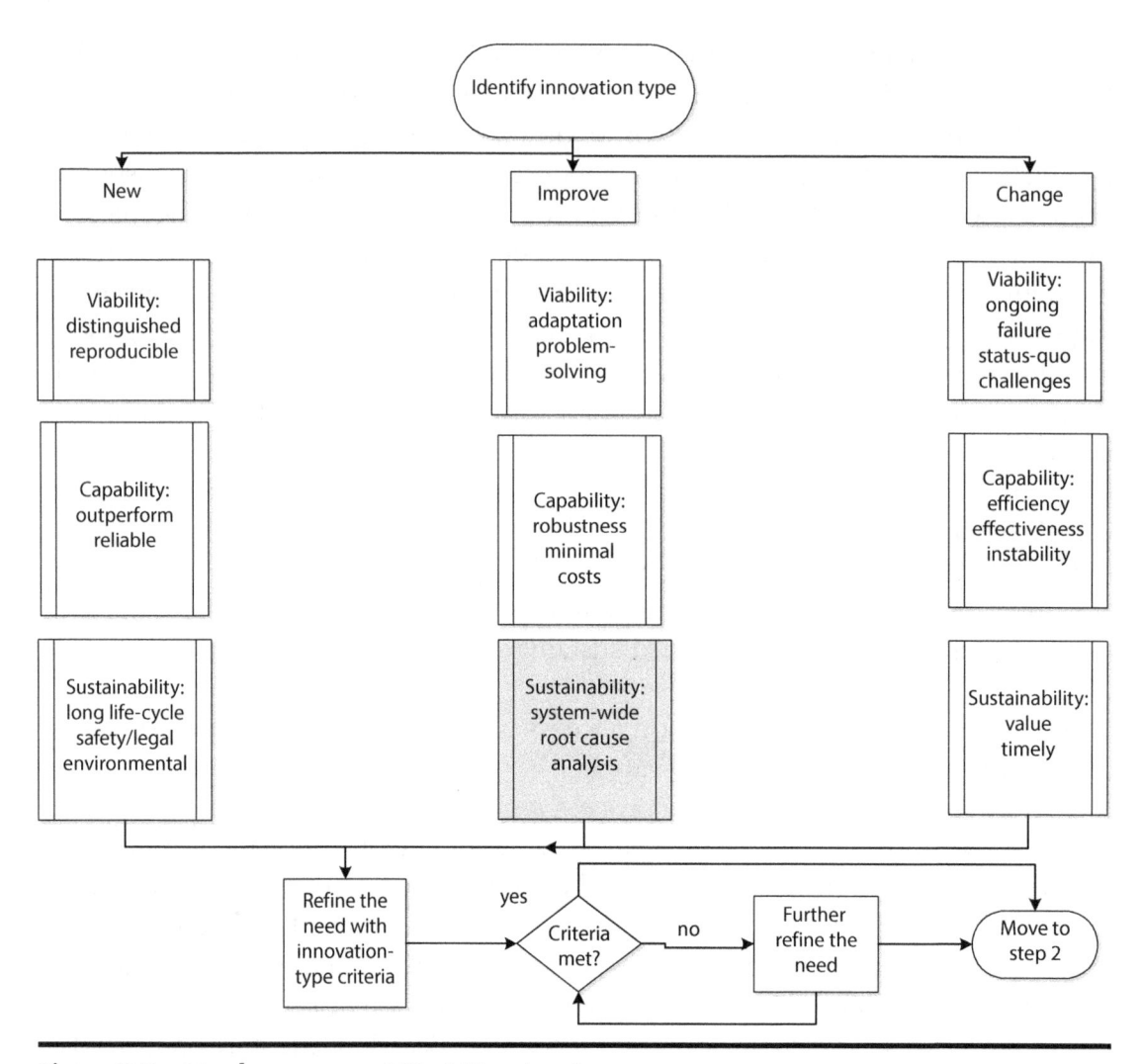

Figure 2.2   Needs assessment (Part 2)—step 1.

The process begins by identifying those characteristics that define viability, capability, and sustainability. Start by rating the characteristics on a numerical scale from 1 to 5 (with 1 being the weakest rating and 5 the strongest). Table 2.1 uses the aircraft procurement example discussed previously.

If the identified criteria are acceptable and meet the overall objective(s), the project can proceed to the next step.

Table 2.1   Needs Analysis and Rating Tool

Measures of Viability	Rating	Measures of Capability	Rating	Measures of Sustainability	Rating
Wear	3	Meets specs	5	Record accuracy	5
Replacement	4	Access time	4	Order time	5
Amount of turns	2	Robustness	5	Delivery time	4
Processing time	4	Flexibility	4	Wait times	5
		Minimize costs	4		

Step 2: Normalize and Nominate

Step 2 involves selecting the right individuals for the project or opportunity by examining their perceptions of the work environment (Figure 2.3).

Work Environment Survey

Presented in Table 2.2 is a work environment survey. For the innovation project or opportunity your innovation team has selected, have each innovation team candidate complete the survey by checking the box that best matches their perception, in

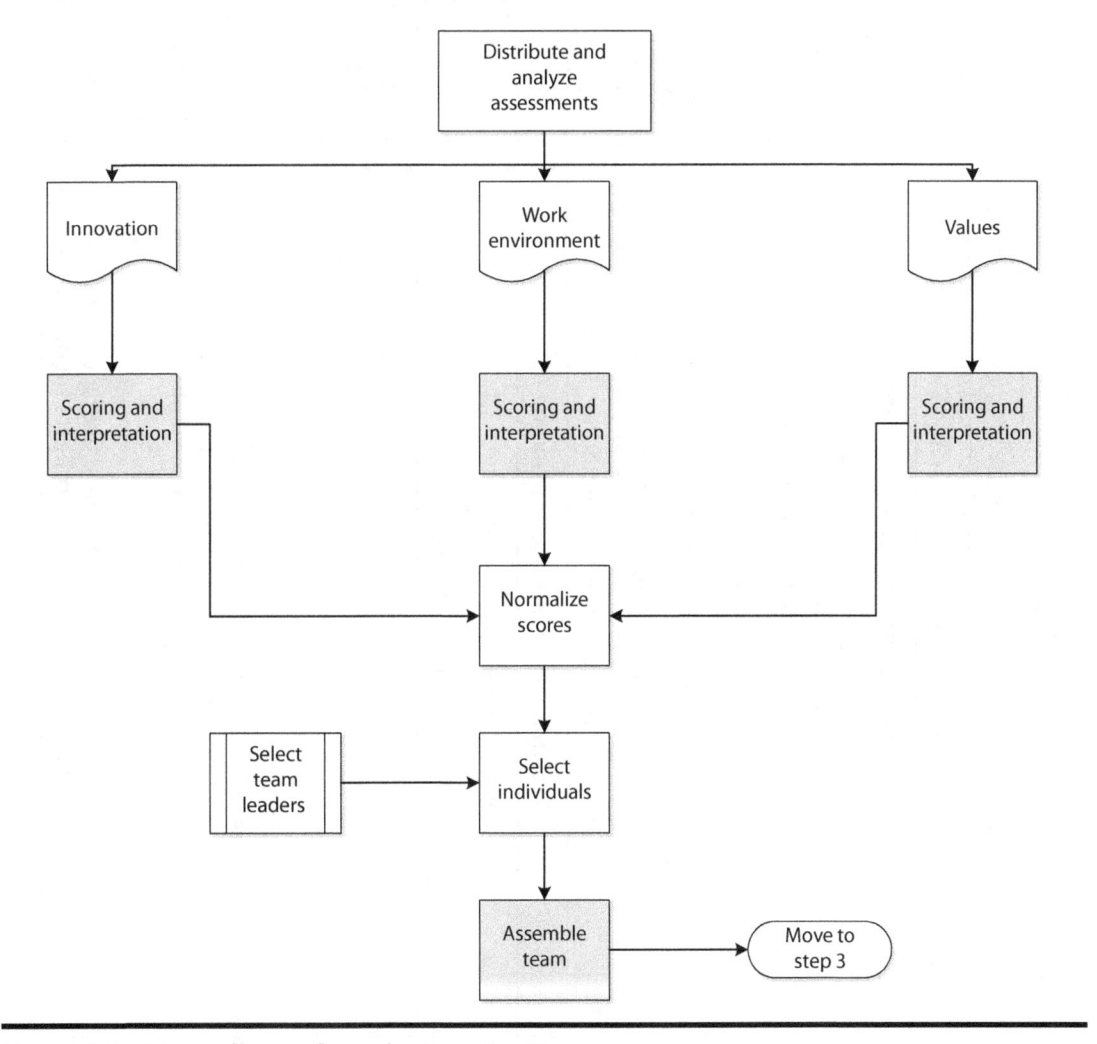

Figure 2.3   Normalize and nominate—step 2.

Table 2.2 Work Environment Survey

Statement Number	Instructions: Select the Number That Best Describes How Much You Agree with Each Statement and Recording That Number in the "My Choice" Column	Strongly Disagree	Disagree	Neither Disagree nor Agree	Agree	Strongly Agree	My Choice
1	The work environment supports creativity	1	2	3	4	5	
2	I have confidence in my own abilities to solve problems	1	2	3	4	5	
3	My workplace provides me with challenges	1	2	3	4	5	
4	The workplace enables me to be creative	1	2	3	4	5	
5	The work environment is open to new ideas	1	2	3	4	5	
6	There is a sense of cooperation among employees	1	2	3	4	5	
7	Management rewards improvements	1	2	3	4	5	
8	Work demands are not overburdening	1	2	3	4	5	
9	My workplace encourages change	1	2	3	4	5	
10	Trust is valued in my workplace	1	2	3	4	5	
Total	Average scores	DIM 1	#DIV/0!	DIM 2	#DIV/0!	DIM 3	#DIV/0!
Total	Range scores	DIM 1	0	DIM 2	0	DIM 3	0

Calculation

Category 1 score = Confidence, challenges, and trust – statements (2 + 3 + 6 + 10)/4; Range = Max–Min
Category 2 score = Creativity – statements (1 + 4 + 5)/3; Range = Max–Min
Category 3 score = Perception of work environment – statements (7 + 8 + 9)/3; Range = Max–Min

Interpretation

Choose the component (item) with the largest average score. The higher the score the more the individual values a particular "value" of innovation. Large ranges (greater than 1.5) indicate inconsistency and therefore reduces reliance on a particular value.

terms of agreeing or disagreeing with the statement as it relates to the work environment. Transform the response into a numerical rating (1—Strongly Disagree, 2—Disagree, 3—Neither Disagree nor Agree, 4—Agree, 5—Strongly Agree).

Scoring

Concept Structure	Statements
Concept 1: Confidence, challenge, and trust	2, 3, 6, 10
Concept 2: Creativity	1, 4, 5
Concept 3: Working conditions	7, 8, 9

Calculate the average scores for concepts 1 through 3 for each individual and then calculate the range. Highest averages indicate greatest amount of agreement to the concept. We also recommend the innovation team pursue additional and more sophisticated analysis of this data, if possible, especially if trying to compare groups and build the correct team composition.

EXERCISE 2.2: WORK ENVIRONMENT SURVEY

Distribute the work environment survey. Choose 20–30 individuals randomly. Calculate the averages and ranges for each concept. Compare the 20 pairs. With what concept do most individuals align? Look for differences in gender, age groups, and position.

The values survey (Table 2.3) is scored in a similar way, except that there is only one concept. Therefore, calculate an average and range for all questions. The larger the average, the stronger the set of values demonstrated.

Values Survey

The time has come to assemble the innovation project selection team, name the team leader(s), and assign responsibilities (operating within the available resource constraints). Once team members identify with a particular innovation type (Chapter 1; or combination of types), they are selected based on their perception of innovation to best achieve the innovation project or opportunity objective. Individuals (team members) who score the highest on the "improve" dimension (based on the case study) would be considered your primary candidates. By choosing candidates with similar perceptions, the team leader encourages participation and productivity, focusing energies on improvement and the project or opportunity objective(s). Adding team members occurs when a particular experience or knowledge set is missing. Use those not aligned with the "improvement" philosophy as resource members or subject matter experts at the appropriate time and place in the innovation opportunity project.

Table 2.3 Values Survey

Statement Number	Instructions: Check the Box That Best Matches Your Understanding of How Innovation Is Defined by Each Statement	Undefined	Poorly Defined	Marginally Defined	Defined	Well Defined	My Choice
1	A new discovery	1	2	3	4	5	
2	New or novel (unique) products and services	1	2	3	4	5	
3	Making something better	1	2	3	4	5	
4	Replacing what does not seem to work	1	2	3	4	5	
5	Improving products and services over time	1	2	3	4	5	
6	Improving something to make it better	1	2	3	4	5	
7	Changing what does not work	1	2	3	4	5	
8	A new invention or patent	1	2	3	4	5	
9	Improving on something that already exists	1	2	3	4	5	
10	Changing for the better	1	2	3	4	5	
	Scores	New	#DIV/0!	Improved	#DIV/0!	Change	#DIV/0!
	Scores	New	0	Improved	0	Change	0

Interpretation

Enter a number in the "My Choice" column that represents your perception. Use the following formula to construct an average and range value.

New: Average: (Statements 1 + 2 + 8)/3; Range = Max–Min
Improve: Average (Statements 3 + 5 + 6 + 9)/4; Range = Max–Min
Change: Average (Statements 4 + 7 + 10)/3; Range = Max–Min

The largest average value (with a range less than 1.5), indicates the innovation type the individual. Large ranges indicate inconsistency and indecision.

For this case study scenario, choose a team size of five to seven individuals with emphasis on knowledge and experience in supply chain purchasing and inventory systems management. Building a diverse team and workgroup is critical, so consider adding personnel who can "think outside of the box" while focused on your ultimate objective.

Step 3: Objectify

The third step (Figure 2.4) begins the process of defining the objective. What will the project accomplish, what is expected, how long will it take? Defining an objective comes only after the finalization of the needs and requirements. This also assumes that organization's management selects the best individuals rather assembling a team of diverse employees. Important to note here, poor alignment of team members derails many innovation efforts.

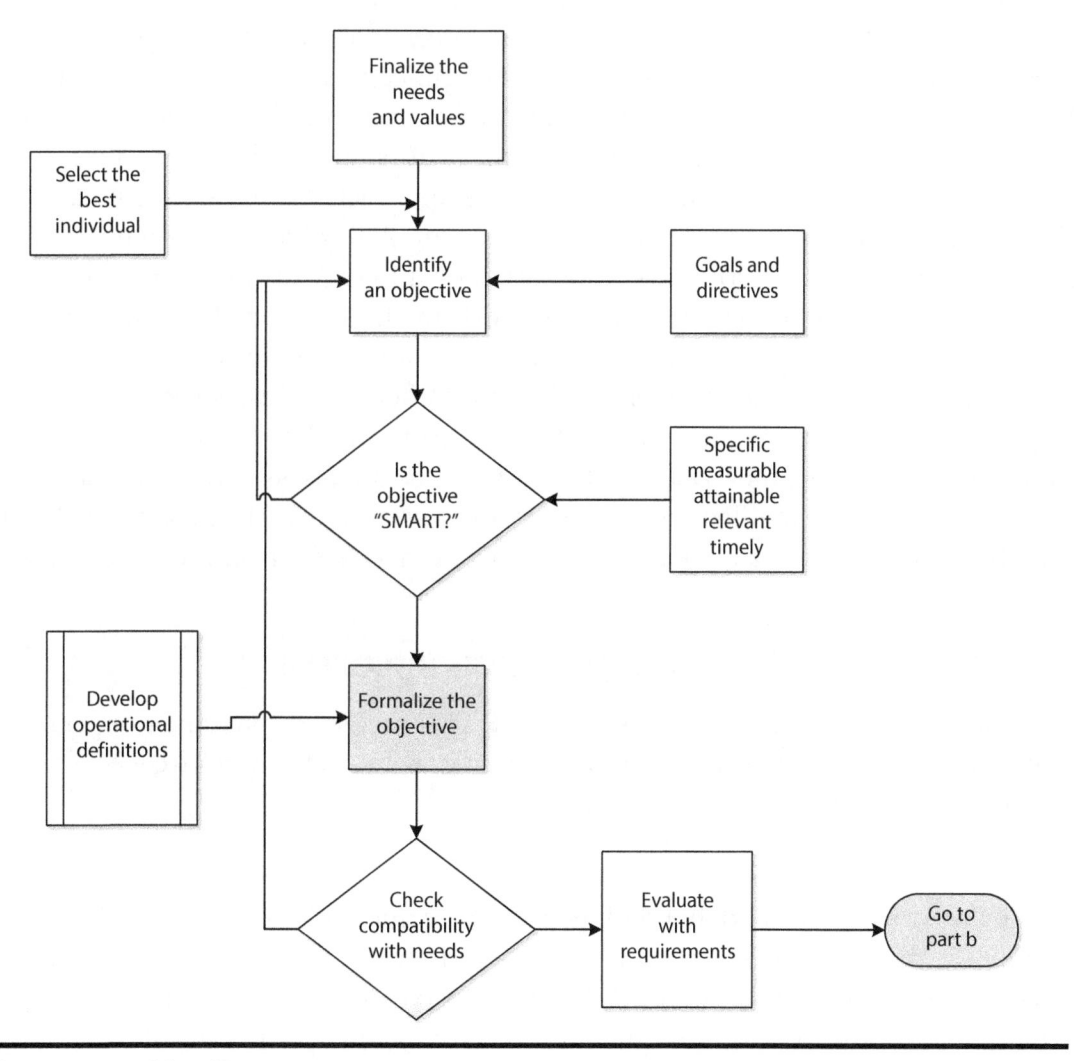

Figure 2.4   Objectify—step 3.

Identifying the objective is the next step. Most innovation projects and opportunities have multiple objectives (values), focused on use, purpose, and intent.

Specific, Measurable, Achievable, Relevant, and Time Objectives

To develop an objective, use the specific, measurable, achievable, relevant, and time-based (SMART) criteria. For this example, there are three SMART objectives for this scenario's procurement process, based on a set of established values:

1. In-place and operational within 60 days
2. Cost effective (within budget)
3. Flexible and reliable

All of these descriptions (of the objective) require an operational definition. An operational definition is one that describes the word and identifies parameters and measures. The term "cost effective" requires an operational definition. For this scenario and innovation opportunity project, a cost-effective procurement system (process) is one that is, at minimum, capable of operating within budget and is at a cost of 10% less (maintenance, personnel, distribution, warehousing, etc.) than the current legacy system. That is, the total monthly (and quarterly) costs are 10% less than the previous approach and version. Similar definitions for flexibility and reliability must occur. A flexible procurement system may be one that can accept parts with partial or missing part numbers, provide some minor diagnostics, tag and identify problematic parts, etc. Reliability (consistency, repeatability) of the replacement parts is a major quality issue and has serious implications if the availability of parts is affected by catastrophic events requiring unscheduled maintenance activities. Assessing these objectives requires more than identifying their outputs. It also requires an assessment of intent. Often, this is one of the first tasks of the team. For any objective, use the SMART criteria: poor or inaccurate measures will have a major effect on project success.

> ### EXERCISE 2.3: SMART OBJECTIVES
>
> Create a set of SMART objectives for a potential innovation project or opportunity within your organization. Indicate how each objective meets each of the five SMART criteria. Comment on the results.

Finally, verify that the defined objectives are compatible with the need. Obviously, the procurement system must be a dramatic improvement over the existing process to satisfy the need. If not, then return to searching for the system that meets the needs (or requirements) of the agency or organization.

The next step is to verify and validate the project (Figure 2.5).

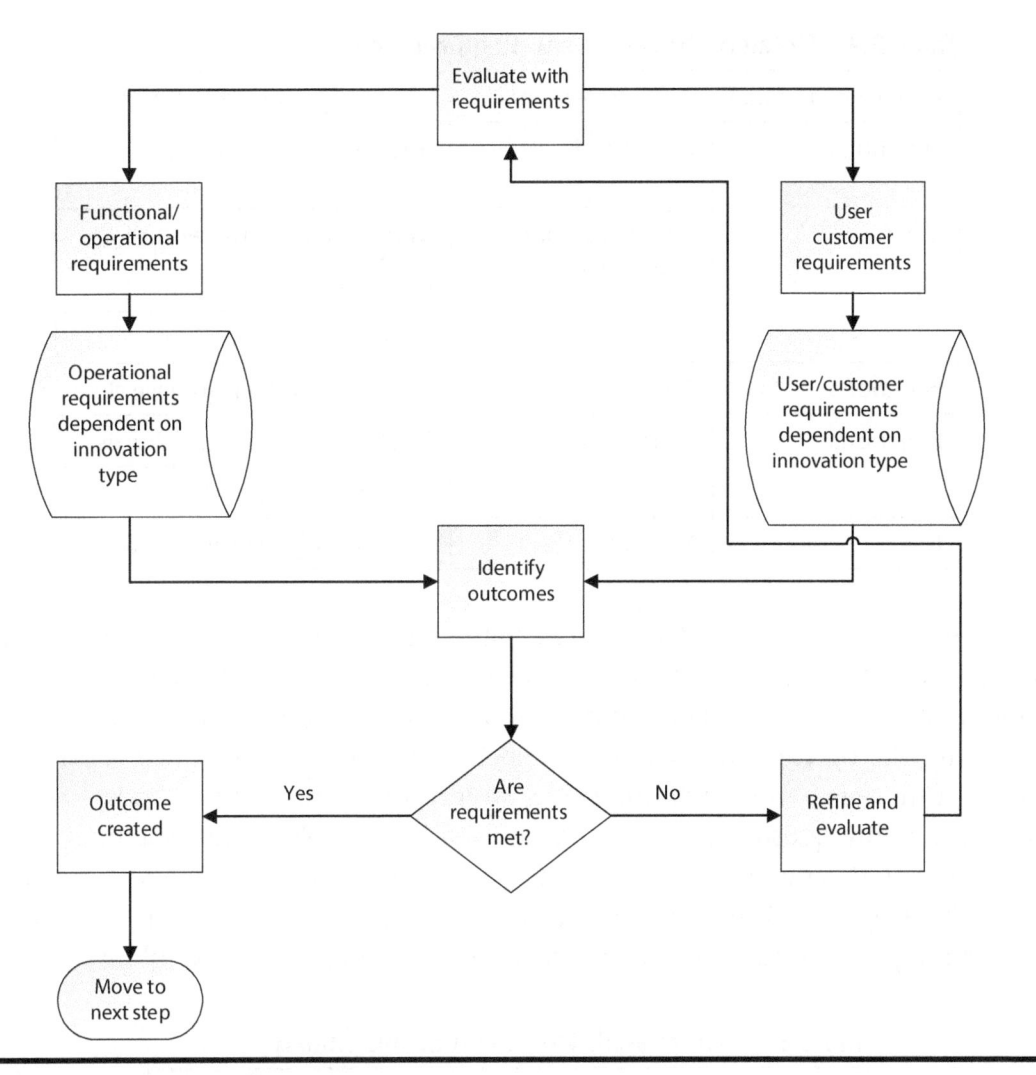

Figure 2.5   Operationalize—step 3.

Detail of Process (Item) Requirements

Upon completing the objective, define the requirements (both functional and user; Table 2.4). Here, the word "requirements" relates to the operational setting and controls. At the innovation project or opportunity selection phase, these can be high-level requirements.

As the project unfolds, develop a more definitive set of requirements. An ongoing challenge is to understand the relationship between user and functional requirements. Table 2.5 provides a mechanism for evaluating these relationships. Strong or medium-sized relationships require full exploration (Table 2.5). A relationship exists when a functional and user characteristic change one another. A change in a functional requirement could influence the user, and vice versa. The strength of these relationships may directly influence the innovation project or overall opportunity outcome.

For example, consider the aircraft parts procurement scenario case study (Table 2.5), where functional and user requirements are an issue. The team wants to

Table 2.4 Detail of Process (Item) Requirements

User or Functional	Requirements	Established Parameters
Functional	Integrated	Interfaces with existing systems and hardware
User	Simple to operate and navigate	Minimum training required
		Windows-driven
		Accessible help screens
Functional	Easy to track	Parts tracked by purchase date
Functional	Reliability indicator	Tracks time between failures
		Estimates failure rates
User	Maintainable	Internal IT personnel certified

evaluate how three success factors (associated with the objective—viability, capability, and sustainability) relate to these functional concerns. This matrix provides a method of examining relationships from a basic and personal perspective.

Finally, the outcome (the objective matched with its requirements) is established. If there is a mismatch, the potential innovation project or opportunity becomes highly questionable. For the case study example, if the system is not fully integrated, simple to use, and easily maintainable then the project may not satisfy its objectives. If the team reaches an unsatisfactory conclusion, then the project may require further refinement or be considered incompatible with stated

Table 2.5 Functional, User Relationship Matrix

	Customer or User Characteristics		
Functional	*Maintainable*	*Navigate*	*Ease of Use*
Reliable	S	S	S
Simple to track	S	M	S
Interfaces	M	M	S
History	W	W	M
Detail	S	S	N
Comprehensive	S	S	S
Adaptable	S	M	M
Auditable	W	W	S
Accuracy	S	S	M
Start up	M	S	S

Note: Assign priorities: Strong relationship—"S"; Medium relationship—"M"; Weak relationship—"W"; Negative relationship—"N."

objectives. If the assumption is that the innovation project or opportunity meets its objectives, the team can proceed to the next step.

> ### EXERCISE 2.4: DETAIL OF PROCESS (ITEM) REQUIREMENTS
>
> Consider a potential innovation project. Using Table 2.4, identify a list of customer and functional requirements and then rate those requirements using Table 2.5 as an example.

Step 4: Validate and Verify

Once the outcome is accepted, it is time to validate and verify. Making a rash decision, based solely on an outcome may eliminate potential innovation projects or opportunities while increasing risk and failure. It is best to enter into this step with the mindset and goal of determining if the outcome is truly worth the overall investment of time, resources, and effort. The beginning stages of this step require an objective evaluation of major assumptions and limitations (Figures 2.6 and 2.7).

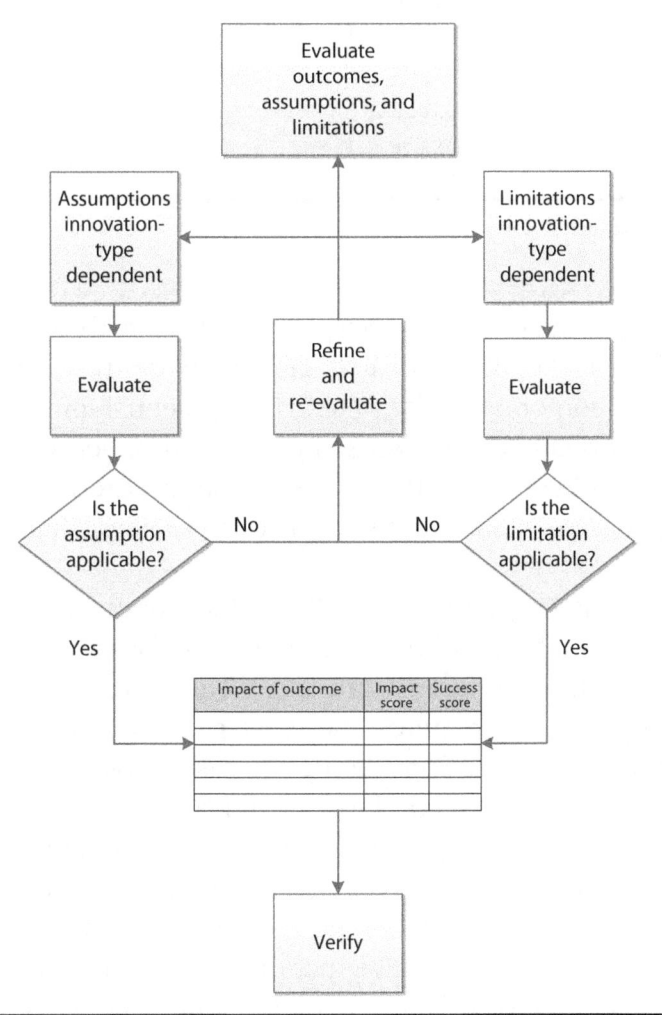

Figure 2.6   Validate—step 4.

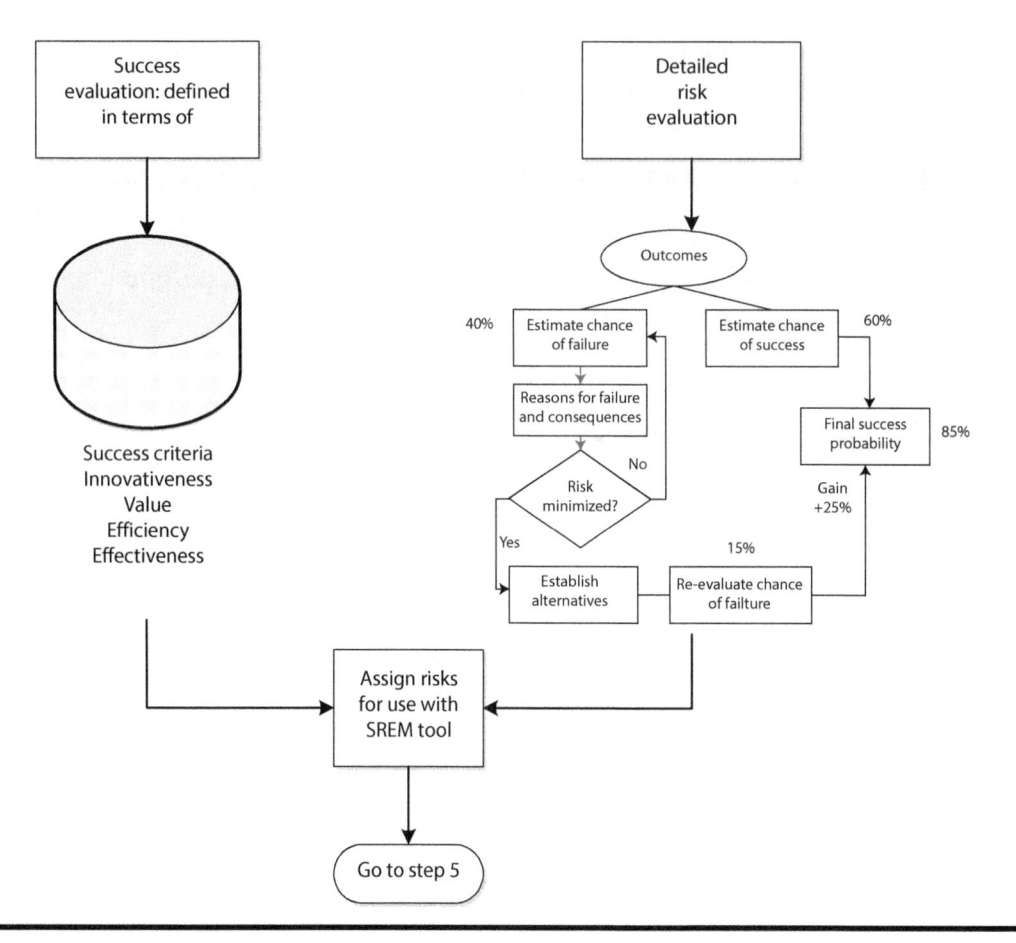

Figure 2.7 Verify—step 4.

"A limitation is that which prevents, deters, or interferes with performance" (McLaughlin and Caraballo, 2013a, p. 102). Limitations restrict performance and therefore any innovation opportunity potential. A potential limitation for this example is that the original system works but is based on legacy or antiquated technology (circa year 2000). We offer that even the most robust supply chain systems are subject to limitations and may encounter compatibility and system integration delays.

Assumptions, at this stage, are essentially an intangible, based on available information, perception, fact, and opinion. Future performance will validate all assumptions (but not their impact or influence). The more assumptions an innovation project or opportunity requires, the greater the need for viable alternatives, given the higher risk of failure. Considering the case study scenario, a typical assumption is the ease of which employees will learn a new process. We assume a short training and acclimation period, but what if that assumption is flawed. If the innovation team misses or incorrectly identifies critical assumptions, the delay could be devastating and/or costly. The team needs to identify the assumptions for evaluative purposes. It is imperative that the innovation team checks each limitation and assumption for validity. In addition, limitations and assumptions may vary over time as the process changes.

Table 2.6 Evaluative Criteria for Assumptions/ Limitations

Determinants of Effect	Measures of Importance
Strong	Critical
Moderate	Moderate importance
Weak	Unimportant

Limitations restrict performance and therefore may act as a barrier to the innovation project or opportunity. The innovation team will need to determine the boundaries within which the item operates. Limitations also define future opportunities such as how a new technology or process can overcome the existing limitation. It is best to know what you can and cannot do before implementing a project.

Evaluative Criteria for Assumptions/Limitations

Check whether the assumption or limitation is viable and determine its overall influence on the outcome. You can accomplish this by objectively evaluating all assumptions and limitations. Evaluate each critical assumption and limitation (team and management can decide which fits this criteria) (Table 2.6). Detail how the assumptions or limitations are measured (or determined), even if it is an opinion or perception. Evaluate the objective effect on the assumption or limitation. Reach a final decision on its importance and document all positions across your innovation team's membership. By reviewing assumptions and limitations (use Table 2.7) and applying evaluative criteria, the innovation team can reach a level of consensus on the state of the outcome. Again, this is a time to decide whether to move forward, revise, or scrap the potential project. It is simple to demean or dismiss this step; but the information gained will far outweigh the time invested.

Once you complete an evaluation of both assumptions and limitations, consider the overall impact on the innovation outcome.

Table 2.7 Evaluation of Assumptions/Limitations

Assumption/ Limitation	How It Is Measured	Effect on 60-Day Timeline	Effect on Cost Effectiveness	Effect on Objective Flexibility and Reliability	Overall Importance
L—Older technology	Date of inception	Strong	Strong	Moderate	Critical
A—Ease of use	Perception/ mistakes and failures	Strong	Strong	Strong	Critical

> **EXERCISE 2.5: ASSUMPTIONS AND LIABILITIES**
>
> Consider the assumptions and limitations of a project. Compare at least one limitation and one assumption to the SMART objectives developed in the previous exercise. Evaluate the impact, using the logic developed for Table 2.7.

Finally, begin the process of determining the overall impact of the innovation outcome (Figure 2.7). Assessing the impact on the expected outcome requires an estimation of the chance of success and the risk of failure. Success and failure are not mutually exclusive—one aspect can succeed, another fail. This is why the innovation team needs to maximize the chance of success.

Outcome Impact and Success Evaluation

Outcomes are a tangible statement of results which meet some (if not all) of the stated objective(s). Suppose the team arrived at three outcomes, listed in Table 2.8. In addition, the team evaluates the overall impact and success using a rating scale of 1 (low) to 5 (high) (Table 2.8). The team can convert these numbers to a chart (i.e., outcome impact and success evaluation) to identify the best possible choices (Figure 2.8). Worthy of note, the size of the "bubble" is proportional to the ratings.

Score using the impact versus success evaluation table with the following rating scale:

1—Low or no impact; 1—Low chance of success
2—Minimal impact; 2—Small chance of success
3—Moderate impact; 3—Medium chance of success
4—High impact; 4—Good chance of success
5—Superior impact; 5—Excellent chance of success

> **EXERCISE 2.6: CREATE AN OUTCOME IMPACT**
> **AND SUCCESS EVALUATION GRAPH**
>
> For each outcome, identify one or more unique impacts. How does that impact affect overall success?

Continuing the validation stage requires further verification. Validating outcomes require a detailed risk analysis and evaluation. Evaluating risk takes on a

Table 2.8 Impact versus Success Evaluation

Impact of Outcome	Overall Impact	Chance of Success
Customized solution	1	5
Off the shelf purchase	3	3
Upgrade of software/hardware	4	4

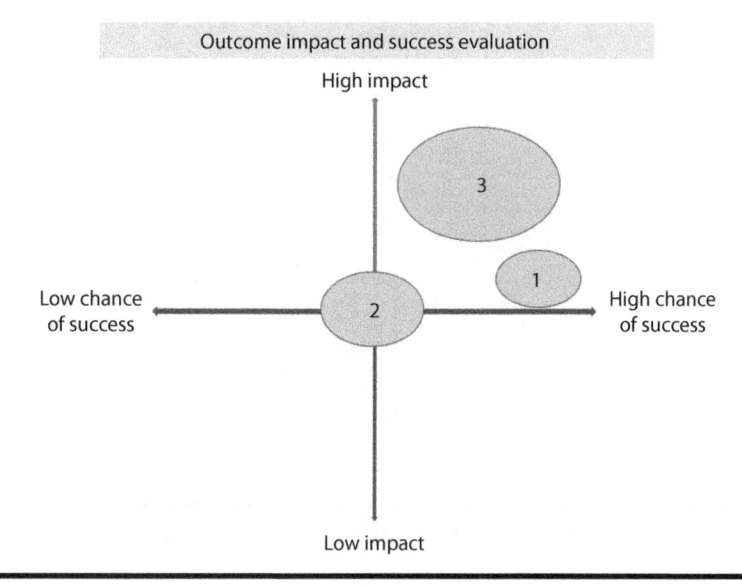

Figure 2.8   Outcome impact and success evaluation.

complexity that exceeds the purpose of this book. Yet, to evaluate an innovation opportunity project, the innovation team must evaluate risk from a basic, if not, more complex approach. Risk accumulates as the potential for failure (reduced performance) increases. One excellent method is the use of failure modes and effects analysis (FMEA), described in another book in this series, *ENOVALE: How to Unlock Sustained Innovation Project Success* (McLaughlin and Caraballo, 2013b)?

Success, Risk Evaluation Matrix Analysis

Another, simpler approach is to assign a probability of success and failure, as shown in Figure 2.9. Finally, an alternative approach is to create a success, risk evaluation matrix (SREM) diagram (Table 2.9). Locate the particulars on this technique in our text—*Chance or Choice: Unlocking Innovation Success* (McLaughlin and Caraballo, 2013a). Extract those successful outcomes from the impact success evaluation and complete the SREM format.

The SREM quadrant analysis (Figure 2.9) exposes success measures (determinants) to various and critical risks. The SREM quadrant analysis can evaluate multiple risks versus an outcome success to assist in deciding whether to continue to pursue the project. Figure 2.10 details the preliminary results of the analysis

Table 2.9   Success, Risk Evaluation Matrix (SREM) Analysis

Success	Risk	Quadrants	Number
Upgrade of software	Incompatible technology—Low	Strength	2
Customized solution	Time to implement—High	Weakness	4
Off the shelf software	Cannot handle special or unusual situations—Moderate	Status-quo	3

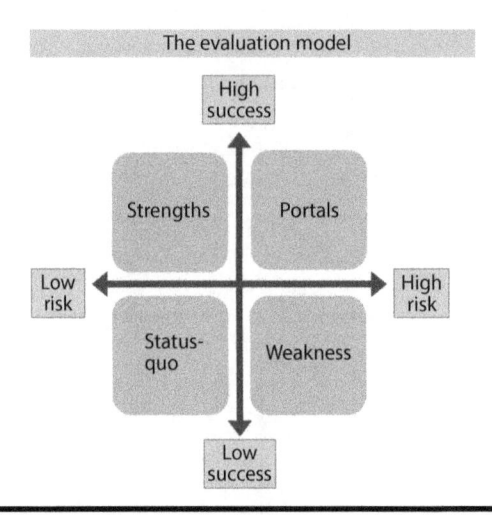

Figure 2.9   Success, risk evaluation matrix (SREM) quadrants analysis.

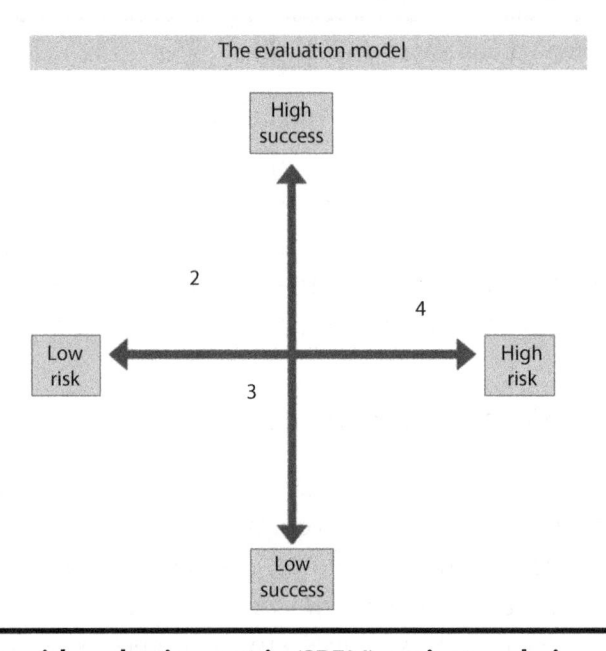

Figure 2.10   Success, risk evaluation matrix (SREM) project analysis.

suggesting that the upgrade of software and hardware may be the best solution, given the three unique objectives.

Step 5: Alignment

Upon accepting the outcome, the team examines the human impact of the proposed project. Examining the human impact involves a determination of how well the project aligns with the organizational (individual) goals and values. Alignment begins with the ability to associate the innovation project or opportunity with organizational values, culture, and scope (Figure 2.11). Overall, attaining value for the organization and user is the ultimate prize. If the project can demonstrate value and competitive advantage over time, it is a project worth pursuing.

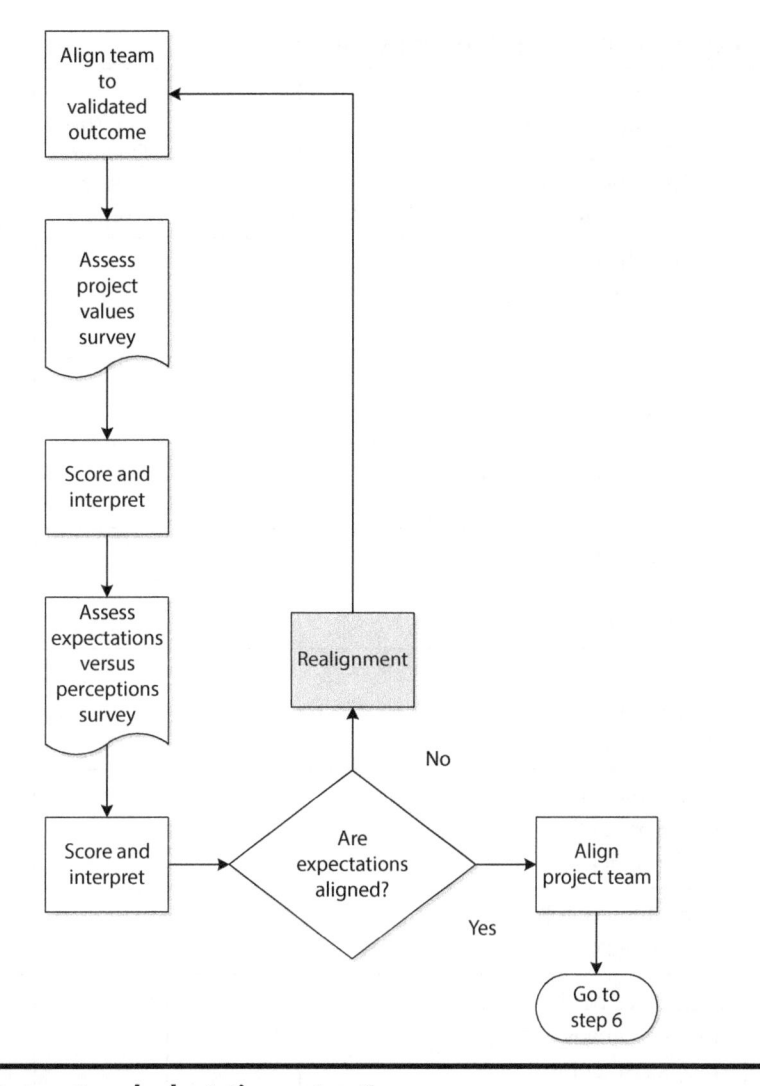

Figure 2.11   Alignment and adaptation—step 5.

One efficient method to measure individual and organizational alignment is through perceptual surveys, interviews, or focus groups. The expectations and perceptions survey (Table 2.10) measures these concepts for overall alignment. There are five pairs of data (1, 2), (3, 4), (5, 6), (7, 8), (9, 10) and five concepts: project objectives, project performance, management contribution, team performance, and project outcomes (Table 2.10). Respondents either agree or disagree at varying levels with the paired statements provided in the survey tool. The designated responses are labeled as: 1 = Strongly Disagree, 2 = Disagree, 3 = Neither Disagree nor Agree, 4 = Agree, or 5 = Strongly Agree. Subtract the even numbered statements from the odd numbered statements.

Expectations and Perceptions Survey

For example, select the project objective statements (statements 1 and 2, from Table 2.10, Expectations and Perceptions Survey). If an individual scores Statement 1 a "4" and Statement 2 a "2" then the score is " –2," if expectations

Table 2.10 Expectations and Perceptions Survey

Statement Number	Instructions: Check the Box That Best Matches Your Agreement (Disagreement) with Each Statement	Strongly Disagree	Disagree	Neither Disagree nor Agree	Agree	Strongly Agree
1	I expect the project outcome to remain the same					
2	The project team is performing well					
3	The project continues to perform as expected					
4	Individuals are committed to the success of the organization					
5	I expect my support to remain unchanged through the project					
6	Team members contribute to the project's performance					
7	I expect to contribute to the project's success					
8	There have not been any major changes to the project outcome					
9	The project team has performed as expected					
10	The project is successful up to this point					

greatly exceeded perceptions (reality). This indicates that the individual was expecting more than what truly exists. This would signal an alignment problem. Negative values indicate that the individual's reality does not coincide with their overall expectations. Averaging the responses will only remove the natural variation. Do examine the frequency of the scores. Aligned teams should score between zero and +1. A poorly aligned team with negative scores indicates disappointment with reality as compared to their original expectations. Misaligned individuals can disrupt a team and its progress.

The process of realignment helps team members to adapt to project and program realities. We recommend that all team members recommit to the project outcomes/objectives. One useful suggestion is to place the outcome/objective in a conspicuous space, so that team members can constantly realign themselves to this concept. Use it as a header or footer on all e-mails. A focused team is aligned and adaptable.

Since innovation is often a "learn as you go" endeavor, adaptive individuals make the best team members. Adaptive individuals are ones who can easily adjust to changing realities. Often what seems reasonable one day may seem ludicrous the next day. Changing priorities are to be expected. That said, those individuals who can easily adjust to change would accept innovation willingly, especially if the benefit is obvious. The acceptance of change survey (Table 2.11) recently validated and proven reliable provides one way of evaluating an individual's perception of how well they accept change.

Acceptance of Change

When change takes place, people need to adjust, align, and adapt (see Table 2.11). Change can be painful or pleasing, depending on the situation and the people involved.

- Acceptance of change is a measure of acquiescence—accepting the change as something permanent is accomplished when:
  - Minimizing obstacles and barriers
  - Developing opportunities for growth
  - Developing a new "role" for employees
  - Minimizing fear, anxiety, and a feeling of loss

Respondents either agree or disagree to some level with the statements presented in the acceptance to change survey instrument. To score the survey instrument, assign a numerical response as follows: 1 = Strongly Disagree, 2 = Disagree, 3 = Neither Disagree nor Agree, 4 = Agree, or 5 = Strongly Agree. To obtain a change acceptance score:

- Calculate an average (range) for statements 1–4, 10 = Organizational change
- Calculate an average (range) for statements 5–9 = Personal aspects of change
- For each individual's average score <3.0; they have problems adjusting to change
- For each individual's average score >4.0; they openly accept change

Examine the range for each innovation team member's (individual) overall score. High variation indicates a poor agreement between individual responses. This suggests that change has been an upheaval for individuals, due to varying feelings.

Table 2.11 Acceptance of Change Survey

Statement Number	Instructions: Check the Box That Best Matches Your Agreement (Disagreement) with Each Statement	Strongly Disagree	Disagree	Neither Disagree nor Agree	Agree	Strongly Agree
1	When change occurs, I am one of the first to embrace it					
2	When my company announces a change, I believe it will be positive					
3	The outcomes of change are generally positive					
4	My organization does not create barriers to change					
5	My organization helps its employees to accept change					
6	Change can be positive when barriers are reduced					
7	I would accept change if there were additional opportunities					
8	Accepting change can me made easier if management communicates					
9	If change reduces stress and anxiety, I would accept it					
10	People who embrace change quickly are better adjusted					

Those resistant to change will often find innovation to be frustrating. Yet, innovation requires an open mind, dedication to empirical evidence, and an ability to maneuver around obstacles and barriers. Most employees or associates have this ability, when guided properly and trained, to deal with ambiguous situations. The ability to deal with changing priorities and prosper from these situations is a key trait for adaptation.

> **EXERCISE 2.7: ADAPTATION SURVEY**
>
> Choose either the expectations/perceptions survey or the acceptance of change survey. Distribute to a group of 20–30 individuals, score the instrument, and interpret the findings by looking for similarities and differences. Remember these surveys are for a quick evaluation only.

Step 6: Tabulate and Track Performance

A critical aspect of any innovation project is whether it can deliver a decent payback over time. Organizations invest in innovation for a specific reason, for example, cost efficiency, value, or effectiveness. Every project must yield a benefit so that its value is established. For profit-driven businesses, return on investment (ROI)—what is invested is a fraction of the benefit obtained. Profit is generally driving the project. Additionally other benefits received may also support and help to implement the project. The project may provide additional benefits (both tangible and intangible). Any estimate is generally an educated guess and the accuracy of that guess depends upon the history and experiences with similar processes.

Figure 2.12 describes the process for tabulating and tracking performance. Since the project is still in the formative stages, it is critical to establish the performance measures (recall the discussion of success factors) that define its identity. At this stage, we estimate the benefits and those financial, operational, and strategic measures associated with the project. For this hypothetical case study, this includes measuring the benefit, projected costs, and unique measures that define the project.

> **EXERCISE 2.8: FINANCIAL INDICATORS**
>
> Establish three to five financial indicators that relate directly to performance (or value). Describe the process of measuring these variables. What are the characteristics that make these capable and sustainable? Will these measures provide the financial information on a real-time basis?

The team, with management support, reviews the performance measures. Establish the goals that constitute success. Additional work should clarify these measures and establish operating guidelines and appropriate systems to capture the benefits of success.

For this example, we use the three objectives and establish a measure of recurring benefit for predictive purposes. The efficiencies gained with the procurement systems should outweigh present difficulties. Some reasonable payback period is part of the overall solution. Benefits should be observable within 3–6 months; therefore, the accounting systems need to be robust enough to track and document this progress. Calculating a benefit depends upon the ability of the accounting and financial systems to track performance on at least a quarterly basis. If the

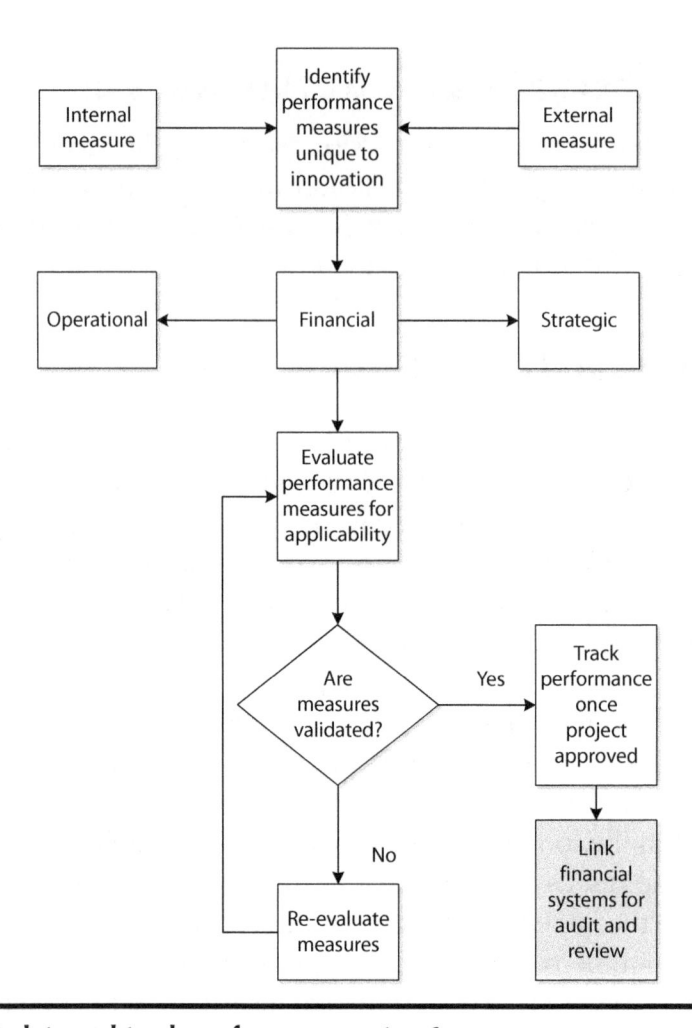

Figure 2.12 Tabulate and track performance—step 6.

team and management feel that the improvement is possible and the outcome/ objective attainable, then decide to go ahead with the project. Before executing the project, the team and management will need to devise a reasonable set of expectations regarding benefits value, ROI, payback, and/or resource allocation.

Step 7: Execute and Evaluate

Finally, at this stage, management will make a final decision (Figure 2.13). Plans can begin to implement the project. This is an excellent time to review the project outcomes, objectives, and to create a plan for implementation. It is especially important to review and solidify those project measures used to identify benefit in step 6 (tabulate and track performance). More than likely, a new team is required to move the project forward. Decide what type of innovation works best. For this example, an improvement type is warranted. The process uses a modified version of N^2OVATE^{TM}, especially designed for the type of innovation and the client organization.

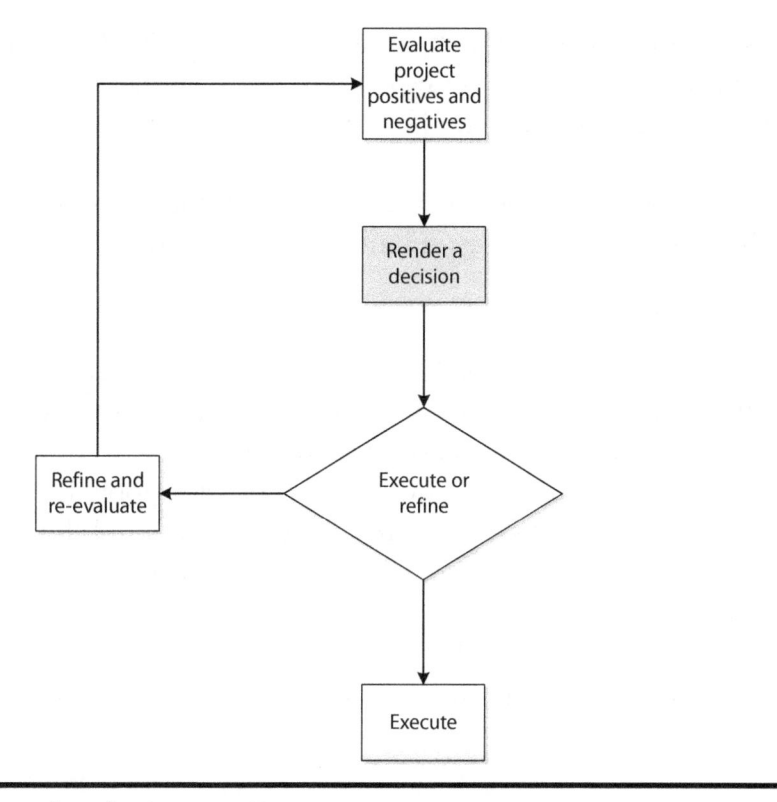

Figure 2.13   Execute and evaluate—step 7.

Summary

This chapter introduced an operational process to select an innovation project. Generally, the process takes 1–2 days to complete. Selecting a project generates a tremendous amount of valuable information concerning the project and the next (implementation) phase. This chapter was an overview of the project section process; those who want to investigate the methodology in more detail can contact the authors. As with any innovation project, the process flowcharts are a place to begin. We expect some modification for each project submitted for acceptance based on agency or organizational culture and propensity toward innovation. These flowcharts give the reader a detailed process in which to select a project. Given the amount of knowledge gained, this entire process is worth executing each time a macro (large) project requires approval.

DISCUSSION QUESTIONS

1. Choose a term and define it operationally. Note: an operational definition is one that describes its criteria, measurement, and decision. An example is "hot temperature"—which is defined as the observation made when reading a thermometer that exceeds 95°F.
2. Discuss 3–5 needs that your organization or businesses faces today. Is there any potential for any of these needs to be an innovation project?

3. Discuss the concept of risk, as you understand it. How does risk become a factor in evaluating (selecting) an innovation project?
4. Discuss when, where, and how management will interface with the N²OVATE™ process.
5. Discuss the importance of individual contributions to an innovation project. Which steps rely heavily on human contribution?

ASSIGNMENTS

1. Discuss the process of validating a set of needs (requirements). Remember, at this point requirements are product specific, based on a contract or agreement. Use an example to do through the process.
2. Choose an objective (be sure it is measurable), apply the SMART criteria to the objective and discuss the results. How much did the objective change?
3. List those financial measures that a project must address to be selected for implementation.
4. Discuss how the N²OVATE™ process could be used by an individual to select an innovation project. What steps would be eliminated, what others would be added?

References

McLaughlin, G. and Caraballo, E. 2013a. *Chance or Choice: Unlocking Innovation Process.* Productivity Press, Boca Raton, FL. ISBN: 9781466581869.

McLaughlin, G. and Caraballo, E. 2013b. *ENOVALE: How to Unlock Sustained Innovation Project Success.* Productivity Press, Boca Raton, FL.

McLaughlin, G. and Kennedy, W.R. 2015. *A Guide to Innovation Processes and Solutions for Government.* Productivity Press, Boca Raton, FL. ISBN: 978-1-4987-2157-8.

Chapter 3

Building an Effective Initial Innovation Opportunity Profile

Introduction

Before describing how to implement an innovation opportunity, we first need to evaluate the opportunity at hand. An unsatisfied need can lead to an innovation but the need alone might be insufficient to initiate a project. As we have mentioned in prior discussion, stakeholders, shareholders, and consumers (or users) must recognize the need as a priority and be willing to act on it. They must be willing to pay for the innovative item and that item must be of sufficient quality (or reputation) to attract and keep the customer's interest. The process from need definition to the realization of an actual product, process or service may require, (1) a great deal of creativity, (2) significant resource and capital investment, and (3) commitment across the consumer base and enterprise. The process can be complex and convoluted, so tracking and monitoring its progress may be beyond the capability of the organization. Innovation opportunity profile (IOP) is both a guide and tool for undertaking an innovation opportunity project. Unlike a project charter that monitors the process of implementation, the IOP is a management tool for assessment, decision making, and benefit evaluation.

The IOP form (Figures 3.1 and 3.2) provides a single document for converting an innovation opportunity into a potential innovation project. This is not a standalone tool, but one that can be employed across the spectrum and types of innovation opportunity projects. We encourage organizations and innovation teams to use the IOP tool as you begin to investigate the merits of the potential innovation opportunities available to your organization. Figure 3.3 describes the process of organizing the information needed before a project begins.

This chapter describes how the IOP instrument is used and how the information can best prepare an organization for an innovation opportunity project. Of course, simpler projects may not need to complete all sections of the IOP and may require only the innovation team project charter (Figure 3.4), briefly introduced in

Executive Summary			
Note: Highlights key information from the 11 sections in the profile; provides high-level discussion on recommendations with supporting benefits considerations, exceptions, limitations, and assumptions, associated risk matrix or factors; and identifies any associated appendices and attachments (target length — 1 page). Identify related core competency(ies), associated functional needs assessments (FNAs), and functional solution analysis (FSA), applicable certifications, standards, and waiver requirements, budgetary documents, test plans, etc.			

Section I. Operational Profile Key Points of Contact			
Name	Title and Position	Department	Contact Number /E-mail
1.			
2.			
3.			
4.			
5.			

Section II. Operational System Requirements Statement			
1. Key Performance Parameters	First Tier	Second Tier	Third Tier
2. Key Performance Indicators	First Tier	Second Tier	Third Tier
3. Key Performance Measurements	First Tier	Second Tier	Third Tier
4. Critical Success Factors	First Tier	Second Tier	Third Tier

Section III. Customer/User Profile Types User Profile (Person, group or business unit operating or using the system or capability)	
Customer Type	Intended Use (Statement of key user requirements)
1. User 1	
2. User 2	
3. User 3	
4. User 4	

Section IV. System-Mode Profile (Manner or way system or capability can operate)	
System or Capability Mode	Mode of Operation
1.	
2.	

Figure 3.1   Innovation opportunity profile—side 1.

Section V. Functional Profile (Evaluation specific essential functions in system or capability modes identified in Section IV)

System or Capability Mode	Essential Function (Requirement)
1.	
2.	

Section VI. Certification, Standards, and Waiver Requirements (Internal/external offices, groups or agencies, and/or standards guiding implementation and adoption)

Entity Title	Internal or External	Certification and Testing Requirements	Standard and Designator	Waiver Requirements

Section VII. Operational Profile (Elements, Architecture, and Test Plans — likely be in attachments and appendices)

Elements, Architecture and/or Test Plan Title	Applicable Functional System and/or Capability	Attachment or Appendix Number

Section VIII. Data Management and Resource Sharing Plans (Describe how information is managed, and how results are shared and disseminated)

Responsible Agency	Plan Title	Justification Statement

Section IX. Project Budget and Financial Information (Justification)

Responsible Agency	Account/Budget Code	Amount	Justification Statement

Section X. Coordination and Approval

Name	Title	Approved /Disapproved	Date
Comments:			

Name	Title	Approved /Disapproved	Date
Comments:			

Section XI. Appendices and Attachments

Attach core competencies source documents, functional needs assessments, functional solution analysis, budgetary documents, architectural and system drawings, certification and guiding standards, waiver processes, test plans, data management plan, resource sharing plan, etc.

Figure 3.2 Innovation opportunity profile—side 2.

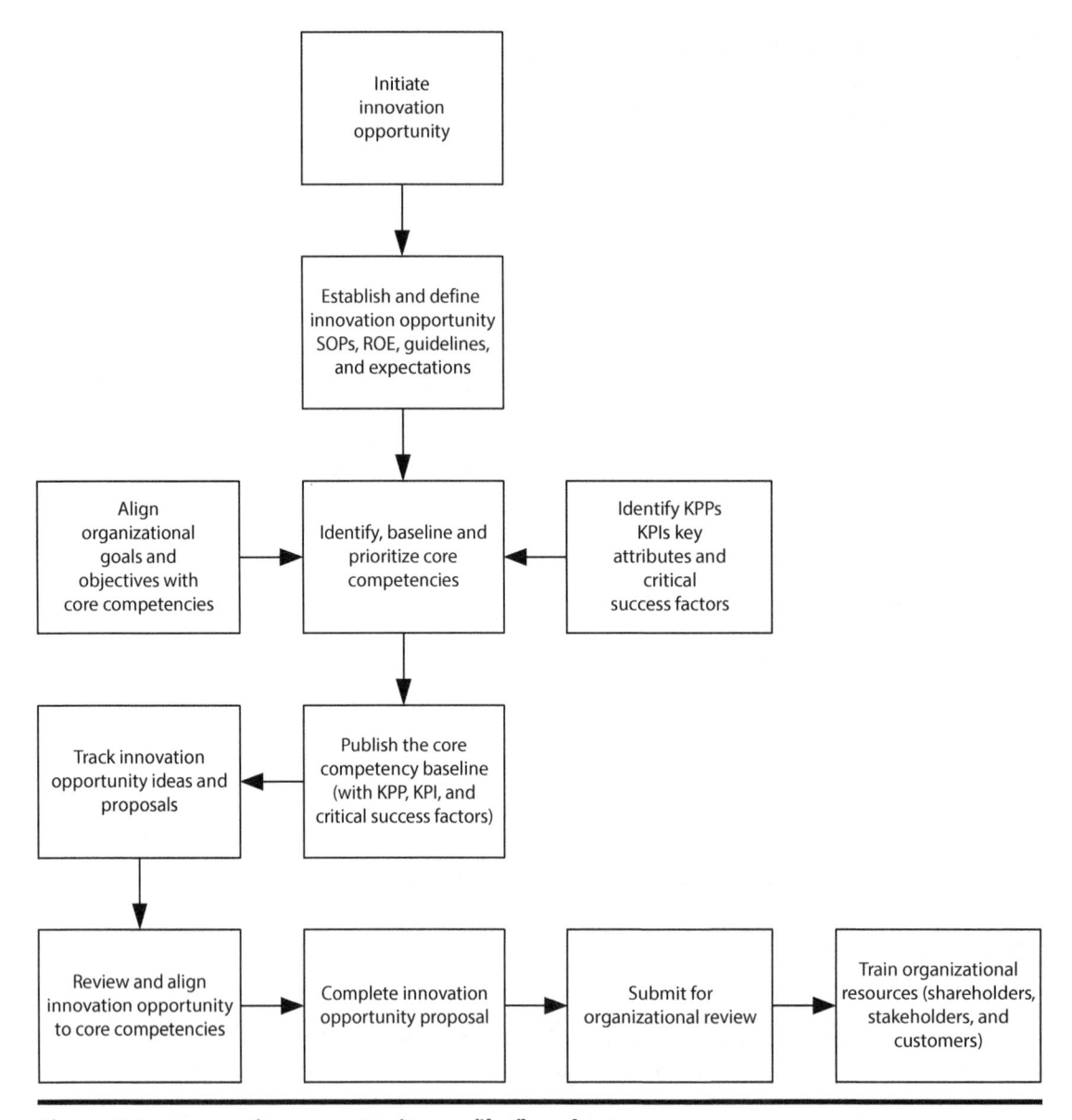

Figure 3.3 Innovation opportunity profile flowchart.

this chapter to achieve a positive innovation outcome (the project charter is covered in more detail and an example provided in Chapter 7). More, complex projects may require an extended version, available from the IPSinnovate.com website.

Completing each process (and subprocess) step in order will result in a completed IOP form. The remaining information in this chapter will help build the document, explaining each element of the form.

Establish the Organization Innovation Management System

Within an organization, it is advisable the organization develops and evolves a repeatable and sustainable innovation management system (processes, procedures, guidelines, and expectation). This approach should be wired into the

Innovation Team Project Charter (Tracking #: _____)

I. General Information

Project Title	Short title of the incremental innovation project				
Project Description	Short description of the incremental innovation you wish to achieve.				
Prepared By	Team leader name				
Date	DD/MMM/YY	Version	1	Expected Completion Date	DD/MMM/YY

II. Project Objective

Detailed description of the innovation project objective.

III. Assumptions and Limitations

Identify known assumptions and limitations. Up date as required.

IV. Project Scope

Identify the focus, objectives and time line in as much detail as possible. Include the boundaries of the innovation project.

V. Project Milestones

Identify inch stones and milestones that are critical in achieving your objective(s).

VI. Impact Statement

Potential Impact	Affected Domains (Departments, Activities, etc.), Processes, Machine Centers, etc.
Identify potential initial perceived benefits and add others as the project proceeds through each of the steps.	Identify areas that will be affected by your innovation project. For example, all departments, activities, and machine centers.

VII. Roles and Responsibilities

Sponsor (Decision maker) **Name and Position**	Provides overall direction on the project. Responsibilities include: approve the project charter and plan; secure resources for the project; confirm the project's goals and objectives; keep abreast of major project activities; make decisions on escalated issues; and assist in the resolution of roadblocks.
Innovation Team Lead (Project Manager)	Leads in the planning and development of the project; manages the project to scope. Responsibilities include: develop the project plan; identify project deliverables; identify risks and develop risk management plan; direct the project resources (team members); scope control and change management; oversee quality assurance of the project management process; maintain all documentation including the project plan; report and forecast project status; resolve conflicts within the project or between cross-functional teams; ensure that the project's product meets the business objectives; and communicate project status to stakeholders.
Team Member(s) — Others have requested to be added but approval from their respective department head is required.	Works toward the deliverables of the project. Responsibilities include: understand the work to be completed; complete research, data gathering, analysis, and documentation as outlined in the project plan; inform the project manager of issues, scope changes, and risk and quality concerns; proactively communicate status; and manage expectations.
Subject Matter Expert(s)	Provides expertise on a specific subject. Responsibilities include: maintain up-to-date experience and knowledge on the subject matter; and provide advice on what is critical to the performance of a project task and what is nice-to-know.

VIII. Resources, Project Risks, and Success Measurements. These areas will be captured in the next version of this plan.

Figure 3.4   Innovation team project charter (basic).

organization's DNA and culture with recurring training and awareness sessions, leadership buy-in and support, and subsequently formalized and recognized as an organization best practice. In sum, everyone in the organization should be familiar with how to submit an idea or innovation opportunity. After identifying an innovation opportunity, the organization's established management system should facilitate the training, initiation, tracking, determination, implementation, and follow-on phases of sustaining the potential opportunity. We must reiterate that training and awareness should also focus on shareholders, stakeholders, and customers, and include feedback services as an essential tool throughout all steps of the innovation process.

This book will provide essential tools for implementing innovation. We present new tools and an example provided to assist in associated exercises. The first of the new tools offered to support identifying (and capturing) an innovation opportunity is the IOP tool (Figures 3.1 and 3.2).

Innovation Opportunity Proposal

Developing an internal procedure for soliciting, identifying, and submitting innovation proposals internal to the organization is an instrumental tool regardless if the organization has a closed or open innovation culture. This process does not have to be complex in nature but there are some key areas important in recognizing and validating any innovation opportunity. Figures 3.1 and 3.2 display the IOP (side 1) and the IOP (side 2), respectively. Completing the form is relatively straightforward and each section is self-explanatory.

Overview: Innovation Opportunity Profile (IOP) Form

In Section I, Innovation Champion (Initiator) and Contact Information, the individual who is proposing the innovation opportunity (need/idea) or a sponsor (supervisor, someone knowledgeable of the process, etc.) will provide their specifics. The assignment of tracking numbers is the responsivity of the organization's innovation management point of contact (this may vary by organization). The next step is to complete Section II, Innovation Opportunity Proposal, which should provide as much detail as available on the proposed improvement or gap, the goals and objectives, assumptions, limitations, and known constraints. For our airborne communications scenario in this chapter, some example assumptions and limitations are:

- Aircraft will use commercial beyond-line-of-site and ground entry points (GEPs) necessary to reach their home domain
- Sufficient bandwidth will be available across the global information grid (GIG) to support semiautonomous and autonomous access to worldwide telecommunication networks, upgrading the current aircraft communication systems will improve maintainability, reliability, and availability

Some additional examples of constraints might be aircraft or airframe type (i.e., space, weight, and power capabilities), interoperability with GEPs during international travel, standardization, and interoperability in the GIG.

Identify information as objective (i.e., factual, source from, reference, etc.) or subjective (i.e., perceived, estimated, no specific reference available, etc.).

Consider continuation sheets and attachments are included as required. In Section III, Key Shareholders, Stakeholders, and Customers, list all those instrumental to this specific proposal. Management can add members to the continuation section (Section V) or as an attachment. Key players are typically executives (C-Suite), department heads, process owners, clients, suppliers, etc. In Section IV, the IOP is validated with the assigned or owning sponsor of the proposal reviews the previous sections and all supporting materials and makes a determination on whether to pursue the proposal (i.e., move toward establishing an innovation team lead and members). The sponsor/owner then may request additional supporting materials or further review by another source (i.e., key stakeholders, shareholders, or customers), or simply decides not to pursue the proposal and closes it out. Section V, Continuation, is self-explanatory.

As previously mentioned, tracking, recording, and reporting innovation proposals are an essential step in the innovation process. If it is determined, the proposal is:

- Not a requirement
- Will not add significant improvement
- Does not reduce waste
- Does not add assessable value at the time it was submitted, it may be worth considering later and filed for future reference

Further, as with other forms and tools offered in this handbook, this tool can be automated online (Internet or intranet) or placed in convenient location (hard copy) throughout the facility.

Executive Summary

The executive summary highlights key information from the ensuing 10 sections in the profile. It provides a high-level discussion on recommendations with supporting benefits considerations, exceptions, limitations and assumptions, associated risk matrix or factors, and identifies any associated appendices and attachments. By necessity, the executive summary builds as the ensuing sections are populated and information becomes available. In essence, it should be the final piece of the profile before submission for review and approval.

As an example lead-in for the executive summary, consider the following: Business travelers today require a full spectrum of communication services when traveling by air. An executive summary for this potential innovation project may be similar to the following:

> With the dynamic nature of the world and international business environment and the emerging movement towards a net-centric environment, senior executives and their support staffs require the same information interchanges while traveling as they have in their primary offices and

operations centers. Meeting the growing communication capability needs of across an organization must include an airborne environment, consisting of voice, video, and data support to Business Enterprise (BE) communications systems, shareholder, stakeholders, and clients.

The executive summary provides a mechanism to define the project and its potential outcomes. The executive summary frames the subject in terms of the expected outcome.

The dynamic nature of the environment reinforces the immediate need for information and decision-making superiority. While fulfilling the organization's strategic policies, business, and goals throughout the spectrum, senior leaders oversee, evaluate, decide, and direct the full range of government and joint military operations to ensure national security. The remainder of the executive summary would capture the key takeaways of the aforementioned considerations and supporting documentation in a short concise manner.

> ### EXERCISE 3.1: INITIATE THE DRAFT OF THE EXECUTIVE SUMMARY
>
> Using the definition and example above, initiate the build of the executive summary. This exercise will be ongoing throughout the chapter. Consider accuracy, brevity, and clarity when building this summary. At the end of the chapter and when your summary is complete, share your draft with your class members.

Core Competencies

Core competencies represent the strengths, competitive advantage, and profit potential of businesses or organizations. The business or organization excels at these tasks. These businesses hold a distinct advantage over their competition. The organization must recognize these core competencies and use these to its advantage.

Core competencies have several key elements that assist leadership at all levels bind their resources toward common goals and objectives. They also help provide a means of prioritizing the most important functions (products, services, and processes) where innovation opportunities might prove to carry the best value added when adopted and implemented. Some of those key elements are key performance parameters (KPPs), key performance indicators (KPIs), critical success factors (CSFs), and key attributes (KAs). A brief definition and an example relative of our airborne communications scenario presented in this chapter follow.

- ◼ KPP—Identifies key operational and performance requirements in terms of measurements or ranges (thresholds and objectives) that support measures of performance or measures of effectiveness. In our airborne communications scenario, examples of KPPs might fall in the categories of system engineering, open architecture and seamless interoperability across multiple domains (architecture), information assurance, and analysis

- KPIs—Critical measures that assess how a product, service, or process performs. These are primary concern in step 3 (Operational Assessment) and they should assist the innovation team in answering questions of how something is happening, what is happening, and why it is happening. In our airborne communications scenario, an example might be *how* a new component changes the equipment configuration and measurements taken to assess the performance against a KPI

- KAs—There are measurable and testable criteria a product, service, or process must have and are best captured or displayed as key steps in a process map. They also are instrumental in supporting KPPs, KPIs, and CSFs. In our airborne communications scenario, example attributes of the system and components could be operated in global environment by effectively transferring data between sender and receiver, and supported in basic communication requirements for all business elements

- CSFs—Unique to each organization, these are critical factors that defined procedures, processes, or activities that a business depends on for survival and are typically directly linked to the organization's core competencies. They are also instrumental to achieving the organizations goals, objectives, business strategy, and plan. A possible example for our airborne communications scenario is the improvement of overall communication system performance and reliability while continually reducing the space, weight, and power (SWaP) requirements that limit cargo and passenger size for smaller tube aircraft

> **EXERCISE 3.2: IDENTIFYING CORE COMPETENCIES, KEY PERFORMANCE PARAMETERS, KEY PERFORMANCE INDICATORS, AND KEY ATTRIBUTES**
>
> Using the definitions and examples above, identify one core competency within your organization. After identifying the core competency, identify three KPIs, and three KAs.

Sources of Innovation Opportunity

As you might imagine, there are many sources both internal and external to your organization that can generate potential idea and candidates for improving capabilities that already meet or exceed the organization's expectations or defined standards for performance. By no means a complete list, we provide the following sources for consideration (based on your organizational climate and innovation culture):

- Shareholders, stakeholders, and customers (internal and external to organization)
- Expos, consortiums, and industry trade shows
- Professional organizations, memberships, and training events
- Cross-industry relationships and knowledge shares (short-/long-term strategic, operational, and tactical agreements)

- Alliances, mergers, or acquisitions
- Genba walks, bug walks, or Kaizen events
- Professional and academic research, reports, and publications

EXERCISE 3.3: SOURCES OF INNOVATION OPPORTUNITY

Using the above sources as a starting point for identifying innovation opportunities, build your own list as it relates to the industry and organization where you work. What can be added to the list above? Prepare to discuss your findings in a group setting.

Section I. Operational Profile Tracking

This section captures the operational profile tracking number, title, team lead (key team members by department and roll; also include contract and third-party support [by company]), project start date, estimated completion date, sponsor information, audit agency, and date of recurring audit. Examples related to our aircraft communications scenario in this chapter would be the executive traveler and their support staff, aviators and their support staff, and home office or organizational support entities.

EXERCISE 3.4: IDENTIFYING OPERATIONAL PROFILE TRACKING INFORMATION

Using the definition and example above, identify the following for a project you are working within your organization: team lead (key team members by department and roll; also include contract and third-party support [by company]), project start date, estimated completion date, sponsor information, audit agency, and date of recurring audit. If all are applicable, simply enter an "N/A" for not applicable. Share the statement with your class members.

Section II. Operational Systems Requirements Statement

In this section, you are looking to capture the operational system requirements statement (also include KPP, key performance measurement [KPM], KPI, and CSF) for your innovation improvement opportunity. An example for our scenario in the chapter could be "Deliver a scalable, modular, interoperable, survivable, and integrated voice, video, and data communications system for commercial-derivative and specially equipped executive support aircraft to support all organizational mission areas of responsibility while they are traveling by air." First, second, and third tier (priority requirement) KPPs, KPIs, KPM, and CSFs are those required, and desirable elements and factors that improve the existing performance elements and factors meeting expectations.

EXERCISE 3.5: IDENTIFYING OPERATIONAL SYSTEMS REQUIREMENTS STATEMENT

Using the definition and example above, complete a system requirement statement for a project you are working. Consider accuracy, brevity, and clarity when building this statement. Share the statement with your class members.

Section III. Customer Profile

In Section III, the customer profile (customer types), your goal is to capture all individuals, groups, or business units operating or using the system or capability. You will identify the intended use by each user identified. In our example, potential individual users could be the chief executive officer, chief financial officer, department head of business unit, or C-suite official within the group or organization. For an example of the group, this could be the collective lead manager's of each group within the organization of perhaps special groups assigned in different departments that are organized in a matrix to achieve a certain goal or objective that require communications capability while traveling by air transport. An example for a business unit could be marketing, business development, or the sales business unit as they often find themselves traveling to meet with clients or attending trade shows which may require airborne communications capabilities and access to the organization's business enterprise (BE) communication systems.

EXERCISE 3.6: BUILDING THE CUSTOMER PROFILE

Using the definition and example above, complete a customer profile table for a project you are working within your organization. Share the results with your class members.

Section IV. User Probability Profile

In identifying an effective user profile for the set of user types identified in Section III, Customer Profile, the goal is to identify who will use the product, process, or service and the probabilities of them using the product, process, or service. An example for our airborne communication system scenario is provided in Table 3.1. For our airborne communications scenario, estimates on probability

Table 3.1   User Probability Profile

User or Customer Type	Probability of Use
Executive travelers	0.98
Executive support staff	0.90
Employees within the organization	0.45

of use of voice, video, and data communications can be typically be acquired from the organization's IT department or the contracted individual service provider servicing the organization. Targeted organizational surveys and interviews can also be used to assess probability estimates.

> ### EXERCISE 3.7: BUILDING THE USER PROBABILITY PROFILE
>
> Using the definition and example from Table 3.1 complete the user (customer) probability tables for a project you are working and share your work with class members.

Section V. System Mode Profile

Per Musa (1993), the system-mode profile defines the way the product, process, or service can operate. An example for our scenario in this chapter could be the manner in how the airborne communication system supporting voice, video, and data communications can operate in the autonomous or semiautonomous mode to ensure services are provided. Depending on your selected project and concentration (product, process, or service), your modes of operation may vary significantly.

> ### EXERCISE 3.8: IDENTIFYING THE SYSTEM MODE PROFILE
>
> Using the definition and example above, complete a system requirement statement for a project you are working. Consider accuracy, brevity, and clarity when building this statement. Share the statement with your class members.

Section VI. Functional Profile

In this section, the innovation opportunity lead and team will evaluate each system mode identified in Section V with a focus on functionality testing, efficacy, and purpose. There are a number of tools discussed beginning with the next chapter that will help define and build the innovational opportunity profile.

Section VII. Certification and Waiver Authority

In building the certification and waiver authority profile, the goal is to identify who will certify your functional profile findings and to what established standards and expectations. Further, identifying any potential waiver authorities for your current product, process, or service performance standards when expectations are not met. For example, in our scenario on the airborne communication system, this could manifest itself in system configuration requirements to meet storage capability and airworthiness testing, and proposed system configuration changes that do not meet standard practice for airborne platforms. For our scenario in this chapter, certification and waiver authorities could be the Federal Communication Committee, the Federal Aviation Authority, any recognized airworthiness certification agency, etc.

> **EXERCISE 3.9: BUILDING THE CUSTOMER PROFILE**
>
> Using the examples cited above, identify potential certification and waiver for standards and guidelines that apply to a project you are considering.

Section VIII. Operational Profile

In this section, simply identify any elements, architecture and engineering drawings, guiding requirement documents, and test plans associated with the innovation opportunity you are considering. Referring to our example in this chapter, examples could be:

- Current and proposed airborne system architecture drawings
- System operations, user and maintenance manuals
- Electrical and communications systems schematics, engineering changes or modification proposals that impact the structure or airworthiness of the aircraft platform
- Quantified SWaP requirements and associated drawings, etc.

> **EXERCISE 3.10: BUILDING THE OPERATIONAL PROFILE**
>
> Using the examples cited above, complete as much of the operational profile as possible on your own for a product, process, or service innovation opportunity you are currently working or a new proposal. After completing this exercise, did you find a need to revisit any prior sections on the form to add fidelity or change previously documented information? If so, what actions did you take and why?

Section IX. Budget and Financial Profile

As most innovation opportunities are measured in value added against cost or resources committed to achieve the innovation, the need for budget and financial estimates are significantly important. In our example scenario, the objective was to capture the proposed cost to perform the upgrade or modification, recurring costs to maintain proposed performance improvements—one-time cost or recurring (monthly, quarterly, semiannual, or annual basis); estimated cost of maintenance and sustainment (annual), percentage increase on current system or performance cost and the difference pursuing the proposed improvement. Remember, budgetary estimate profiles can be an ongoing affair, as they often require significant coordination with shareholders, stakeholders, and customers to ensure accuracy.

> ### EXERCISE 3.11: BUILDING THE BUDGET AND FINANCIAL PROFILE
>
> Using the examples above from our airborne communication system scenario, develop a budgetary and financial profile estimate for a project you are working on or may propose.

Section X. Coordination and Approval Authority

Achieving a smooth coordination and approval process through the right authorities can also be a lengthy process. As your IOP is routed through the organization (also include sections requiring shareholder, stakeholder, and customer buy-in or approval), questions for additional information might certainly arise at any level in the routing process.

> ### EXERCISE 3.12: ROUTING YOUR IOP FOR APPROVAL
>
> Consider a project or IOP you are working. Identify three primary leaders, decision makers, or business units within your organization you feel are seminal to the decision on your project or proposal. Why did you cite these individuals or business units? Explain their purpose in achieving an approved innovation opportunity.

Section XI. Appendices and Attachments

The final section on the IOP form is self-explanatory. This will be your essential reference list for all supporting documentation and correspondence that support your case for approval. This section should also identify any dissenting or alternative positions and comments received during the routing process. Further, alternative views should also be captured in the executive summary so when you reach this stage, we suggest you revisit your executive summary and ensure these comments are included and the owning individual or business unit identified in each statement. Conversely, you should also consider adding a list or comment capturing the key individual(s) and business units that are in full agreement with the profile as presented.

Functional Needs Assessment

In its basic sense, the functional needs assessment (FNA) is a process that helps identify capability gaps between existing and desired wants or requirements (needs). The focus is to capture the wants (perceived and expressed) and needs (requirements). An example of a common FNA is the strengths, weaknesses, opportunities, and threats (SWOT) analysis (Figures 3.5 and 3.6).

Figure 3.5 SWOT (strengths, weaknesses, opportunities, and threats) analysis.

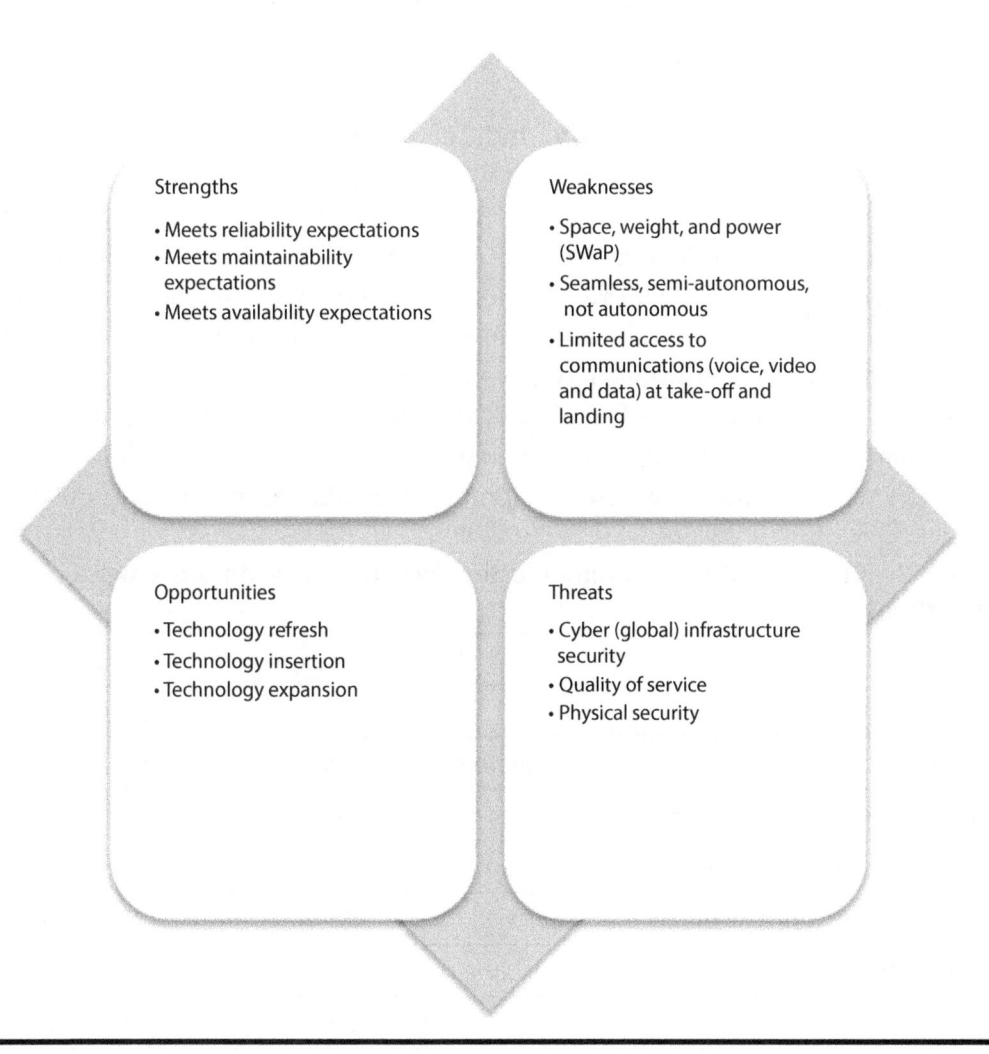

Figure 3.6 SWOT (strengths, weaknesses, opportunities, and threats) analysis—example.

Functional Solutions Analysis

The functional solutions analysis (FSA) is an important step in identifying potential innovation opportunities and helps construct the operational profile. The FSA will also help the innovation team identify if there are material and/or nonmaterial opportunities for improving the current products, services, or processes that meet or exceed expectations. Relative to our scenario, Tables 3.2 and 3.3 provide two examples of charts and tables that contribute to the overall operational profile.

The focus is on improving reliability, maintainability, and availability posture of the airborne communication systems supporting voice, video, and data communications for executive travelers on a small-tube aircraft platform.

> ### EXERCISE 3.13: FUNCTIONAL NEEDS ASSESSMENT
>
> Consider a project or IOP you are working. Use the SWOT analysis example in Figure 3.6 as an example and build your own basic SWOT a project you are working or might propose.

The FSA, for our example scenario, indicated that there were no nonmaterial approaches that would significantly improve or resolve these capability gaps. Most systems considered are tactical in nature and do not provide the quality of service required by the executive leaders to/from and aboard the aircraft. Additionally, although it was concluded that organizational changes will have little impact on reducing the identified communication gaps, restructuring roles and responsibilities for communications support may have administrative benefits.

In some cases, delays are a function of the aircraft's configuration and the lack of equipment needed to support a particular type of organizational-level communication service request. Where equipment is available, the average delay is

Table 3.2 Current Airborne Communication System Delays (Improvement Opportunity)

Types of Aircraft Communication Delays	Delay to Be Expected in Minutes			
	Voice		Data	
	Minimum	Maximum	Minimum	Maximum
Executive request processing	≥1	≤16	≥1	≤9[a]
Nonsecure equipment availability	≥0	<8	≥0	<5[a]
Secure equipment availability	≥0	<8[a]	≥0	<5[a]
Bandwidth availability	≥0	<5[a]	≥0	<4[a]
Total	≥1	<29[a]	≥1	<18[a]

[a] Equipment necessary to support this communication service is not available on all aircraft platforms.

Table 3.3 Operational Priorities Matrix

Position	Home Domain			VTC		Commercial	
	Voice	*Data*	*Networking*	*P2P*	*Broadcast*	*Internet*	*TV*
Executive	1	2	3	4	5	6	7
Executive staff support	2	1	3	NR	NR	4	5
Mid-level supervision	1	3	2	4	5	6	7
Employee	1	5	2	4	3	7	6

Note: 1 = Highest priority, 7 = Lowest priority, NR = Not rated by survey participants.

due, in part, to flight attendant, deck crew, and ground operator interventions currently required by the equipment and the equipment/system configuration. The operator (i.e., attendant/flight deck, ground) delay is compounded by current equipment limitations aboard aircraft platforms and the type of bandwidth supporting the communication process to/from the aircraft.

The conclusions derived from the analysis are that:

- Current equipment does not allow for sufficient bandwidth management to support executive or organizational-level communications adequately
- Some aircrafts do not have any executive-centric communications capability installed, forcing the travelers to rely on limited flight deck communications
- Executive communications should be automated as much as practical to reduce delays in communications
- Automation will improve the quantity and efficiency of airborne communications
- Current equipment will not support increases to traveler communications automation
- Some executive communication systems aboard the aircraft are also labor and knowledge intensive for travelers to operate (e.g., International Maritime Satellite [INMARSAT])

For our scenario, the potential approaches for adding value for improving service capabilities specific to voice, video, and data communications in this innovation opportunity are determined as material (i.e., technology refresh, insertion, or expansion) versus nonmaterial (i.e., policy, organizational, management or personnel, education, training, etc.). Example material approaches include:

- *Technology refresh*: Modifies the existing system to the greatest extent that is practical. Senior leader communication operations remain essentially the same
- *Technology insertion (minimal on aircraft communications equipment)*: Installs the most practical amount of equipment/systems compatible with ground equipment/systems, providing travelers with required communication

capabilities. The services provided and the quantity of services will be dependent upon the size of the aircraft (in our scenario, the small tube or 7–15 passenger size capabilities)

■ *Technology insertion (airborne switching)*: Replaces equipment with ground network compatible secure/nonsecure voice/data switches and bandwidth management devices. Ground-based networks are extended directly to the appropriate terminals aboard the aircraft. Communication operations, for the aircraft traveler, are partially integrated with their permanent ground office infrastructure

■ *Technology expansion (autonomous traveler)*: Replaces the existing system with a ground network compatible secure/nonsecure voice switches, secure/ nonsecure Internet protocol (IP) servers, commercial cable television equipment, and a bandwidth management device. Aircraft traveler communication operations are integrated with but dependent on their permanent ground office infrastructure but capable of distributed operation

---

EXERCISE 3.14: FUNCTIONAL SOLUTIONS ANALYSIS

Consider a project or IOP you are working. Use the SWOT analysis example in Figure 3.6 as an example and build your own basic SWOT a project you are working or might propose.

Innovation Team Project Charter

The innovation team project charter (ITPC) is a common project management tool that can help identify, synchronize, monitor, and report innovation team efforts (i.e., objectives, responsibilities, and outcomes). The ITPC is briefly introduced in this chapter as the tool can be employed in support of any type of innovation opportunity, we present throughout this handbook (see Figure 3.4).

In Chapter 7, we provide an example scenario from the manufacturing and production industry that helps further clarify the purpose of each section within the tool. Further, additional tools and exercises are provided that walk the reader through the major steps in developing their own charter for an innovation opportunity project within their organization.

Summary

In this chapter, we briefly introduced two tools that can be employed across the spectrum of innovation opportunities—the ITPC and the IOP tool. We described how the IOP instrument is used and how the information can best prepare an organization for an innovation project. To reiterate, simpler projects may not need to complete all sections so the reader must use their best judgment as not to bring unnecessary complications that can slow the innovation opportunity decision. When the process becomes complex and convoluted, tracking and monitoring its progress may be an important function that should not be overlooked. The IOP is both a guide and tool for undertaking an innovation project. Further, unlike the ITPC that monitors the process of implementation, the IOP is a management tool for assessment, decision making, and benefit evaluation. Finally, consider using the IOP tool as you begin to investigate the merits of the potential innovation. More, complex projects may require an extended version, available from the IPSinnovate.com website.

DISCUSSION QUESTIONS

1. Following the IOP flowchart (Figure 3.3), select an innovation opportunity project within your organization and pencil down some initial thought as the project relates to each step.
2. Name two (2) innovation opportunity tools from this chapter's discussion. Explain their use and discuss the three (3) key elements in each tool. How are the elements you chose important to the innovation opportunity performance acceleration process?

ASSIGNMENTS

1. Identify a process, product, or service that has the potential to become an innovation opportunity project. Using the information gathered during the exercises, complete the IOP executive summary section and submit your final product to another class member for review and feedback. Discuss the feedback in a short discussion and update your executive summary accordingly.

Reference

Musa, J.D. 1993. *Operational Profiles in Software Reliability Engineering*, IEEE Software Magazine, March 1993.

Chapter 4

New Products/Services with Existing Resources

Introduction

New products, services, and technology are the readily identifiable innovation opportunities to recognize. These innovation opportunities are unique, yet meet an unsatisfied need (requirement), and are usually one of a kind. This perception of new can vary by generation (age) group, job function (technical vs. nontechnical), and/or gender (Caraballo and McLaughlin, 2012). As previously mentioned, "new" types of innovation opportunities are subdivided into four categories:

- New discoveries and breakthroughs (may or may not use existing resources)
- New unique and original (uses existing resources)
- New application or uses
- New approaches

Because of our intended project focus, new discoveries and breakthroughs are outside the scope of this discussion but are manageable with repeated success using the N²OVATE™ methodology. Further, discoveries and breakthroughs often come from the organization's creative process but are extremely rare events compared to incremental innovations which most companies are most familiar with. They are also often discrete and unplanned events considered creative in nature. The goal and objective of this handbook, focuses on categories 2–4 above, as these are much more common, predictable, and within the span of control of the organization to act on with a better chance for innovation outcome success. Finally, the types of innovation opportunities we discuss are proactive and supported by an established innovation management strategy to develop and pursue innovation opportunities in an organized, empirical, and repeatable manner.

In Chapters 4 through 6, we provide established project plans (processes) for implementing aspects of new innovation opportunities, beginning with those innovation projects or opportunities that require more development time. The project scenarios throughout this handbook employ the N²OVATE™ process (since this methodology establishes high-level or first pass objectives, outcomes, requirements, limitations, and assumptions). If not then the innovation team will generate this information during the early phases of project implementation. We will use a simple example to lead the reader through each of the new types of innovation opportunity projects. There are new tools, embedded exercises in the text, and a more extensive set of flowcharts to assist the reader in applying the N²OVATE™ methodology though an innovation project of their choosing. We begin with a discussion of how these concepts have evolved over time.

Evolution

The materials published in 2013 (Caraballo and McLaughlin, 2012), represent a high (strategic) level approach to innovation. Figure 4.1 describes the initial seven-step process that continues to evolve, as it is applied across multiple industries and situations. The only different step was that of originality, which distinguished the three new types of innovations. Operating at strategic level did not prepare the organization to implement the innovation from concept to finished product, service, or technology. This is not to insinuate the ENOVALE™ process was lacking, but rather, to strengthen and enhance and evolve its capabilities to the system and culture levels. Consider Figure 4.1 as an enhancement of the ENOVALE project selection criteria (McLaughlin and Caraballo, 2013).

The evolution and significant modifications to the ENOVALE methodology for innovation opportunity projects begins with the realization that the seven-step process must adjust to the cadre of different innovation opportunity types. Words such as "validation" or "verify" (value building) are appropriate no matter what innovation opportunity type your organization is considering. The N²OVATE™ project implementation process begins after the project selection process is complete. We realize that many will want to skip this front-end process, so we begin

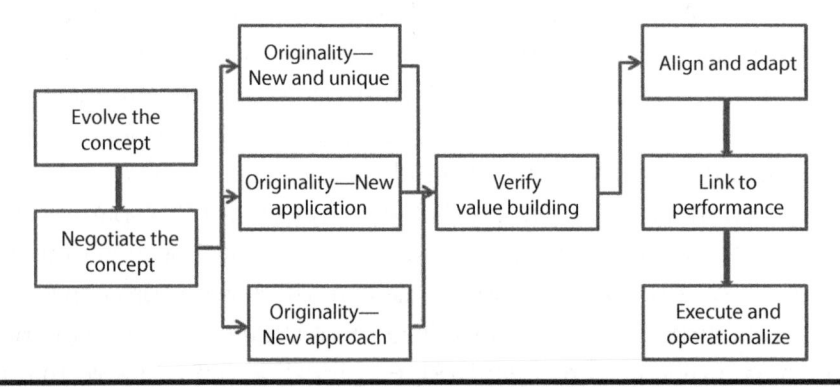

Figure 4.1   Original ENOVALE process for new innovation projects. (From McLaughlin, G. and Caraballo, E. 2013. *ENOVALE: How to Unlock Sustained Innovation Project Success.* Productivity Press, Boca Raton, FL. With permission.)

by capturing, classifying, and analyzing needs or requirements. Clearly identifying and defining the needs (or requirements) is so critical that it is the first letter of our new methodology (process). For each letter, there is corresponding concept with its own process. However, each new type of innovation opportunity has its own version of N^2OVATE^{TM}. Thus, each with a tailored emphasis which is more than a generic process as is featured in Figure 4.1. We feel the changes and additional tools we have developed specifically for the N^2OVATE^{TM} methodology will assist our clients and customers achieve repeated innovation outcome success, more frequently, and in a much shorter cycle time.

This chapter describes the process of creating a new type of innovation from existing materials and resources. This innovation type is common to many organizations, since it introduces a new product, service, or technology not previously seen as a unique offering to customers (users) at present. It also satisfies an unmet need (requirement). Of the three new types presented (Chapters 4 through 6), this is the most complex of the three. It is also the riskiest of all three types since there is a possibility the best plans might possibly lead to a dead end or a decision by the organizational leadership not to pursue or invest in a particular innovation opportunity at this moment.

> ### EXERCISE 4.1: N^2OVATE^{TM} METHODOLOGY
>
> What key principles (concepts) does N^2OVATE^{TM} adhere to in terms of innovation success? Why do the three middle initials (OVA) rarely change?

New and Unique Innovation

This is truly an original innovation, using existing resources, as it is something that no one has experienced previously either internally or externally to the organization. These types of innovation opportunities not only satisfy a need (requirement), but one that is outstanding and game changing. For example, manufacturers have been striving to invent a battery that can both hold a charger longer while delivering consistent performance without the need for exotic materials. This is an example of this particular type of innovation and that would be a boon to whoever devised such a battery. Figure 4.2 details the seven-step process transforming ENOVALE into $DRDOVATE^{TM}$ (a derivative of the N^2OVATE^{TM} process). Notice that the most comprehensive stage is the first stage. Each step further divides into a mini or subset of more definitive processes.

Develop the Concept

The first step requires an understanding of the main drivers (or inputs) for the innovation opportunity. This type of innovation requires a modification to the N^2OVATE^{TM}

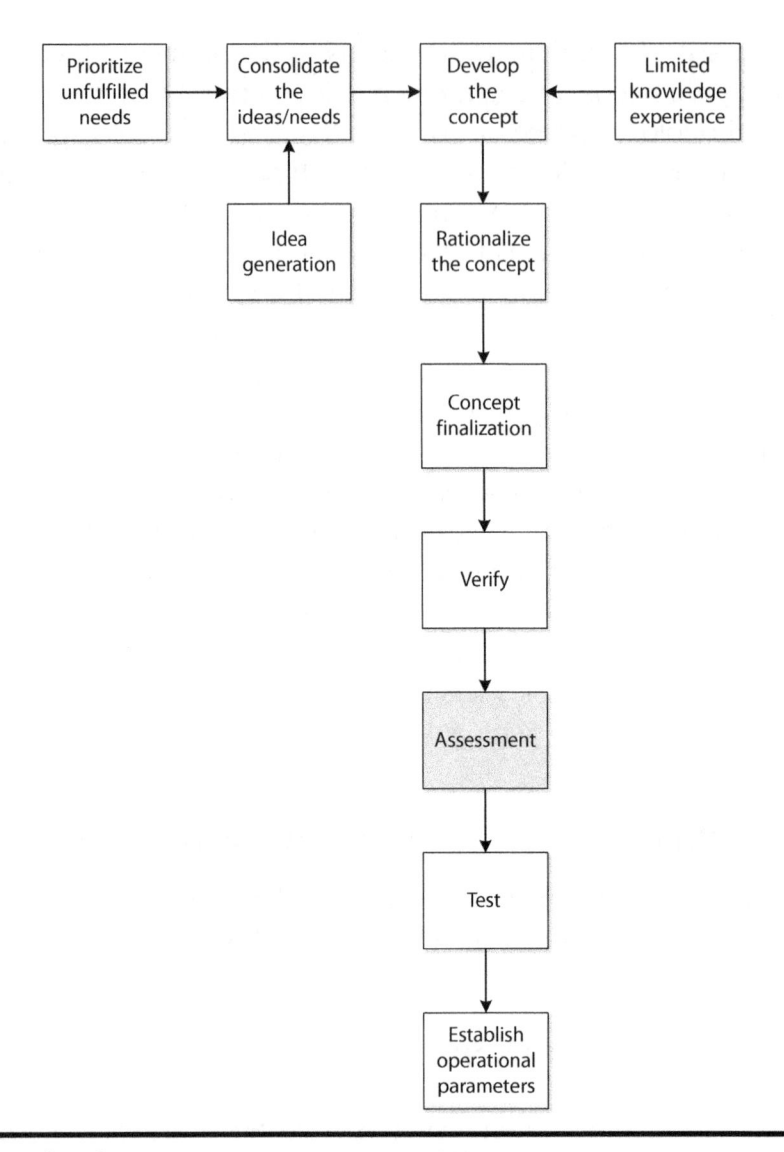

Figure 4.2 Updated process (ENOVALE to DRDOVATE).

process. After presenting the seven-step process, we introduce an innovation project implementation strategy designed specifically for this type of innovation opportunity. To date, it is the only innovation type requiring a modification of the N²OVATE™ process. Therefore, the process begins at the "unsatisfied needs" stage.

Unsatisfied needs for this stage may not be evident and therefore the idea/ need generation may provide an excellent opportunity to expose potential needs (requirements) not previously known or understood. Ideas, alone, will not provide sufficient information to make an innovation opportunity decision. Thus, developing "idea/needs" pairs are critical components at this particular stage. There are numerous idea-generating methods already available in the business community today. Choosing the best method is a topic left for others to address. We suggest the organization choose the method that best suits their current business operating style, protocol, and the needs (requirements) vetting process. That said, we feel the best approach is to gather as many idea/needs pairs as

Table 4.1 Idea/Needs Decision Tool

Needs (Requirements)	Technically Possible	Customer Appeal	Existing Resources	Cost Concerns	Benefits	Decision
No chemical reaction	Unknown	Medium	Uses some	Many	Sig	Major concerns
Safe (no risk of fire)	Yes	Very strong	Uses some	Many	Sig	Some concerns
Does not overheat	Yes	Strong	Uses few	Some	Many	Some concerns
Holds a charge for 24 h	Not at this time	Very strong	Uses some	Sig	Sig	Major concerns
Fast charge—15 min	Not at this time	Very strong	Uses many	Many	Sig	Minor concerns
Dimensions— 1″ × 1″ ″0.25″	Yes	Medium	Uses all	Few	Some	Go
Weight, <1 kg	Yes	Strong	Uses all	Few	Some	Go

possible. Consider the idea of a new battery that holds a charge for 24 hours; it is safe (no risk of fire) and chargeable in less than 15 minutes; and it is comparable in size to present batteries. Table 4.1 describes how to examine the idea/needs pairing and whether it holds promise as a future innovation project.

EXERCISE 4.2: IDEA/NEEDS IDENTIFICATION

Use the idea/needs decision matrix on a possible innovation (could be macro or micro in size), determine whether the innovation is worth further consideration.

At this stage, it is prudent to note, decisions made represent a "best guess" estimate, given the large number of unknowns. This is why knowledge and experience are useful contributors since these represent the human side of innovation.

In the early development stages, there is a great need for human intuition, based on organizational knowledge and experience. Many of the innovations we simply cannot live without today were born out of an idea based upon a gut feeling, an observation, a suggestion, or a complaint. Humans rely on their internal beliefs and values, developed through their knowledge and experiences. These internal beliefs, values, knowledge, and experiences then become the catalyst that can drive innovation at this stage. As a cautionary measure, temper the ideas with sound, objective reasoning, and intuition. If an idea meets an unsatisfied need (requirement), it is capable of being economically produced or created, fills a gap or adds significant benefit (value), and then it is an innovation opportunity candidate. Subsequently, do not let a single criteria or individual influence your innovation opportunity decision process.

Step 1: New and Unique

Developing the concept (Figure 4.3) begins with assembling the innovation team. Seek to identify those candidates who perceive new as the most identifiable (recognizable) type of innovation opportunity as team members. This is a key element in aligning the innovation team to the task at hand. Next, create a developmental plan for the concept. Primary elements of the developmental plan include (at a minimum):

1. First stage concept
2. Feasibility (sustainability, capability)
3. Second stage concept verification
4. Confirmation
5. Approval to move to next phase

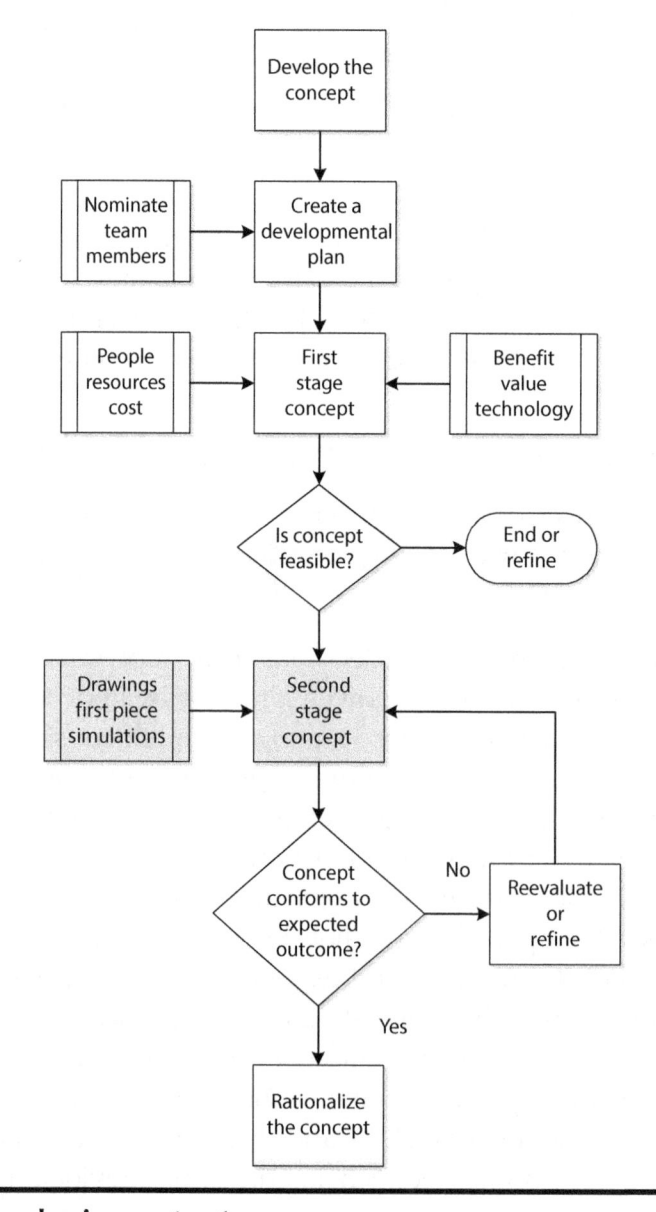

Figure 4.3   New and unique—step 1.

First Stage Concept

Begin with expanding the idea/needs decision matrix (Table 4.1), includes the following:

- People
- Resources
- Various fixed and variable costs
- Benefits (intangible)
- Value

Again, the purpose here is to evaluate using the knowledge and experience of the organization's work force (i.e., shareholders, stakeholders, and possibly the customer). Of course, any data collected and interpreted can also add to and enrich the first concept review. Think of the first concept as an initial decision point to pursue this potential innovation opportunity. For example, when planning a holiday (vacation), you consider the needs and wants of the family but in context with the amount you are willing to spend. It is truly a balancing act. Just to recap, no firm arrangements have been made and nothing yet reserved as this is a preliminary stage—no final decisions yet made. The first stage enables the team to become comfortable with the concept and examine its potential innovation opportunity from a very human perspective.

Second Stage (Feasibility)

Next, the innovation team must consider whether the idea/need is feasible from both a customer and an internal organizational perspective. There is always a risk that the feasibility could have a short life cycle and not be a viable candidate for innovation. In addition, it is easy to comprise compatibility if the organization, its resources, and funding are not well matched to the organization's strategic or operational goals and objectives. Finally, sustainability is a key for competitive advantage or lasting value. Three seminal questions to ascertain or estimate up front:

- How long will it take the innovation to payback on the initial investment?
- What is the estimated return on investment?
- When will competitors have a viable alternative?

Third Stage

Please note the time between these stages will vary depending on the innovation opportunity (product, service, or process). Depending upon the item's DNA (i.e., process, service, technology, etc.), the stage involves creating everything from a first piece (for a product) to a drawing (flowchart for a service, CAD/CAM output for a product, etc.), or simulation (for technology or service). The preliminary point is to bring the concept "to life," enabling the innovation team to use their knowledge, experience, and objective senses to experience, evaluate, and reach a decision on the item's viability (feasibility).

Fourth Stage

Fourth stage is the confirmation stage. This stage focuses on evaluating the item from a human perspective. This stage compares differences between expectations and what actually occurs (at least from a first piece/pass perspective). If the item meets or exceeds expectations, it is worthy of moving forward; if not, then the project ceases to exist or requires further modification.

Fifth Stage

Fifth stage is the decision stage. The innovation team and organizational leadership decide whether to pursue development, reevaluate, or end the project. The innovation opportunity decision occurs from the results of the first piece analysis (includes results from drawing, simulations, etc.). It should combine both empirical information with human intuition and experience with the goal of providing actionable information in a timely manner to the right level of decision making within the organization.

The completion of all five stages results in a rationalization of the innovation opportunity concept. If the decision makers agree, the concept passes from idea to reality. At times, this is the greatest hurdle, other times the most disappointing is when a good idea fails to produce sufficient benefit. Never discard the idea/ needs pairs, as there are numerous incidences of where timing and packaging become an issue. The impossible can become the possible when timing and packaging remain fluid and responsive.

EXERCISE 4.3: DEVELOP THE CONCEPT—STEP 1

Consider one of the five stages discussed in this section. Prepare a detailed plan to address this stage. Include recommendations and suggestions to check for validation.

Rationalize the Concept

Figure 4.3 describes the process steps in this second phase. This step brings the concept from proposal to reality. This step involves evaluation, negotiation, and finally a reality test. Concepts that cannot pass these criteria must either disappear or reappear in a different form. After accepting a concept (e.g., a drawing), there are often many modifications and adjustments made that produce a number of alternatives to consider.

Step 2: New and Unique

The COCO tool, described in, *ENOVALE: How to Unlock Sustained Innovation Project Success* (McLaughlin and Caraballo, 2013), is an excellent method to evaluate some closely aligned alternatives (Figure 4.4). Should conflict arise in reaching a decision, apply the COCO (Table 4.2) dimensions for comparison purposes:

- "C"—Clarity: Full and complete understanding of how the concept will apply to perceived need
- "O"—Originality: Originality of concept; ability to stand apart and fend off competitors
- "C"—Customer demand: Meeting/exceeding the needs of the customer/user over the entire life cycle
- "O"—Objectives met: Meets profit and financial objectives

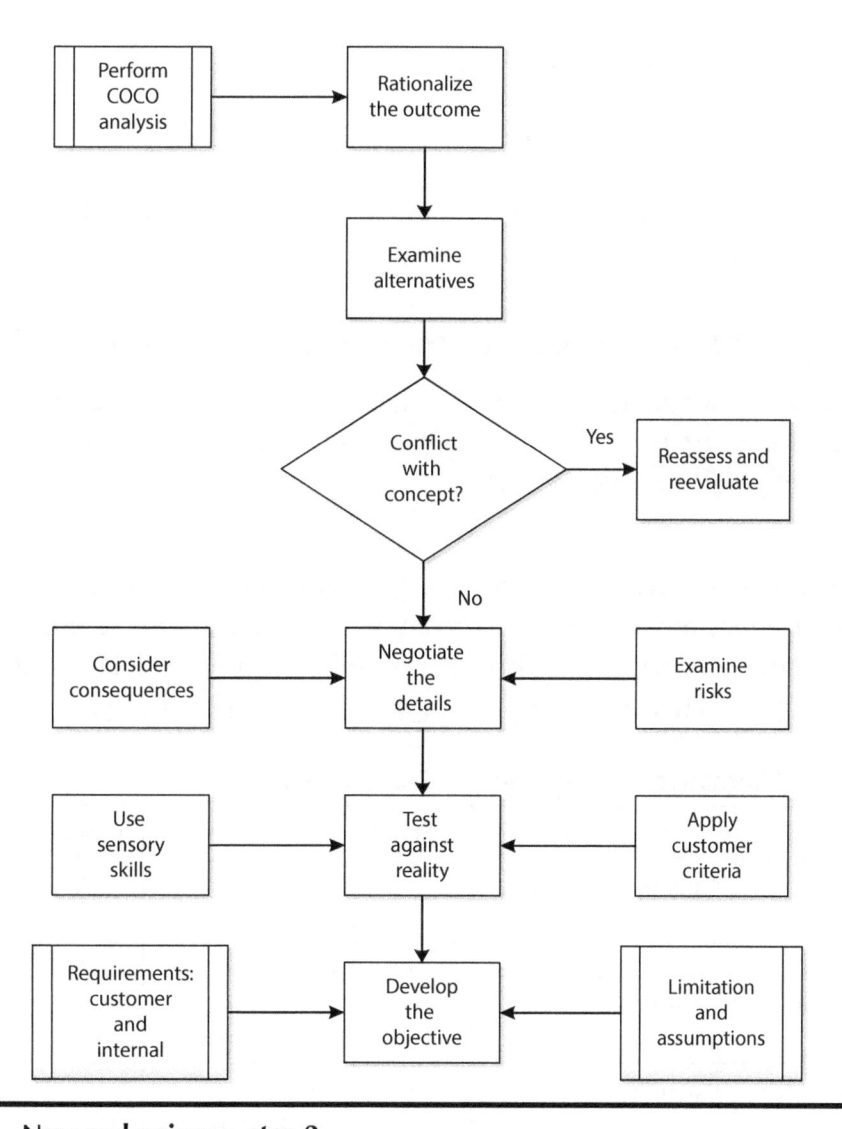

Figure 4.4   New and unique—step 2.

Table 4.2   COCO evaluation Scale

COCO Criteria	SMART Chip	Zero Inventory	Supplier Control
Clarity	Neutral	Neutral	Favorable
Originality	Favorable	Favorable	Neutral
Customer demand	Favorable	Neutral	Neutral
Objectives met	Favorable	Neutral	Favorable

To update this technique, the authors added a scale to assist in differentiating the concepts. The scale measures expected performance based on each of the four dimensions. For example, if clarity was better than expected, then the concept feasibility would increase. Conversely, if customer demand is less than expected, the project is reevaluated or halted.

There are three simple situations: better, as expected, or less than expected performance.

Favorable: Better than expected
Neutral: As expected
Unfavorable: Less than expected

Further, a team or management differentiates the instrument with additional criteria and a scale that reflects more detail or refinement.

> **EXERCISE 4.4: COCO EVALUATION SCALE**
>
> Complete a COCO analysis for any concept that you are considering or have considered in the past. Does this thought process help you to realize the differences between concepts? Explain.

Next, examine alternatives (Table 4.3). Alternatives consist of any enhancement, modification, replacement, or substitute for an existing concept. However, any alternatives carry with it a consequence and require a simultaneous rating.

We use the hypothetical battery example described previously.

Table 4.3   Alternative Consequence Evaluation Tool

Alternative	Benefit	B Score	Consequence	C Score	Ratio
Graphene battery	New technology	5	Added cost Availability	1	5.0
Extended capacitor	Uses existing resources	4	Heat Needs fan Replacement	5	0.80
Solar battery	Existing technology	1	Slow High price	2	0.50

Alternative Consequence Evaluation Tool

Scoring

Benefit score (1–5): 1—No benefit; 2—Minimal benefit; 3—Some benefit to the
outcome; 4—Benefits the outcome; 5—Maximum benefit to the outcome
    Consequence score (1–5): 1—No consequence to the outcome; 2—Minimal
consequences affect the outcome; 3—Some consequences affect the outcome;
4—Consequences affect the outcome; 5—Severe consequences affect the outcome
    Ratio = Benefit score (B score)/Consequence score (C score)

Interpretation

If the ratio >1, the potential innovation is viable, a ratio <1 requires reconsidera-
tion. Only choice 1 is viable at this stage.
    After calculating the ratio, reevaluate and reassess for completeness. Carefully
assess all concepts, alternatives, and consequences looking for conflicts and
discrepancies, especially at this stage. Negotiate with all concerned parties. The
timeline can vary from very short to very long for this stage. It depends upon
what is at stake for acceptance (negotiable items, consequences, and/or risk).
Better to solve problems now than during the operational (production) phase.

EXERCISE 4.5: ALTERNATIVE CONSEQUENCE EVALUATION TOOL

Consider some alternatives (characteristics, functions, appearances, outcomes,
etc.) to an existing innovation and their associated consequences. Be sure that
performance is clearly identified (measured) and apply the risk that the consequence will affect that performance.

Finally, test for reality. The seven functions involved in any test for reality (for
a new concept) are:

1. Management buy-in (leadership)
2. Finance and accounting (money people)
3. Customers and stakeholders (who we must satisfy)
4. Operations (who must make this work)
5. Human resources (training, new hires)
6. Sourcing (resources)
7. Competitive assessment (who we must outperform)

Do not try to attempt your reality check too early in the process. Ideas can
fool even the most pragmatic people. Use your intuition and experiences to
evaluate the product, service, or process.
    Formalize the objective(s) (include customer internal and external require-
ments, assumptions, and limitations)—all key elements of N²OVATE™. Recall that

for this particular innovation type, we needed to revise the original process to account for the design and development of a new concept.

Step 3: Finalize the Design

Finalizing the design (Figure 4.5) is the objective of step 3. This is the time to add features, highlight certain attributes, evaluate risk, and consider the more esoteric features. The key factor is the value of the resulting product, service, or technology while maintaining or increasing customer appeal. Finally, the product is prototyped, displayed, and fully accepted. The time to prototype may be long or short, depending upon the item complexity. A prototype is a working or functioning item. The prototype is a true necessity for innovative products.

For those businesses with a detailed process, then consider the finalization with the use of a storyboard or simulation. Storyboarding a potential service innovation may provide an opportunity to see the service in action before scheduling an actual attempt to test the service. In any case, a simulation provides an overall evaluation, acting like a prototype. Please note the innovation must perform in a realistic setting.

This step requires a great deal of customization dependent upon the item. The reality check for a service innovation is far different from a reality check for a new technology. Use the simple flowchart (Figure 4.6) to help decide the additional steps needed. Some reality checks are simple; others can be very

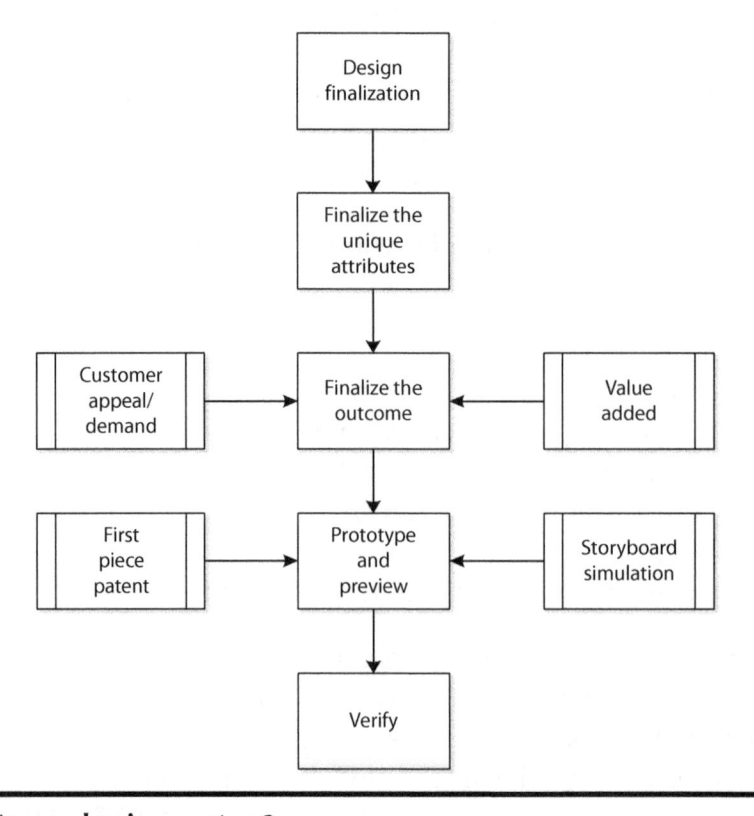

Figure 4.5   New and unique—step 3.

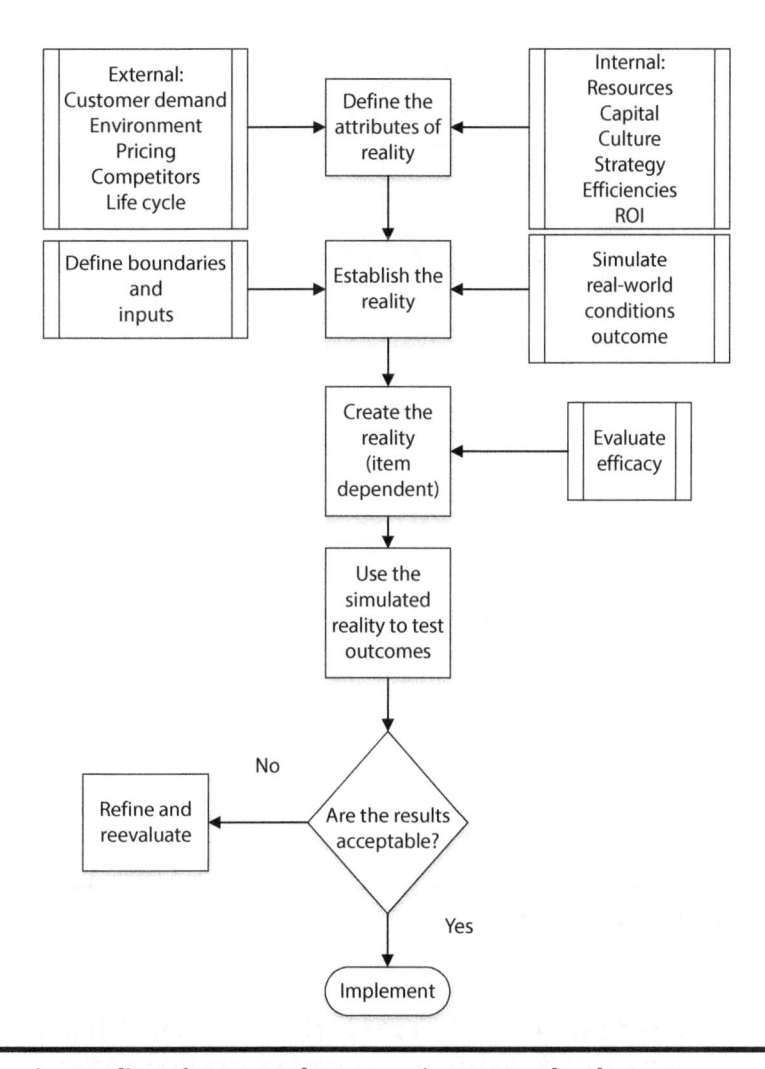

Figure 4.6   Testing reality of new products, services, or technology.

complex. Begin with understanding and modeling the environment in which the innovation exists. Focus on the issues related to the innovation (such a purchasing demand/behaviors, available alternatives/substitutes, performance, overall value, unsatisfied needs, etc.). Create a simulation (via computer is only one type of tool) closest to reality (for the key issues) and observe the outcomes (results). Push the boundaries to determine the capability of the item. Obviously, the better the simulation, the better the information and value added.

Step 4: Verify

The next step is verification (validation) and very similar to the validation phase of the N²OVATE™ or ENOVALE processes (Figure 4.7). During this phase, the team/management verifies outcome performance. Validating performance requires an understanding of risk as influencer and possible game changer. Verification (used interchangeably with validation) must lead to a sustainable outcome. Chapters 5 and 6 provide a number of techniques for validation.

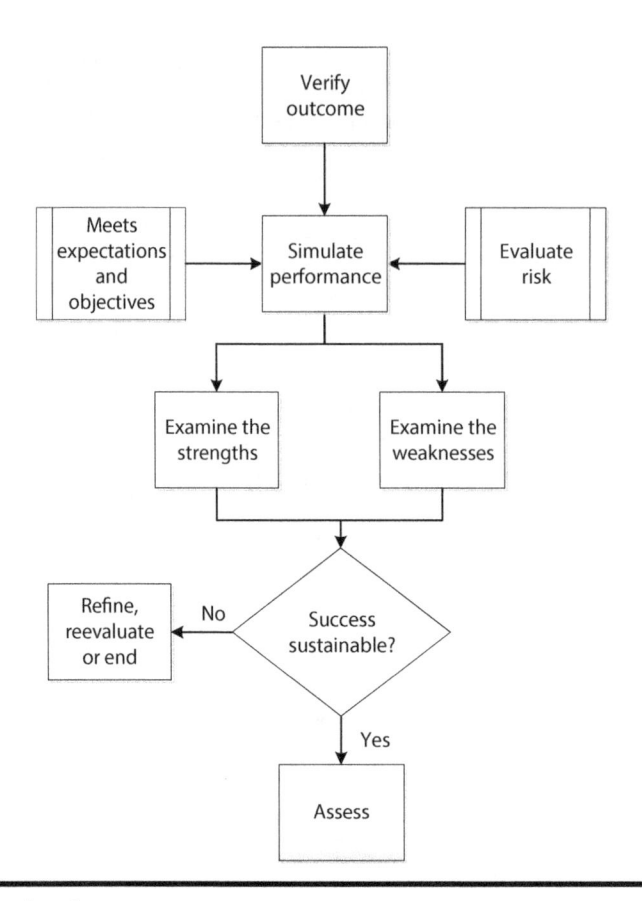

Figure 4.7 New and unique—step 4.

> ### EXERCISE 4.6: TESTING REALITY OF NEW PRODUCTS, SERVICES, OR TECHNOLOGY
>
> Devise a plan for testing a prospective innovative item using the "reality" approach. How do you define reality; how do you test this reality; how do you choose the conditions that define efficacy?

Step 5: Assess

Step 5 (Figure 4.8) again evaluates the outcomes, using the results from previous steps (such as the reality and value checks). After the assessment stage, adaptation and alignment begin. Managers and employees must begin adapting to this new item and aligning themselves to the new reality.

> ### EXERCISE 4.7: DEVISE A PLAN FOR SIMULATING PERFORMANCE FROM A NEW TYPE OF INNOVATION
>
> Explain the environment in which the innovation will need to exist; identify potential strengths and weaknesses. Comment on sustainability.

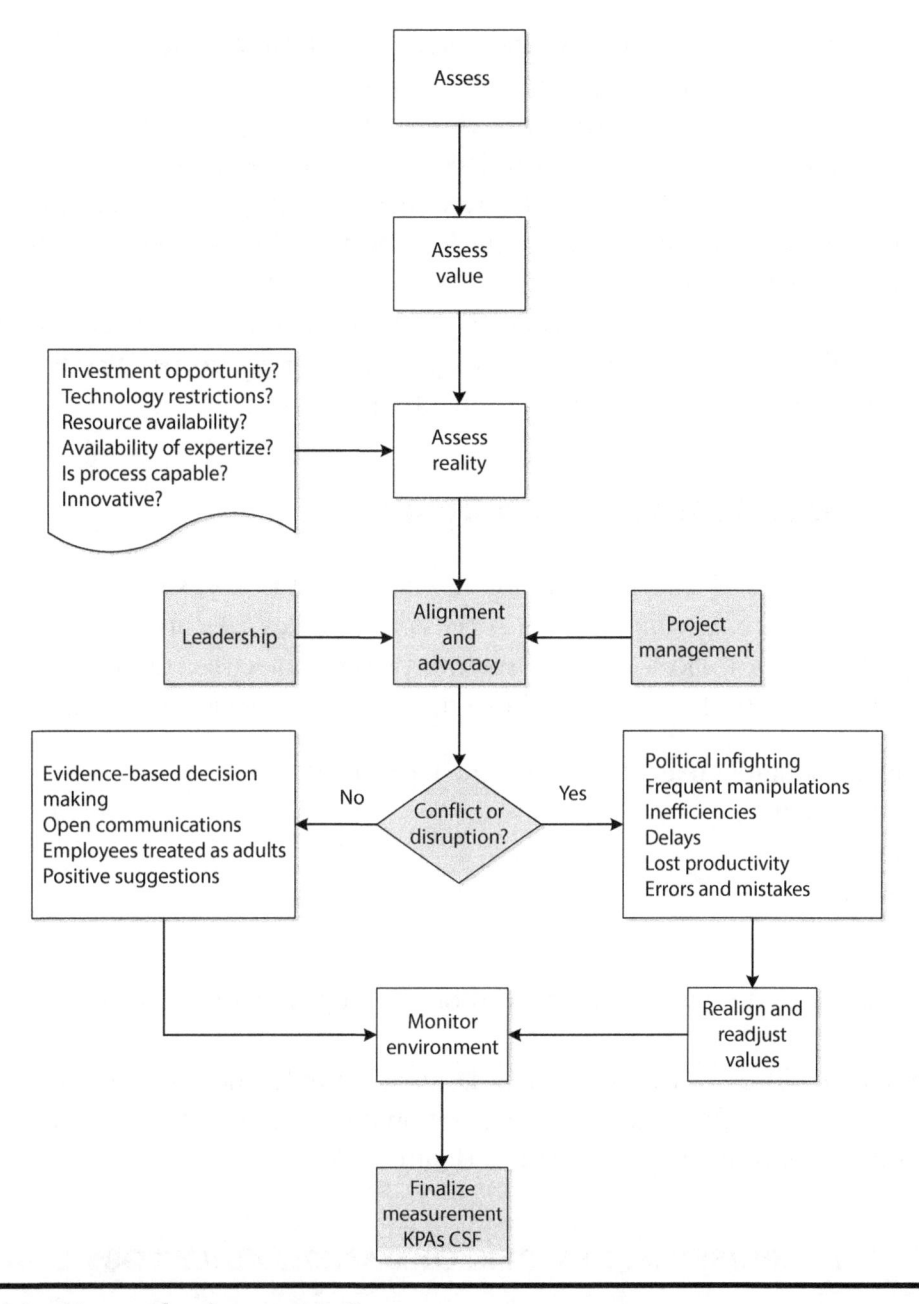

Figure 4.8 New and unique—step 5.

Changes that affect performance goals and expectations require strong leadership and management support. Adaptation is a business-wide activity to communicate and align the business to the new standards of performance. The proposed modifications may require input from other sources and therefore a process of consensus may follow. After initiating the adaptation process, further changes should be simpler to implement. Adaptation is then both an internal and external process (McLaughlin and Richins, 2014, p. 101).

Alignment concerns the team, customers (users), and the organization. Consensus must exist before recognition of any improvement. Alignment is complete, when the innovation is understood as meeting a new set of standards, a new level of success. Communication is fundamental to informing users that the item now consistently meets their expectations. Alignment is "people oriented" and it is successful when achieving consensus (McLaughlin and Richins, 2014, p. 105)

Although hardly ever planned, conflicts do arise and may result in a significant amount of productivity. Conflicts are either conceptual or human driven, dealing with tangible or intangible items. The bottom line—expects conflict and creates a process to detail this process. The goal should be to: (1) identify the process, (2) recognize its implications, (3) deal with conflicts, and (4) remedy the situation. Realignment is a strategy that organizations need to practice to keep employees, managers, and customers fully aligned.

Step 6: Test and Measure Performance

The major objective of this step (Figure 4.9) is to identify measurement points related to performance, which define success. These key performance metrics or key performance indicators (KPI) align to project objectives (McLaughlin and Richins, 2014, p. 136). Five traits of these measures are (Todorvic et al., 2013):

1. Fully accountable (easy to understand), practical
2. Timely, accurate
3. Actionable
4. Relevant
5. Predictive

Creating these metrics is a stepwise process. Step 6 involves both creation and validation.

Step 6 also addresses the number of items to sample and the integration of metrics into existing financial and organizational reporting databases. Locate further information in Chapters 3 and 4 (Figure 4.10).

> **EXERCISE 4.8: KEY PERFORMANCE INDICATORS**
>
> Devise a plan for selecting and testing metrics (KPIs) that evaluate performance characteristics of the new type of innovation. Explain how the process sustains a quality (performance) level over time.

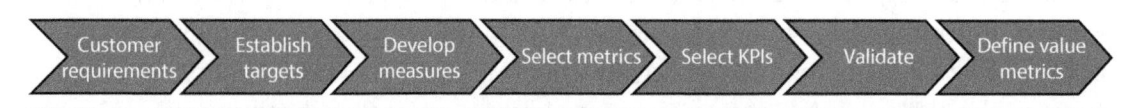

Figure 4.9 Key performance indicator (KPI) creation process. (Adapted from M. Todorvic, Z. Mitrovic, and D. Bjelica. 2013. *Journal for Theory and Practice Management*, 18(68), 41–48.)

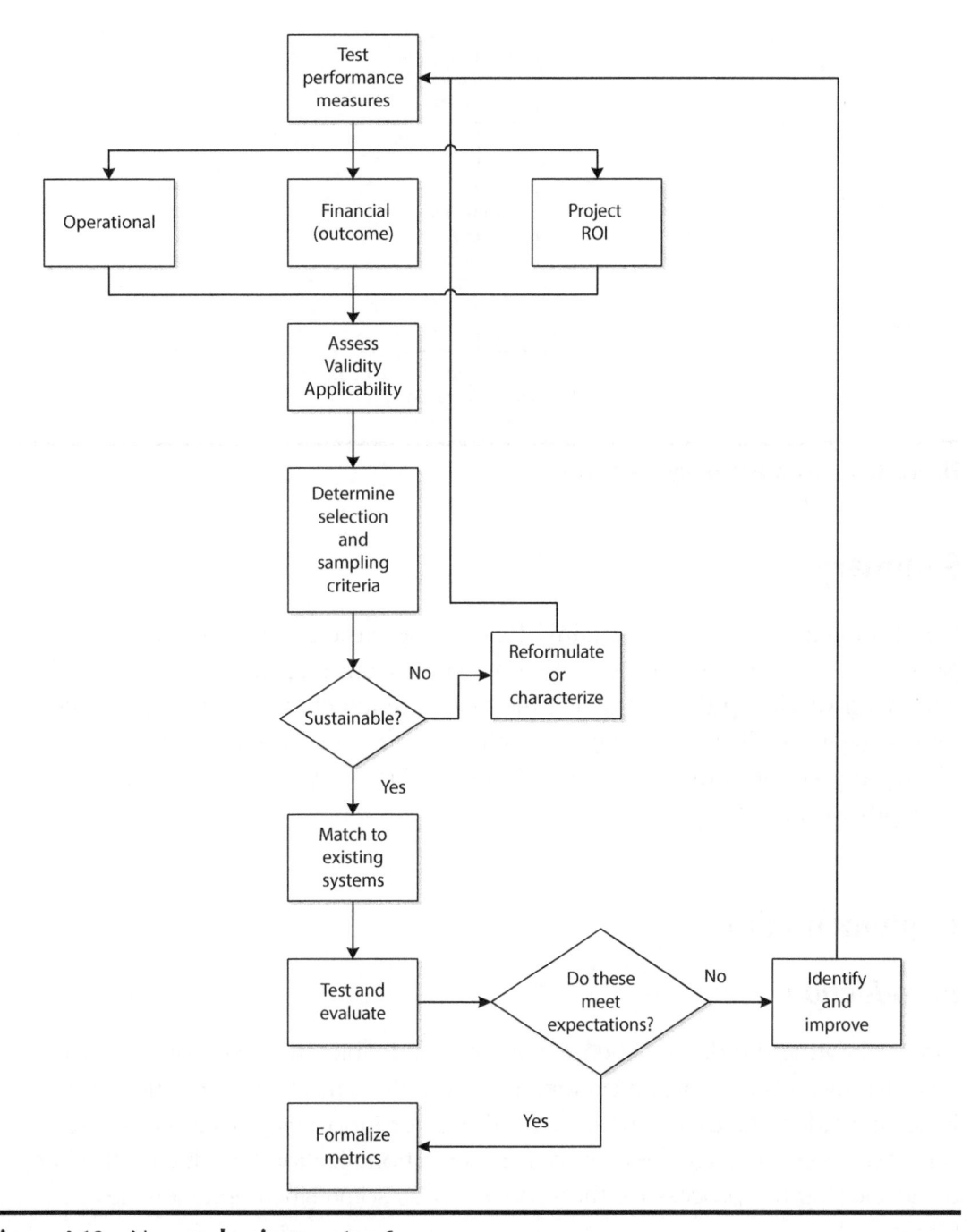

Figure 4.10   New and unique—step 6.

Step 7: Operationalize

To complete the last step (Figure 4.11; establish operational parameters), the team finalizes operational parameters on metrics and places these near the top in terms of importance and meaning to the project. Finally, the project can be moved to commercialization.

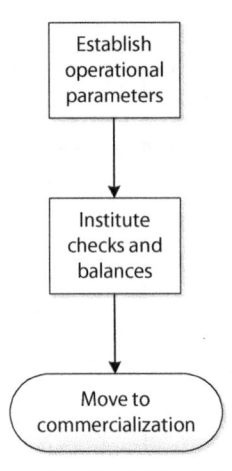

Figure 4.11   New and unique—step 7.

Summary

Developing a new concept certainly follows the basic tenants' of the N²OVATE™ process. The process begins with meeting unsatisfied needs and ends with validating the outcome. Due to its unique characteristics, the concept moves from initialization through a testing phase, and then a rationalization phase, to prove its worthiness. Its unique qualities may require some additional in-depth work.

Implementation

Introduction

After validating the design (the results are sustainable), the decision to move forward involves commercialization. This commercialization is identical to the implementation stages, discussed with the other innovation outcomes, based on innovation type. The next process is operationalization (producing the item or developing the process for the service), or as some say, implementation (Figure 4.12).

The process begins with preparing the infrastructure and ends with a monitoring (evaluation) step. A description of each step in the process (and its subprocess flowchart) follows this introduction. This project implementation process aligns well with the N²OVATE™ derivatives in other chapters. Due to the extensive up-front assessments, evaluations (validations), metrics, and critical success factor development associated with the concept, the authors present a substitute implementation process. We recommend this substitute implementation process, as an alternative, given that the N²OVATE™ derivative selection process preceded implementation. Many of the phases are identical to a N²OVATE™ process for implementation. Phase 1 (Figure 4.13) begins the process.

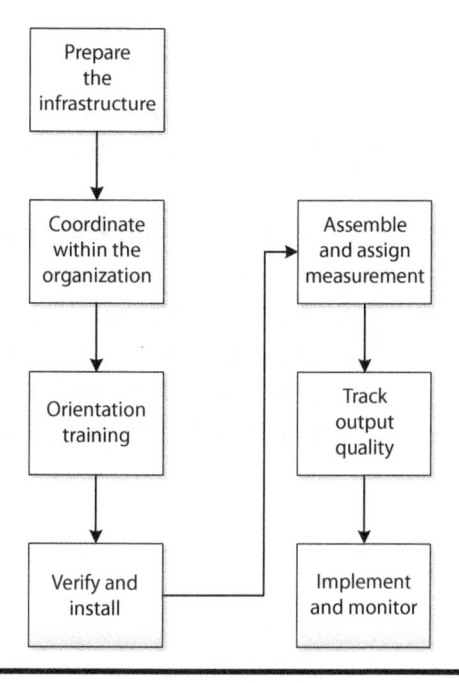

Figure 4.12   Implementation process: New and unique.

Step 1: Prepare the Infrastructure

When rolling out a new product, service or technology, access the resources, personnel, financial, and operations supporting the rollout to ensure a smooth implementation. These organizations (and agencies) must coordinate the rollout with these infrastructure items. One key element of the infrastructure is the coordination of human resources and precisely, the implementation team. For a new type of innovation project, the implementation team is generally different from the innovation or design team. Therefore, the team should consist of those who best understand new combined with experienced project management personnel. This team's objective is commercialization. Management needs to assemble the best team to meet the goal of commercialization in the shortest timeframe.

With any new project, personnel need to be oriented to the objective and receive training in whatever tools seem appropriate. Do not forget that this training must include skills on communications, negotiations, conflict management, and alignment. Orientation can begin as resources come together.

Finally formalize the specific and detailed plans required to execute the project. This step is second nature to any good project manager. The key point is to prepare the infrastructure before launching the project.

> ### EXERCISE 4.9: PREPARE THE INFRASTRUCTURE
>
> Describe any additional detail needed prior to project launch? Which element of the infrastructure will change most (least) and why?

Step 2: Coordination

Once the preparations for the resources and within the organization are completed, the next phase is coordination with leadership, employees, customers, and stakeholders (Figure 4.13).

Coordination begins with leadership (management) and culminates in the preparation of a master implementation (execution) plan. The master implementation plan integrates the four elements (resources, personnel, financial, and operations) into a cohesive working architecture. With the team in-place and management coordinating, the assignment of responsibilities can begin. This is a critical step, with experiencing and knowledge playing a key role.

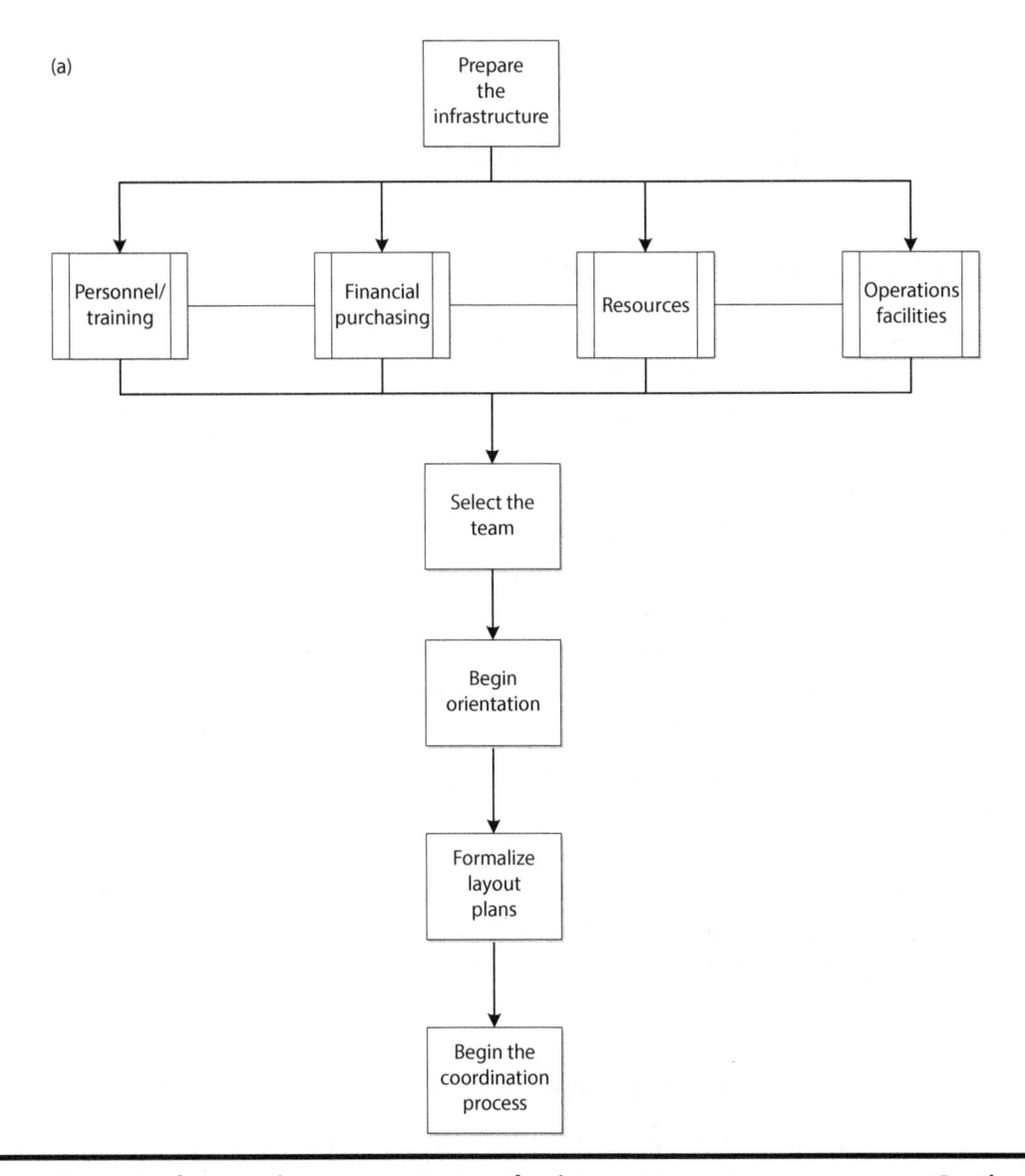

Figure 4.13   Implementation process: New and unique—(a) step 1.   (*Continued*)

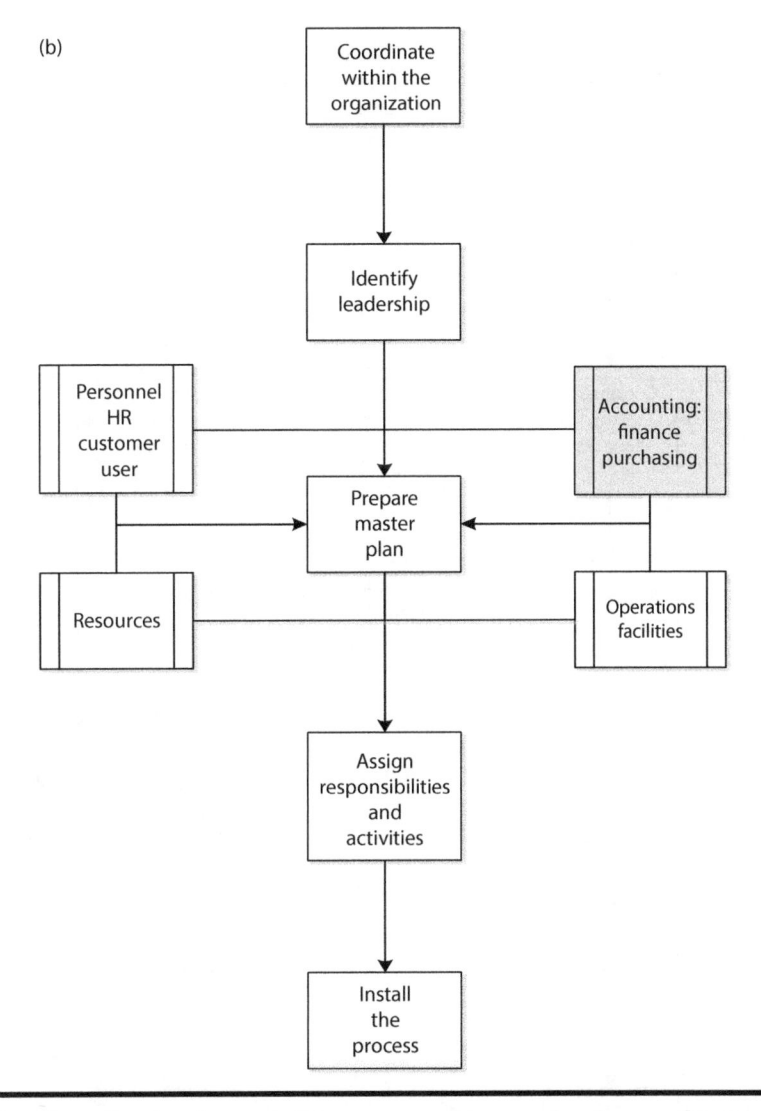

(b)

Figure 4.13 (*Continued*) Implementation process: New and unique—(b) step 2.

Step 3: Install the Process

For the sake of simplicity, we subdivide product and services processes in Figure 4.14. These processes will differ in both the effort needed to make each successful and the time elapsed to complete. Both require certain resources, a master execution plan and coordination between the team, management, and leadership. We will discuss these separately, although realize that many innovative items have both a product and service component.

For products (technology), construction of the process, handling, and storage facilities will most likely require a major investment or expenditure. Construction may take several weeks to several months depending upon various concerns. This could easily entail real estate, refurbishment, or relocation. Next, establish a set of checks and balances with the master execution plan, schedule, and actual workload; and attempt to determine "pain" points and/or slippages in

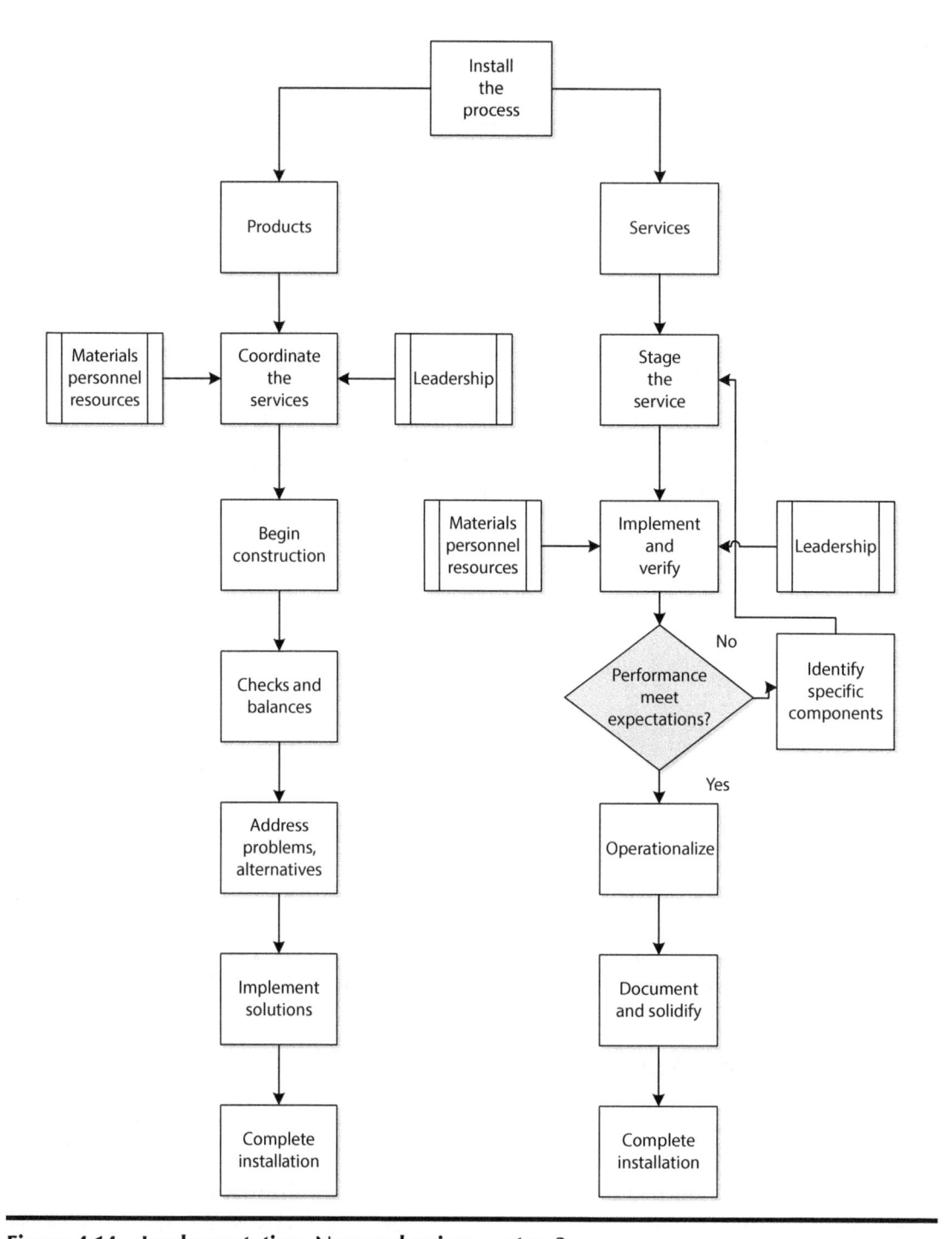

Figure 4.14 Implementation: New and unique—step 3.

performance. Address these problems with alternative courses of action, being aware of the emphasis on consequences derived from using an alternative. Use this process to implement solutions, on as continual basis, until the installation is complete.

For services, stage the service by coordinating resources, personnel, and management (leadership).

Two key questions to consider during this phase are:

1. Does the service meet expectations?
2. Is performance an issue?

Ensure the service can return repeated outcomes. If expectations satisfy the consumer, operationalize the process, document performance, and control features resulting in the installation of the process.

> ### EXERCISE 4.10: CHOOSE EITHER A PRODUCT OR SERVICE APPLICATION
>
> Compare an installation you are familiar with to the process described in (Figure 4.14) were there any differences, which would affect successful and why?

Step 4: Process Orientation and Training

Step 4 now orients (trains) those responsible for operating the process, selling the product, service or technology (Figure 4.15). The complexity of the item will

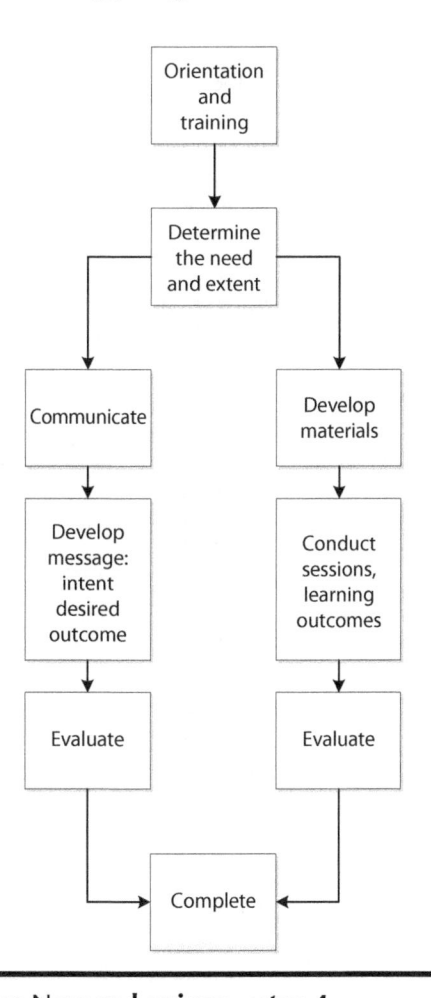

Figure 4.15   Implementation: New and unique—step 4.

guide the amount, intensity, and diversity of training required or made available. Note: Training and orientation are central (key) to any new type of innovation. Finally, evaluate the training for efficiency and effectiveness.

> **EXERCISE 4.11: COMMUNICATIONS PLAN**
>
> Describe a communication plan that will be proactive versus reactive, relaying a clear, cogent message to all involved with the project.

Step 5: Assess and Assignment

Step 5 involves assessment of the project and the assignment of key measurement to evaluate performance. Figure 4.16 details this fifth step. As with the

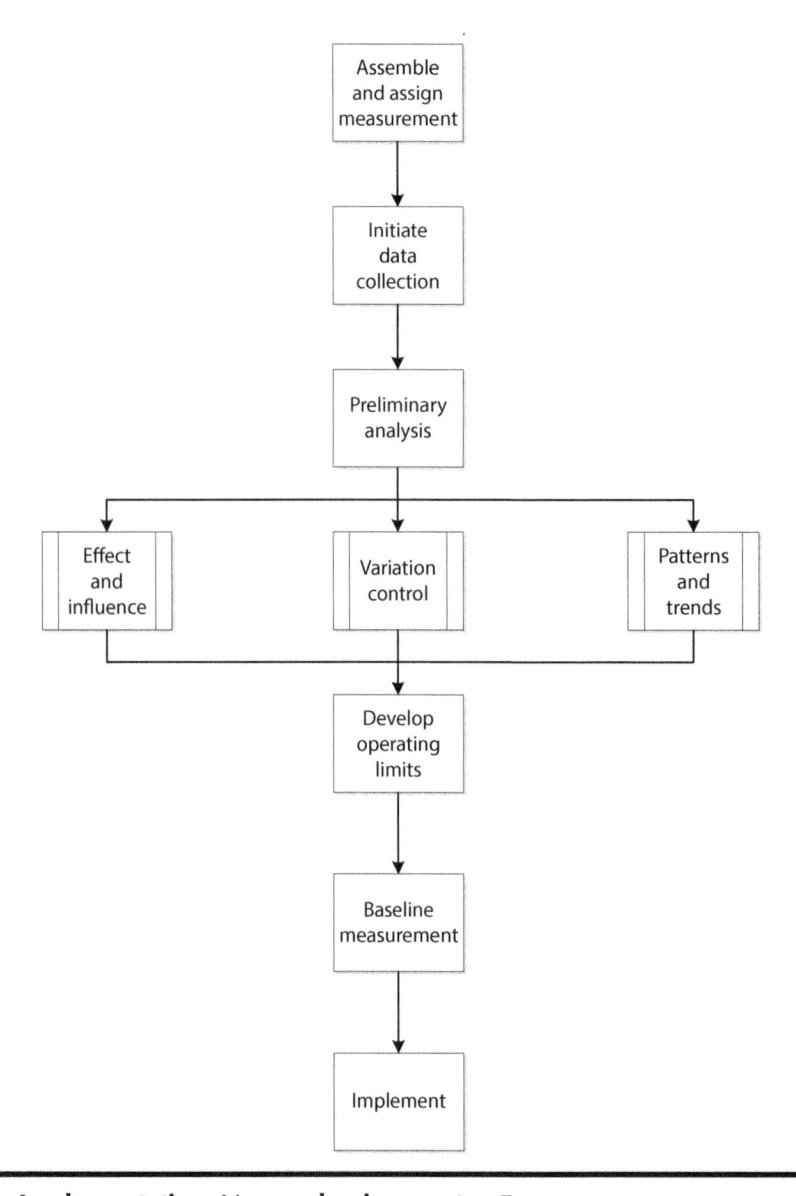

Figure 4.16 Implementation: New and unique—step 5.

N²OVATE™-derived processes, data collection and analysis are the keys. With the process functional (which we referred to as installation), this step reevaluates all measures (especially those related to the KPIs identified for performance) through data collection and data analysis. The results of the preliminary analyzes, examines key product attributes (KPAs) such as consistency (variation), effect and influence, control and predictability; all necessary features for sustained performance.

From these calculations come control points, baseline measurements, and a profile to maintain sustained performance. A number detailed description of these measures is provided in Chapters 5 and 6. This step is a combination of the verify and analyze phases in N²OVATE™ strategy. As a reminder, there is no single approach to accomplishing innovation. Certainly, phases and steps overlap

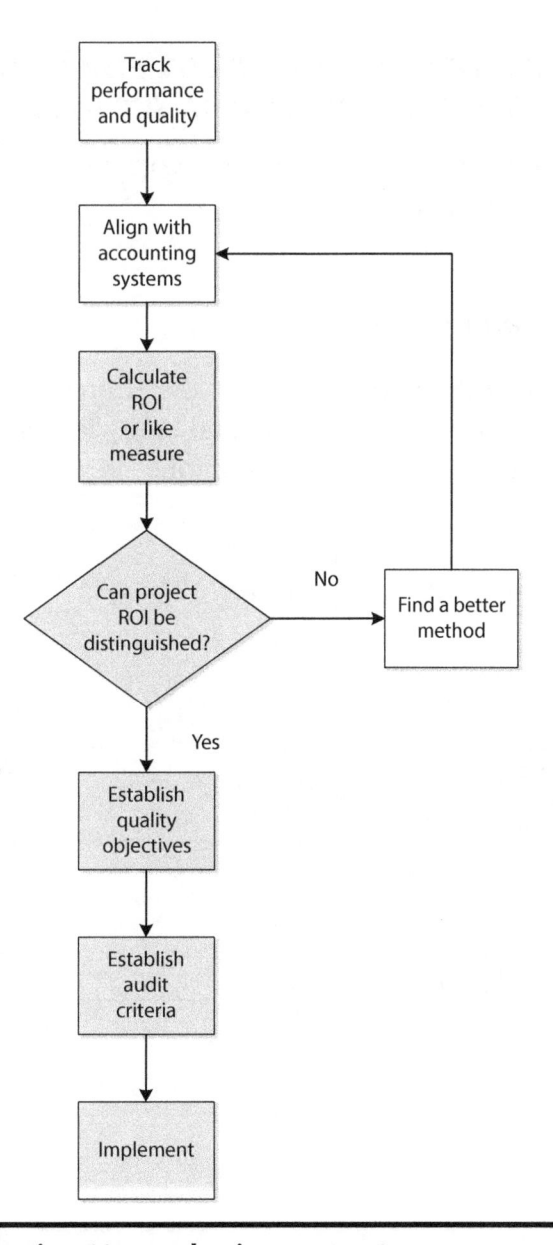

Figure 4.17   Implementation: New and unique—step 6.

as needed, yet the N²OVATE™ strategy (in its many forms) is definitely the foundational building block of project selection and implementation.

Step 6: Tracking Performance

Step 6 is reminiscent of the "T" step in the N²OVATE™ strategy. Figure 4.17 recounts the need to align project tracking with existing systems (accounting, purchasing, quality, etc.) to maintain sustained success. Only the reader can determine if these systems align and provide real-time performance information. Failure to align these systems will doom a project, or worse, become strikingly evident that critical items affecting performance were overlooked and may surface after full implementation. More information is available in Chapters 5 and 6.

> ### EXERCISE 4.12: DEVISE A STRATEGY FOR IMPLEMENTING A TRACKING PERFORMANCE SYSTEM
>
> What key elements would you control? What concerns you most about maintaining consistent performance?

Step 7: Implement and Control

Again, this step (Figure 4.18) is reminiscent of the "E"-related process used in our methodology. The project is now complete and ready for handoff to operations. After meeting all the criteria, the "new and unique" item is now a viable product,

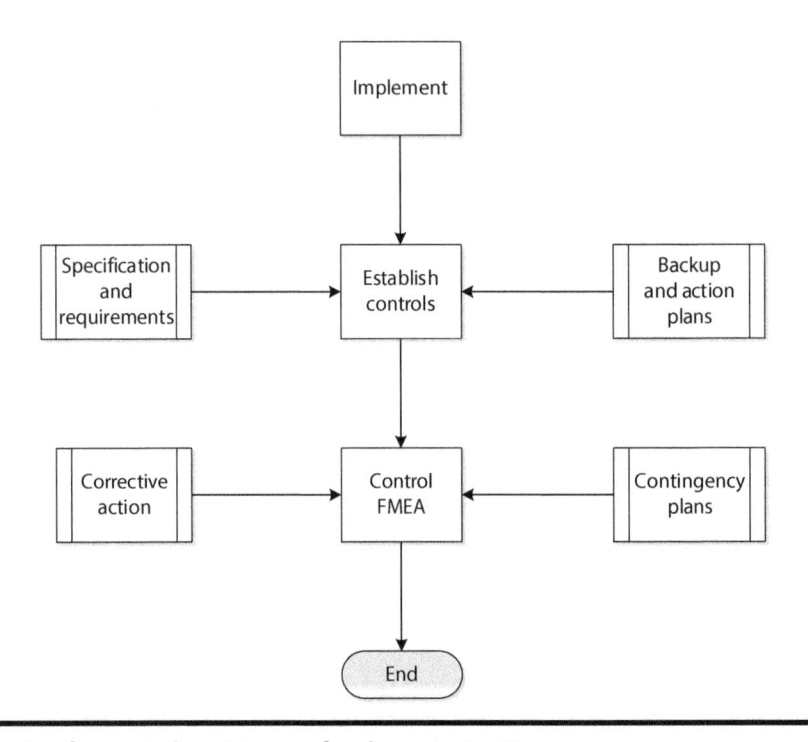

Figure 4.18   Implementation: New and unique—step 7.

service, or technology. This step monitors the performance and establishes effective controls. Further, audit the process on a recurring basis to maintain consistent performance.

Summary

This chapter provided a method for developing a new and unique concept and then provided a second process for implementation. These types of innovations are time consuming given the need to understand and rationalize the concept. Forcing the concept early to meet a set of realistic expectations highlights the need for innovation. Bypassing steps may save time but will lead to problems down line that may prove to be unsolvable. It is best to develop the concept with the objective of sustained performance rather than hope this is an end goal. Flexibility is required in any innovation project and we have provided that flexibility throughout the process.

DISCUSSION QUESTIONS

1. Why is innovation that has never existed before, so difficult to implement?
2. What advice would you provide to management if your department were attempting a new and unique innovation?
3. Given the high percentage of failure, what would you suggest to do prior to a decision to move forward on a project?

ASSIGNMENTS

1. Take a recent innovation and determine if it would be viable using the alternative consequence evaluation tool.
2. Consider an idea that you have (or have seen recently)—what are the steps needed to turn this idea into reality?
3. Discuss the importance of intangibles in making a final decision.

References

Caraballo, E. and McLaughlin, G. 2012. Perceptions of innovation: A multi-dimensional construct. *Journal of Business & Economics Research*, 10(10), 1–16.

McLaughlin, G. and Caraballo, E. 2013. *ENOVALE: How to Unlock Sustained Innovation Project Success.* Productivity Press, Boca Raton, FL.

McLaughlin, G. and Richins, S. 2014. *Unlocking Sustained Innovation Success in Healthcare.* Productivity Press, Boca Raton, FL.

Todorvic, M., Mitrovic, Z., and Bjelica, D. L. 2013. Measuring project-success in project-oriented organizations, *Journal for Theory and Practice Management,* 18(68), 41–48. doi: 10.7595/mangament.fon.2013.0019.

Chapter 5

"New" Applications

Introduction

It is difficult for most businesses and organizations to produce unique products or services on a regular basis. Limiting factors, such as the time, cost, and resources required to pursue innovation opportunities tend to eliminate these types of projects. Businesses (organizations) must search for an alternative that enables these entities to offer new products and services to maintain a technological or competitive advantage. To accomplish this goal many organizational initiative strategic alliances with another company or organization, intellectual property agreements or acquisitions of companies capable of filling the capability and knowledge gaps to pursue the innovation opportunity. Others innovate by introducing a new product or service application without the expense of design and development costs, time requirements, and additional resources. This "new" offering utilizes existing resources and applies a unique approach not yet available in the marketplace.

In this chapter, we offer an innovation strategy for introducing a new product or service without the design and development costs, time requirements, and additional resources. What is proposed is a process that develops new uses or applications for an existing product or service. Consider the following example:

> Proctor and Gamble's (P&G) product "Tide" has gone through many iterations, adjusting to its ever-changing consumer set of needs, appealing to new customers, rebranding itself for improved sales. Yet, detergent is just that, detergent. Its main use is to help in the process of cleaning the fabrics and refreshing the laundry. It has accomplished this purpose since its inception. However, to their credit, P&G has continued to offer new uses and applications of the product (bleach added, softeners added, dies removed, color changes, different scents, etc.). Each new iteration identifies a distinctive application. The product continues to be "New and Improved." In fact, some of the

iterations are in fact innovative, since they met unsatisfied consumer needs. This is an example of what we mean by a new application, or if you prefer a new use.

Some Innovations (new applications) or "firsts" for Tide (Kattan, 2012):

1. The first detergent to advertise on TV
2. The first to provide new samples inside washing machines
3. The first US detergent formulated with enzymes to thoroughly breakdown protein and carbohydrate stains
4. The first without perfumes
5. The first detergent with color-safe bleach
6. The first compact powder and liquid detergent

These "innovations" enabled Tide to maintain brand recognition and leadership in a highly competitive marketplace. Identifying these attributes (except for # 1) as "New and Improved" provided the manufacturer the opportunity to identify the innovations, meet a presently unsatisfied need, and excite the consumer to make a purchase decision.

This chapter will highlight the process of implementing such a project. The assumptions is that the proposed product or services has been selected using the N^2OVATE^{TM} or $ENOVALE^{TM}$ processes. Otherwise, the information generated by these selection processes (requirements, objectives, limitations, and assumptions) forms the basis upon which to build the final stage of implementation.

The purpose of Chapter 5 is to introduce the process for implementing projects with new applications or uses. New uses for products is one means to keep ahead of the competition, one means to achieve technical superiority. The difficulty arises when your competition may be pursuing a similar strategy. New uses can provide improved profit margins and a longer product life cycle. Of course, once introduced, the competition may pursue a similar strategy. Therefore, the strategy provided develops a means of evaluating products and services in their present states and determine, what, if any, opportunity exists.

For new uses (applications), we suggest a seven-step implementation process (Figure 5.1)

The process highlights the need for scanning the existing business and competitive environment. The need (consumer demand) must be strong enough to drive the application throughout its development and implementation stages. This new type of innovation requires quality input including customer, user, and information that express the need or desire for such an item, even if it does not yet exist. Those organizations with access to market research or to customer analytics (informatics) will have an advantage. Without such information, businesses would require customer feedback that expands beyond what most businesses regularly collect and analyze. A functioning analytics department may be the best source of information to determine the efficacy of a new application or use.

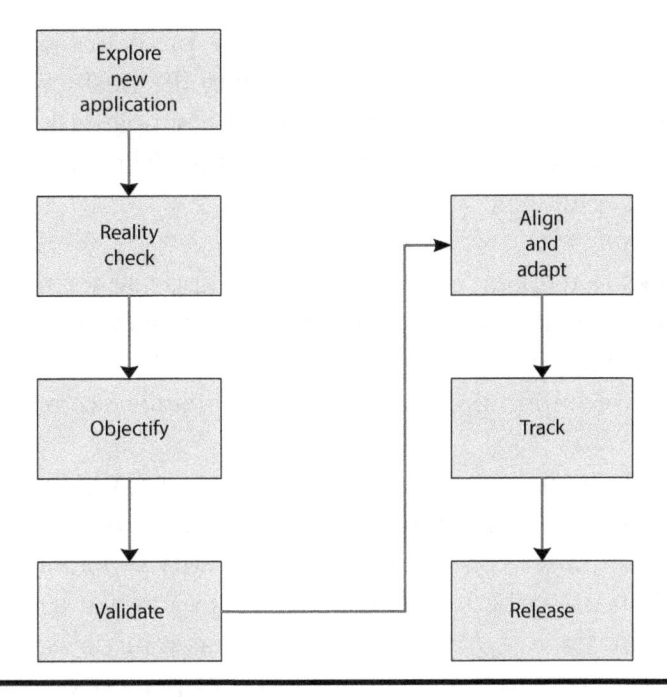

Figure 5.1   New application—7-step process.

The first stage of the process is dedicated to exploring new applications or uses for those products and/or services where management feels there is an opportunity for customers or users to identify the new application as innovative. The process to explore new applications involves both customer feedback, extracted from market research and analytics, as well as information that salespeople intuitively extract from the customer. Companies without large market research organizations or departments may use focus groups to gather information on ideas, wants, and desires that customers may express. However, the customer may not directly tell the business what they want but it may come from an integration of ideas, needs, and desires that customers express they had access to for their own personal use. Here, the project selection (and assessment and diagnostics) are critical to understanding where an organization stands in terms of acceptance of a culture that supports innovation. It is our opinion, that businesses and organizations should institute a program of regular feedback from sales and marketing personnel to discuss pertinent issues. That is, any customer-facing employee must understand their responsibility in collecting information on what the customer wants, needs, or desires. Interestingly, our experience has also shown us that organizations without this candid customer feedback often miss or lose value from the innovation opportunity most new applications can provide those that do.

Second step is one based upon a firm understanding of the reality of the organization, its capability and access to resources. Customers may want or desire something and it is impossible for the organization to deliver given its previous record of accomplishment in developing new use replications for products or services. The reality check is a critical part of this "new" type of innovation as it stands to evaluate potential benefit (value) of the product before commencing implementation.

The third step is the opportunity to develop the project objective. The objective addresses aspects of benefit and profitability to the business or organization given this new potential innovation. This is never a simple task given the complexity of trying to predict so many unknown factors. The success of such a new use or application depends upon factors such as:

1. The customer's perception of innovation and appetite for new application
2. The obvious needs that are satisfied with the product or service
3. Cost and overall appeal
4. Profitability, based upon present costs and availability of resources

The fourth step is similar to previous iterations of ENOVALE™ and N²OVATE™ in that it validates or verifies that the product or service can deliver what is promised. This chapter will discuss how to validate or verify a potential new application or use based on prescribed set of criteria. This particular step is consistent throughout the entire process. Validation is critical as it involves an evaluation that looks at innovation opportunities at various levels of perception and depth.

The fifth step provides guidance on implementation, that is, the rollout of the product or service. The key is to align employees, management, customers, and suppliers to the new application as it offered to the customer. Again, given the strong emphasis of perception, the innovation must satisfy a need and deliver superior performance while remaining competitive with other similar products. The sixth step involves tracking the product requiring both a strong internal and external set of measures or metrics (i.e., key performance indicators, key performance measurements, and critical success factors). It is not only critical to demonstrate the benefit and value of the innovation opportunity, the innovation must also demonstrate how it meets a need which remains unsatisfied up to the point in time in which this product or service becomes available. The final step is rollout to the customer or user.

Step 1: Exploring the New Application

As mentioned previously, this step involves a great deal of gathering and analyzing information to determine the true need for the application. Figure 5.2 provides a systematic process flow chart for this step. Exploring new applications requires an evaluation of four inputs:

1. Customer and user needs (What existing needs remain unsatisfied?)
2. Existing workarounds or substitutions with a positive impact (may become a future standard)
3. Competitive information—(Are outcomes easily achieved?)
4. Acceptance criteria—in the form of performance standards in which to judge performance

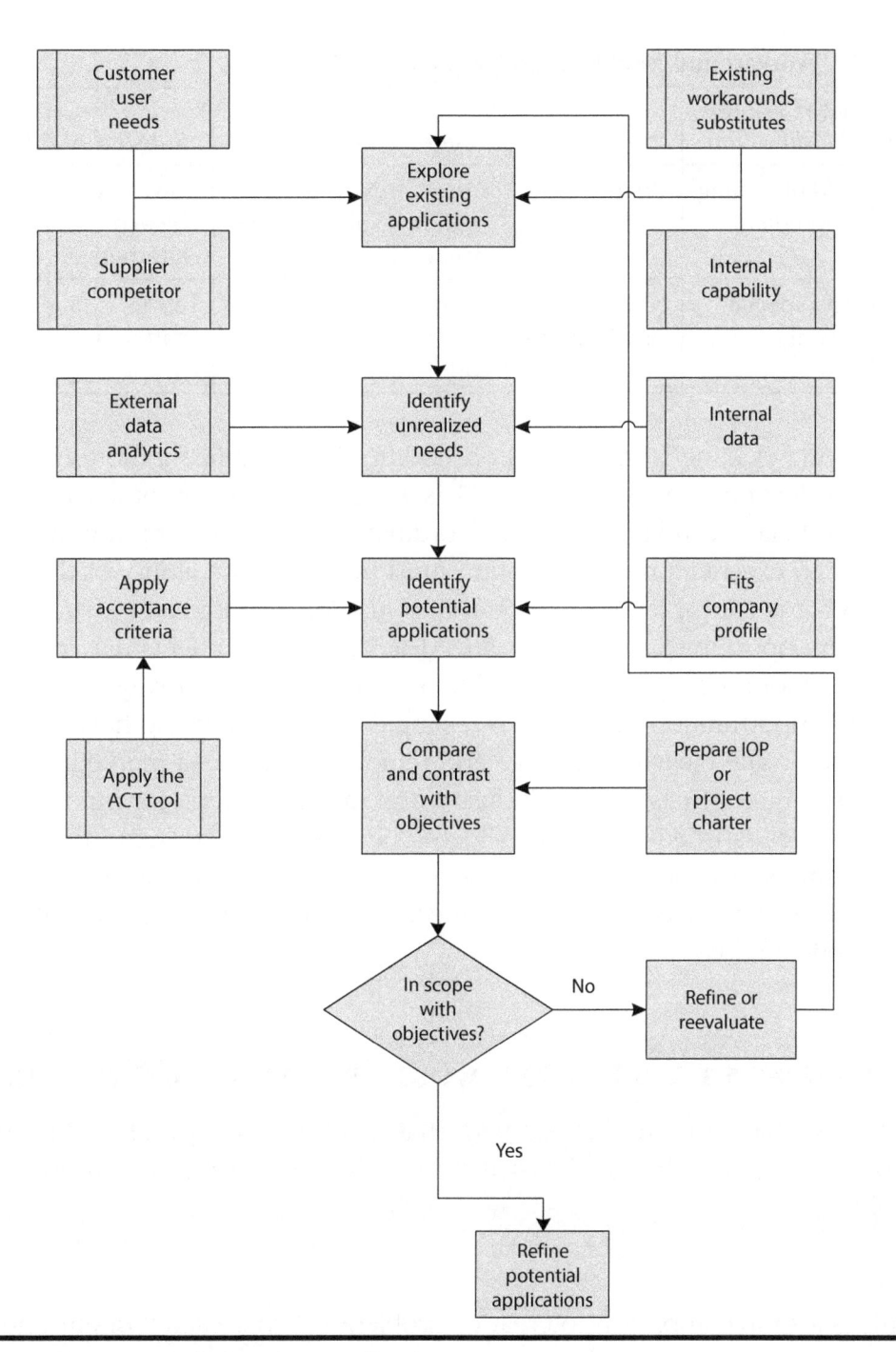

Figure 5.2   Step 1—exploring new applications.

Existing and outstanding customer (user) needs should be frequently reviewed as opportunities for new applications. We advise applying three criteria to determine if an outstanding need is worth considering. The three criteria are viability, sustainability, and capability. For a more detailed description, refer to *A Guide to Innovation Processes and Systems for Government* (McLaughlin and Kennedy, 2015).

Table 5.1   Workaround/Modification Simple Example

Item	Workaround/ Modification	Benefit	Failure	Value to Organization	Substitute	Decision
Tide	Add bleaching ingredient	Brighter colors	Faster fading wear	New applications	Powered bleach alternative	GO
Tide	Add special scents	New applications	Scent wears off	Product extension	Fabric softeners	GO

Reviewing existing workarounds or modifications requires a more comprehensive evaluation. Obviously, Table 5.1 is a simplified version of a set of criteria used to evaluate existing plans. This coordinates with critical input number 2), as the ability to execute a new application must be within the ability of the organization. What is critical is that a workaround may be a candidate for this type of innovation opportunity. Often, specialized or customized effects may provide an opportunity for a new application. Table 5.1 can be used as a way of initiating ideas and opportunities. This table is a simple example showing how Tide introduced a color-safe bleach alternative and removed scents as a marketing tool—both of which are "firsts" for the industry and met the criteria for innovation. Both examples satisfied a need, provided a benefit and were "new" to the industry. Consumers saw the value and purchased the product. Was it innovative from a discovery perspective, no, but it did meet the criteria for being innovative—and greatly benefitted P&G.

EXERCISE 5.1: EVALUATING WORKAROUNDS/SUBSTITUTIONS

Pick a product you are familiar with that has undergone at least one "new" application or use change. Construct a simple table, using the template from Table 5.1.

This is a simple approach to creative problem solving. Each workaround/modification project is a potential micro innovation project.

The third and fourth elements focus on internal systems (capability) and culture that support two-way communications with customers and suppliers. Communications must be proactive (eliciting suggestions, improvements, and recommendations. It is normal and essential to listen to all stakeholder communications. However, there is a need for a system capable of collecting/analyzing customer and supplier communications. One way to capture that information is with a focus group.

A focus group is a small set of individuals (could be suppliers or customers) led by discussion by a skilled moderator (Guidelines for Conducting a Focus

Group). The purpose is to obtain unbiased information relating to a topic or concern. Structured questions provide the mechanism for collecting the data. Discussion is free flowing. The moderator, who presents 12 or fewer questions, leads the group. Questions should be (Guidelines for Conducting a Focus Group, 2005):

1. Short and to the point
2. Focused on one dimension each
3. Unambiguously worded
4. Open-ended or sentence completion types
5. Nonthreatening
6. Worded in a way that they cannot be answered with a simple "yes" or "no" answer

A recorder carefully captures both the vocal and nonvocal responses. Analysis involves both verbal and nonverbal cues that help describe completeness and truthfulness. The purpose is to gather information that other competitors fail to capture, monitor, or react to when conditions change.

EXERCISE 5.2: FOCUS GROUP

Design a set of questions for a focus group. Use the theme of new applications or uses. Be prepared to defend the "theme" that the questions are built upon.

Using focus groups and interviews, as well as supplier perceptual surveys, often provides the information needed to assess the present state of affairs and determine unmet needs (what is possible).

Gather competitive information. Analyze the data; look for distinctive patterns and trends. Identify opportunities, research competitor activities and build competitive profiles. Predict future competitor action; assess against the present state of existing options; be willing to take action before the competition reacts. Table 5.2 compares unique service offerings (Tide

Table 5.2 Competitor Assessment to Objectives (Outcomes) Tool

Unique Attributes	Key Competitor	Cost	Leadership	Brand Recognition	Objective 4	Objective 5
Tide with bleach	Many	1	3	2		
Liquid Tide	Many	1	3	2		
Small packet Tide	Few	3	3	2		

Example) versus existing competitors. Construct Table 5.2 by identifying unique attributes of the service that distinguishes the innovation from its competitors. Identify the Key Competitors and their offerings that could challenge the new application. Rate these against the objectives (or outcomes) established for this project. For the Tide example, we use Cost, Leadership, and Brand Recognition as three potential objectives. With this tool, use the following scale:

3—Competitor value exceeds MT case study objectives (outcomes)
2—Competitor value equals MT case study objectives (outcomes)
1—Competitor value less than MT case study objectives (outcomes)

This simple tool will quickly highlight difficulties or potential opportunities. Do not be afraid to challenge the status quo. Understanding your competitor is more than half the battle of trying to develop a competitive advantage. Yet, many businesses relegate this analysis to a minor role.

Data analysis, whether it be simple or complex (Analytics) should uncover opportunities for the business or organization. Figure 5.3 details the process of collecting and analyzing analytical information on suppliers, customers, and competitors, using Analytics. Analytics is useful for collecting and analyzing consumer information, patterns and behaviors. For innovation, gathering information on unmet needs is critical.

Figure 5.3 details the process of collecting and analyzing analytical information on suppliers, customers, and competitors.

Those organizations without this information (or the capacity to gather such information, i.e., small businesses) can easily brainstorm unrealized needs or use focus groups and surveys to gather this information. Focus group sample questions would consist of:

1. What are your purchasing criteria for a new product or service?
2. If an item is new and innovative, will you purchase it automatically?
3. If the item meets a need, like no other presently available, will you purchase the item?
4. How do you define a need?
5. How do you know if the need is satisfied or not?
6. Would you consider purchasing an item that meets a need?
7. Are you more comfortable with the next generation of an item or would you rather have something that no one else has access to at this time?

Table 5.3 is an example of such a perceptual survey. Answer each statement by selecting a response that best meets your agreement or disagreement with the statement provided and placing the response in the "My Choice" column. Needs are defined as something wanted or desired. Often requirements may take a similar role as needs.

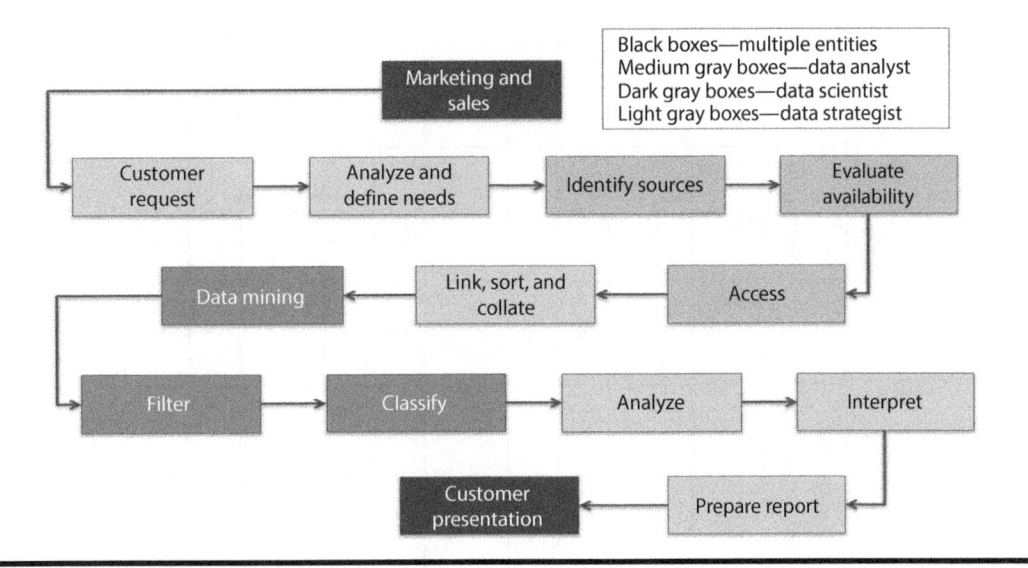

Figure 5.3 Analytics information flow.

Scoring and Interpretation

To score the Perceptual Survey, convert all statement scores into one of three score categories:

- ■ 1—When the respondent scores a positive response—Agree, Strongly Agree
- ■ 0—When the respondent scores a neutral response—Neither Disagree nor Agree
- ■ –1—When the respondent scores a negative response—Disagree, Strongly Disagree

> ### EXERCISE 5.3
>
> Determine a plan (strategy) for collecting in customer, supplier, and competitive information using an "Analytics" or Focus Group/Survey approach.

Try to develop a profile of the statements that received a rating of 1. Examine the variation between those statements that score a 0 and especially –1. This indicates a more complex purchasing process. The purpose of the survey is to determine how needs factor into innovation purchase decisions. In addition to these questions, we suggest adding statements directly related to your product or service.

Finally, the remaining critical sections are finalizing opportunities for identifying potential applications. Use some form of acceptance criteria to evaluate these opportunities. Choose criteria from a broad spectrum of evaluation and do not just focus on financial or cost benefit. Criteria must evaluate the innovation opportunity potential (i.e., sustained success or satisfying a need) and then scale each response in terms of its importance or how it meets some other established performance metric. Begin building the IOP or Project Charter. Begin with the process to choose the criteria. Brainstorm a list of criteria.

Table 5.3   Customer/User Unrealized Needs

Unsatisfied Needs	Strongly Disagree	Disagree	Neither Disagree nor Agree	Agree	Strongly Agree	My Choice
Services associated with my treatment always meets my needs	1	2	3	4	5	
When something I need cannot be easily met, the staff searches for alternatives	1	2	3	4	5	
Information regarding patient's needs should be accessible	1	2	3	4	5	
Patients should be able to suggest potential needs	1	2	3	4	5	
Needs are better voiced through the Internet rather than face-to-face encounters	1	2	3	4	5	
When a service meets my needs, I automatically voice my appreciation	1	2	3	4	5	
I only consider returning if my needs are fully satisfied	1	2	3	4	5	
I am more comfortable purchasing a medical procedure, such as in Dubai, with which I have some experience	1	2	3	4	5	
If my need is impossible to fulfill, I would still be satisfied	1	2	3	4	5	
I base my decision to purchase based on whether my needs are satisfied	1	2	3	4	5	

Brainstorming Rules (Hasso Plattner Design School at Stanford University)

1. *Defer judgment*: Separating idea generation from idea selection strengthens both activities. For now, suspend critique. Know that you have plenty of time to evaluate the ideas after the brainstorm.
2. *Encourage wild ideas*: Breakout ideas are right next to the absurd ones.
3. *Build on the ideas of others*: Listen and add to the flow of ideas. This will springboard your group to places no individual can get to on their own.
4. *Go for volume*: Best way to have a good idea is to have lots of ideas.
5. *One conversation at a time*: Maintain momentum as a group. Save the side conversations for later.
6. *Headline*: Capture the essence quickly and move on. Don't stall the group by going into a long-winded idea.

Remember to keep track of all ideas. Once complete, use a filtering technique such as 10-5-1 Voting. Each person gets 10 votes; they can vote for 10 items each with one vote; they cannot assign more than 5 votes per criteria; they must choose a minimum of 3 criteria and assign no more than 5 votes to a single criteria.

EXERCISE 5.4: BRAINSTORMING

Design a set of criteria to evaluate a potential application. Think critically (using Brainstorming) as a tool. Think from the perspective of the customer— How would you want the item to perform? What need is satisfied, can you confirm an innovation?

Apply the Acceptance Criteria Tool (with rating scale), such as the example shown in Table 5.4. This is an example for the Tide with Bleach Alternative.

This tool uses the experiences and knowledge of employees to examine a product, service, or technology. It is meant to capture the ideas and thinking of a wide range of employees. Given that, individuals decide what is or is not innovative (this tool can capture criteria often overlooked or not considered). The more individuals that recognize the innovative characteristics of this item, the greater the opportunity to reach this audience and generate sustained success.

External influences, used to judge or purchase innovation are needs, customer appeal, and overall affordability. Customers use multiple criteria before selecting a new product, service, or technology. Individuals use numerous criteria (unequally weighted) to evaluate innovation. This tool (Figure 5.5) attempts to rate a set of typical criteria a consumer would use to judge innovation and initiate purchase. Individuals judge the criteria by evaluating whether the criteria equal, fall short of, or exceed expectations. Since each person creates his or her own expectations, the tool captures the amount of influence the consumer will

Table 5.4   Acceptance Criteria for New Application Projects

4CT-Acceptance Criteria Evaluation Tool						
Acceptance Criteria	*Less than Expected*	*Expected*	*Greater than*	*Sustainable*	*Easy to Implement*	*Why*
Uniqueness		X		L	S	
Acceptable profit margin			X	M	S	
Resource capable			X	M	S	
Customer want or desire			X	L	S	
Perceived as innovative			X	L	S	
Brighter colors			X	M	S	
Better value		X		M	S	
Improved competitiveness		X		S	M	
Controllable costs		X		M	M	

Instructions: Develop a set of Acceptance Criteria. Select a "new" application, opportunity or feature. Evaluate the feature against each acceptance criteria and determine whether overall performance expectations would be less than expected, expected, or greater than expected.

Sustainment: Evaluate the sustainability of the feature or opportunity, using the following scale:

Limited (L) = Less than 1 year

Marginal (M) = 1–3 years

Superior (S) = over years

Ease of Implementation: Evaluate the ease of implementing such an opportunity, using the following scale:

Difficult (D) = Involves many departments, requires additional resources, affects many employees

Moderate (M) = Involves 1 or 2 departments, minor resources needed, affects patient positively

Simple (S) = Involves only department, minimal resources, positive impact for patients

use in their purchase and innovation assessment decision. In addition, the team evaluates the sustainability of the new application and its ease of implementation. The authors predict that a strong relationship between expectations, sustainability, and ease of implementation and the amount of influence exerted adequately defines whether a person will decide to purchase or not. The scoring attempts to capture this changing perspective. Rather than capturing an average score, examine the number of items in the Acceptable and Strongly Acceptable categories. These criteria drive consumer behaviors.

> **EXERCISE 5.5**
>
> Compare and contrast like products (e.g., the Apple I-PAD and Microsoft Tablet). List three to five criteria and rate each item. Remember to be unbiased in your evaluation or better yet, get someone else to complete the ACT Tool.

The last elements of Step 1 compare and contrast these ideas (opportunities) among a set of objectives. Create objectives using the SMART criteria (see McLaughlin and Kennedy, 2015). Usually the previous version's established objectives will work for the new version of the product, service, or technology. SMART objectives are metrics (measurements) that drive the business or organization. These are not tactical nor operational measures, but strategic measures used in decision making. If these measures are positive, then management may implement this opportunity. If not, then the opportunity may require further evaluation, refinement, and modification.

If the "New" application meets and completes Step 1, then move on to Step 2 called the "Reality Check" phase. This phase verifies what we know about the "new" application.

Step 2: Reality Check

Step 2 is a critical step as opportunities are vetted, evaluated, and checked for reality. Prior to reality checking the innovation opportunity, the first evaluation begins by understanding how the new application will influence all elements of the business or operation. From Figure 5.4 both internal and external influences affect the "new" application. Internal influences include (but not limited to) funding, resources, and existing priorities. External influences include competitor practices, overall appeal and affordability. The authors developed a new tool to help in assessing the amount and degree of influence. Interchange the word influence with the word "impact" as many influence elements affect the decision whether to proceed or not. This tool has numerous uses, not just at this stage but anytime a number of influencers may modify a decision, but also to "think" in more than the 2-dimensions.

Influence Matrix

The team can begin with the external or internal influences. Rather than looking at these in a linear fashion, consider both a linear and an interactive approach. To begin, consider the internal influences of resources, funding, and priorities on the outcome. Consider the one-dimensional influence separately and then begin to consider two of the influencers together as a contributor. Does priority influence the funding or resources allocation? If this interaction is present, which it is, how does it affect availability? Answer these questions and you can begin to understand the degree of interrelatedness and complexity needed before

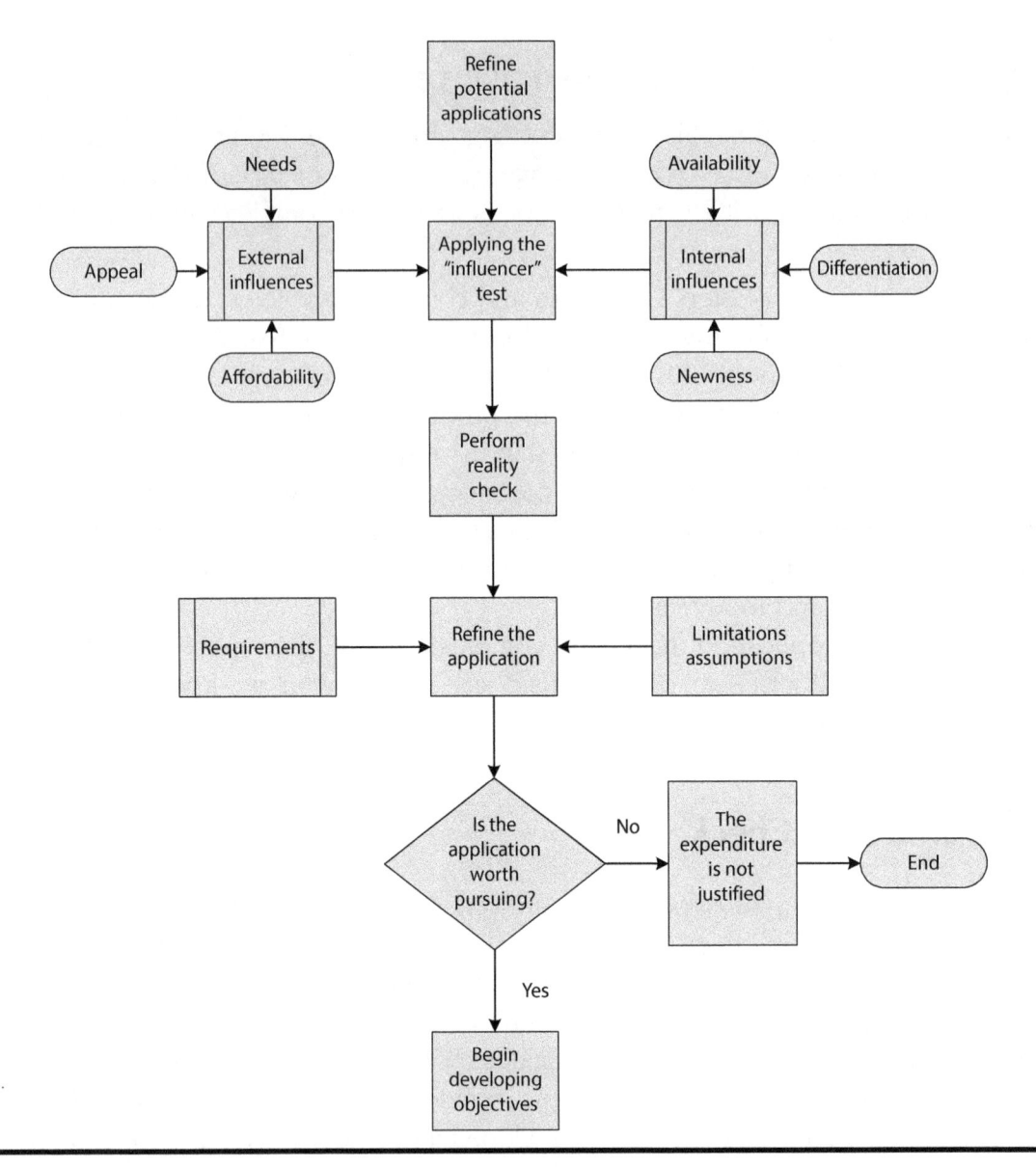

Figure 5.4   Step 2–reality check.

reaching a final decision. Think of these influencers, not individually, but in the context of how these interact with one another (Figure 5.5).

To begin, operationally define attributes (characteristics) that consumers (purchasers) will use to evaluate the product. Consider the following general terms:

Definitions:

Needs: Ability to meet (satisfy) customer or user needs
Applicability: A measure of value and use
Price: Determines sustained profit (ROI) potential
Availability: Supply and demand issues
Differentiation: The degree of difference between the product (service) the application replaces or updates
Newness: Perception (or novelty) of "newness" by the customer or user

Influence Matrix - General

Influence Component	Needs Score	Customer Appeal Score	Price Score	Availability Score	Differentiation Score	Newness Score	Total Score
Ease of Use	2	1.5	2	1.75	1.5	2	31.5
All-in-one Functionality	2	2	2	2	1.5	2	48
Full entertainment experience	1.5	1.5	0.5	1	1	2	2.25
Base model than $750	1.5	1	1	1	1	1	1.5
No need for contract	1.5	2	1	1	1	1	3

Instructions: Choose a Influencer Element, determine how much influence this element will have on purchase behavior. The greater the influence, the higher the score. For a score of "1" (parity) suggests that its influence will be essentially the same as the product it is replacing. Lower scores - less influence; higher scores - more influence.

Definitions

Resource Availability – Resources available without major external support
Priorities – A measure of value and frequency
Funding – Determines financial profile for funding the project
Competitors – activity directly related to products offerings or replacements (substitutes)
Availability - The degree of difference between the product (service) the application replaces or updates
Appeal – Perception (or novelty) of "newness" by the patient or user

Scoring

Resource Availability Scoring:	Low - .25, .5, .75; Medium - 1.0, 1.25; High - 1.50. 1.75. 2.0
Funding Scoring:	Low - .25, .5, .75; Medium - 1.0, 1.25; High - 1.50. 1.75. 2.0
Priority Scoring:	Low - .25, .5, .75; Medium - 1.0, 1.25; High - 1.50. 1.75. 2.0
Competitor Savvy Scoring:	Low - .25, .5, .75; Medium - 1.0, 1.25; High - 1.50. 1.75. 2.0
Affordability Scoring:	Low - .25, .5, .75; Medium - 1.0, 1.25; High - 1.50. 1.75. 2.0
Customer Appeal Scoring:	Low - .25, .5, .75; Medium - 1.0, 1.25; High - 1.50. 1.75. 2.0

Figure 5.5   Influence matrix example.

EXERCISE 5.6: ACCEPTANCE CRITERIA FOR NEW APPLICATION PROJECTS

Create a set of criteria known to influence a potential innovative application. Devise a scoring rubric that enables a measurement of influence of these criteria.

Using this tool (Figure 5.5), the team identified key "influencers" that could or would affect the decision. Figure 5.5 lists the Influencing Matrix evaluations with scoring defined. The largest score suggests the influence element that greatly affects how consumers will choose to purchase the product or service. These general influencers all affect purchase (use) decisions. Every item is unique, so criteria and scoring will vary. Use a low score when the amount of influence is weak. The authors suggest a value less than parity (1.0). Near parity for moderate influence and greater than parity, the influence is strong. These criteria could easily come from a perceptual survey or focus group. Rather than asking the customer or user what they like, ask them what do they need, want, or desire. Ask them to define how they know when they are satisfied and capable of making a decision. The Influence Matrix considers each influence component and then determines a score based on criteria.

Example

Consider the next-generation *i*-Pad or tablet device. Assume that this device can convert from pocket size to full size with a lightweight rollout screen, cloud-based computing, and acting as an "all in one" unit with phone, laptop, and entertainment/media center. Rather than being something very new, this is a new application or new use. Assume the criteria previously developed are applicable with this new product. Figure 5.5 lists the influence elements, for this example.

The results, although simulated, say that ease of use and functionality are the driving influencing factors. These factors (elements or components) represent the loci of attention for the application to be successful. Implementing this tool within the Marketing and Sales functions may provide a unique set of insights into the customer or user desires or feelings. Similarly, using this tool with suppliers may provide a unique vantage point in better understanding their perspectives and approaches. This tool applies whenever factors or elements influence the result or decision-making process.

EXERCISE 5.7: INFLUENCE MATRIX

Create a set of criteria based on a hypothetical application. Associate scoring of the influence factors to correspond to the tools objectives. Identify which element scores the highest and why it is critical for success.

The Influence Matrix is the last of the reality checks that started with Step 1. Once completed, the team begins to review requirements, assumptions and limitations. This is not identical to the requirements developed in the Project Selection stage (which examine the overall characteristics of the opportunity). These requirements, limitations, and assumptions have a distinctive operational emphasis used to refine the application. For example, buying a suit is the first stage, fitting the suit the second, wearing the suit the third. At this point, a decision concerning the viability of the project is forthcoming. Finally, is the project worth continuing? The information collected and the performance observed should predict an outcome from the step. An application worth pursuing is one that generated benefits in spite of the general business environment.

Step 3: New Application

Step 3 continues the process of evaluation, this time the emphasis is on the objective and whether the project remains a viable option. Recall that in the project selection phase, the team and management choose objectives for the project. The team validates those objectives and they become a focal point for the project as it proceeds to implementation. There is a constant need for proactive review and reevaluation, as displayed in Figure 5.6. During the implementation phase, the objectives again come under scrutiny. There is a constant need for proactive review and reevaluation, as we emphasize in Figure 5.7. Step 3 reviews objectives and expectations but also aligns to form project outcomes. The alignment between outcomes and objectives is direct; outcomes include a combination of requirements and assumptions/limitations. If outcomes are not yet developed, use existing project objectives. Meeting or exceeding objectives (outcomes) define the measurement of success for a project. Over time, objectives (requirements) may change to reflect new knowledge or the business environment. Therefore, it is critical to understand why these discrepancies exist and what remedies are possible to bring these objectives into alignment.

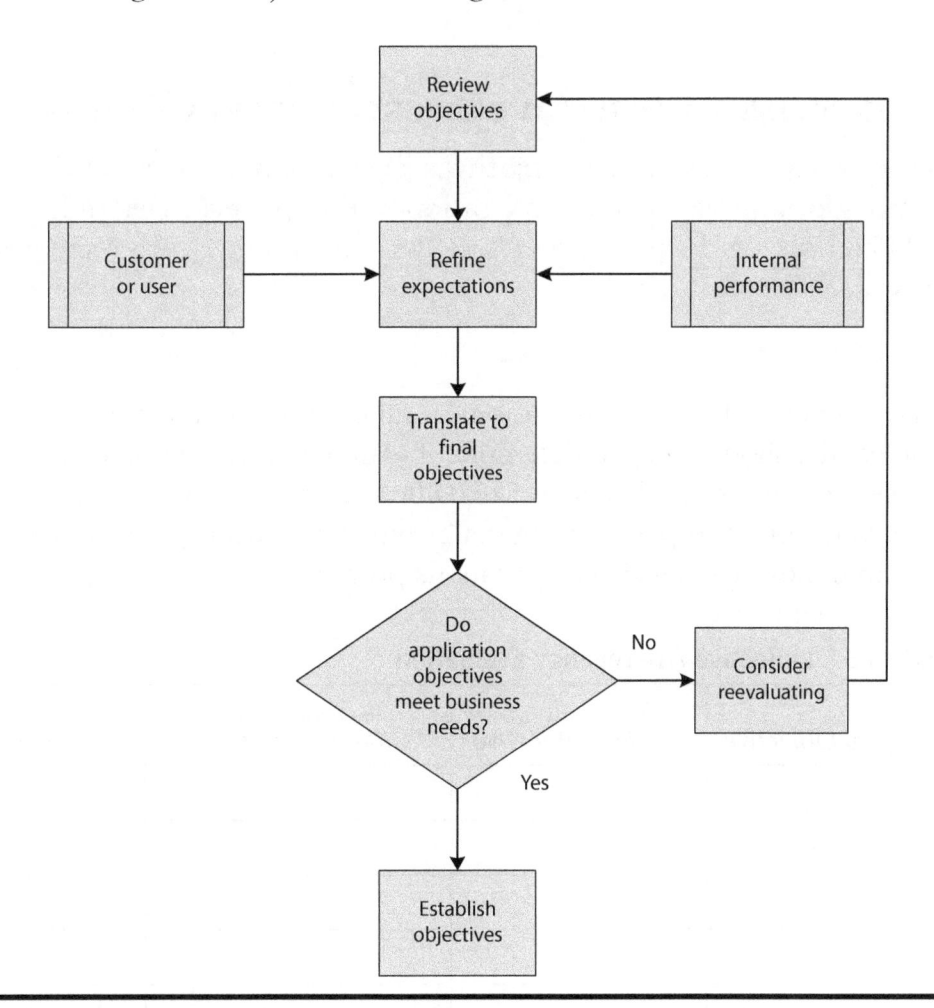

Figure 5.6   Step 3—objectify.

Construct the Objective (Outcome) Discrepancy Evaluation tool (Table 5.5) to determine the causes and potential remedies for aligning old and new objectives (outcomes). Begin with the existing outcomes (objectives) and evaluate these with the modified or new outcome. Describe the discrepancy that exists and identify the reasons for the misalignment. Determine a remedy (or solution) that brings the new outcome into alignment with the requirements and assumptions and limitations of the existing objective. If no discrepancy exists, then skip the tool. Figure 5.6 provides a blank template. Finding a remedy for the discrepancy reduces the risk of misalignment and project failure (Table 5.5).

The purpose of this step is to reach an agreement on the outcomes as the project implementation continues. Failure to address these issues could result in destructive behaviors if disagreements exist and are not resolved. Moving forward requires an examination of expectations as well. Individuals use expectations to develop their beliefs and attitudes that become long-term predictors of behavior.

To understand how consumers rate or evaluate an innovation requires an understanding of expectations as a key for success.

> ### EXERCISE 5.8: OBJECTIVE DISCREPANCY EVALUATION
>
> Analyze a set of established objectives versus a new or revised set of objectives for a project (should be an innovation project). Determine how the differences or discrepancies affect the outcome. Discuss remedies to standardize.

To measure expectations, have customers fill out this short survey.

Complete the short survey to determine if team members and managers have the same expectations profile (Table 5.6). Differing profiles suggest variation in response. Variation in responses suggests inconsistency while a lower average response indicates that negative expectations prevail.

Table 5.5 Objective Discrepancy Evaluation

Original Objective	Replacement or New Objective	Discrepancy Found; Identify the Causes	Remedy

Table 5.6 Project Expectations Survey

Statement Number	Enter the Numerical Value (1–5), in the My Choice Column, that Best Describes How You Agree (Disagree) with the Statements Provided	Strongly Disagree	Disagree	Neither Disagree nor Agree	Agree	Strongly Agree	My Choice
1	The project is expected to meets its objectives	1	2	3	4	5	
2	Implementation is expected to complete on time	1	2	3	4	5	
3	No delays are expected in meeting the timelines	1	2	3	4	5	
4	The project is expected to be successful	1	2	3	4	5	
5	Support for the project remains unchanged	1	2	3	4	5	
6	Performance is expected to remain at similar levels	1	2	3	4	5	
7	Expect that customers or users will perceive item as innovative	1	2	3	4	5	
8	Expect that few changes will be made to the project	1	2	3	4	5	
9	The project team has performed as expected	1	2	3	4	5	
10	Expect management to continue support for this project	1	2	3	4	5	
Total	**Scores**	**AVG** perceptions	**0**	**AVG** expectations	**0**	Difference	0
Total	**Scores**	**RANGE** perceptions	**0**	**RANGE** expectation	**0**		

Examine the difference between the Perception (odd-numbered) and Expectation scores (even-numbered). If perceptions exceed expectations (a positive difference), then the person is satisfied and the reality is better than expected. If the Expectations exceed perceptions (a negative difference) then the person is not satisfied and the reality is less than expected. These persons will not align well with the project.

Scoring and Interpretation

Assign a numerical value to each of the five survey responses, placing the value in the "My Choice" column. Average these over the 10 statements. Keep track of the range of the responses per individual. Interpret the results as follows:

- Average = 5.0 or better—Positive expectations (formed a positive outlook)
- Average = 2.8–3.8—Medium (neutral) expectations (requires some form of alignment)
- Average = 0–2.6—Low expectations (could lead to negative consequences)

A low value indicates disagreement between project expectations and personal expectations, regarding the outcomes. A positive value indicates both agreement and satisfaction with the project outcomes.

If there is a large amount of difference between the averages, this suggests that inconsistencies exist between respondents. This could be as simple as those who "touch" and those who "manage" the process. This requires some form of alignment to bring both sides to a place (space) they can come to an agreement.

Finally, use the information recently captured in the previous exercises to refine outcomes and expectations. Outcomes (objectives) and expectations support the business case for this project. These are measures not typically associated with project management and yet individual differences can lead to infighting, delays, replacements, and even cancellations. Remember the human element is critical in innovation project management. This step considers the team dynamic and the role it plays in overall project success. Failure to address these concerns may adversely affect the overall outcome and influence sustained success. Assuming that agreement on the goals (set by the team) and outcomes (set by management) is always positive or at best, neutral can easily comprise the integrity of the team and its ability to achieve success.

After aligning outcomes (objectives) and expectations, move on to Step 4.

Step 4: New Applications

Validation begins with a formalization of objectives (outcomes) and elements that define the new application. For the Tide example, the objective that meets profit targets and captures market share must coincide with the application (Color-safe Bleach or Bleach Alternative). If the objectives and key components of the application are compatible, then the process can move forward.

Validation is a similar phase (see Figure 5.7), for all project implementations, no matter what the type of innovation. It is the final step before full implementation begins. This step begins by matching outcomes to application elements and assuring these coincide and reinforce one another. Formalization involves a

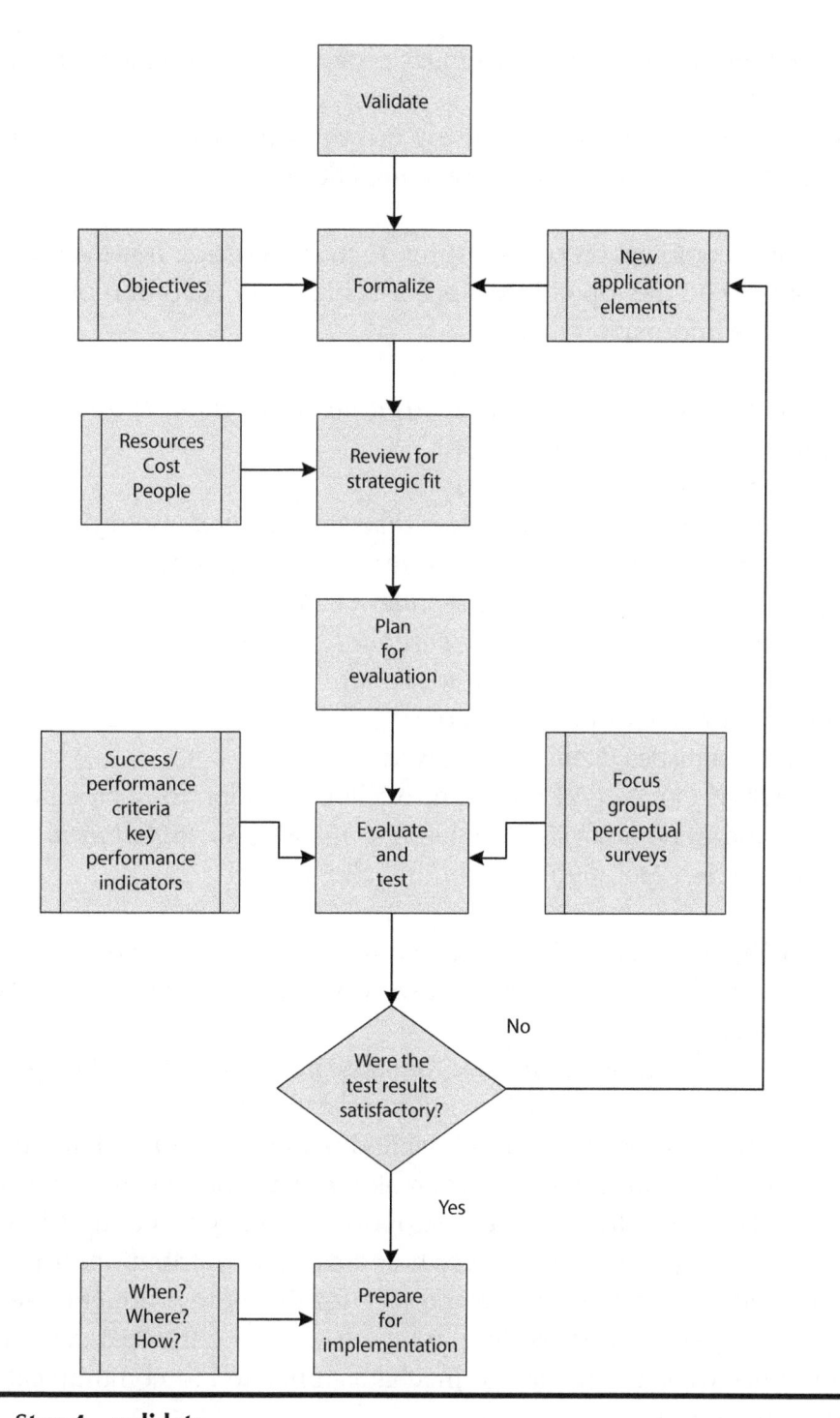

Figure 5.7   Step 4—validate.

review of the outcomes for relevancy and applicability. To meet these criteria, the outcome must include:

1. A consensus (the objectives continue to be relevant and predictive) among management, stakeholder, and consumers
2. Verification via empirical evidence (both from descriptive and inferential statistics)

3. A historical precedence (past similar projects using identical or similar outcomes)
4. Success criteria that is competitively driven (using standard performance information); regularly utilized by competitors)

Often it is a combination of 3–4 of these characteristics; however, empirical evidence should be the top choice since it is bias-free. Helpful tools to view and understand this information include:

- Run charts (*ENOVALE: Unlocking Sustained Innovation Project Success*; McLaughlin and Caraballo, 2013b)
- Descriptive (Exploratory) analysis:
  Exploratory Data Analysis (EDA) is an approach/philosophy for data analysis that employs a variety of techniques (mostly graphical) to maximize insight, uncover underlying data patterns, detect outliers and anomalies, test assumptions, and develop operational settings. (http://www.itl.nist.gov/div898/handbook/eda/section1/eda11.htm)
- Control charts (described in Chapter 6)
- Inferential statistics (Statistical analysis)
- Risk analysis (suggest @Risk as an excellent addition to Microsoft Excel)
- Pattern and trend analysis (*ENOVALE: Unlocking Sustained Innovation Project Success*; McLaughlin and Caraballo, 2013b)

Keep the empirical analysis simple, but instructive. This serves as a predictor of future performance and success; it also serves as a mechanism to detect and act upon change.

The next minor step is the review for strategic significance. Management and leadership reexamine the objectives and application to determine an overall fit with the company or organization's business plan (strategy) and alignment with core competencies. This final decision-making phase permits an overall review of how the objectives align with and support strategic goals and vision. It is an opportunity to judge the project's worth and overall contribution. It is also time to communicate and prepare the workplace for this new product or service line extension. This permits leadership, the time to examine the real value to the company (business), and begin the mechanism needed to communicate and support such an effort.

The "test" portion of the Validation phase involves "proving the concept." By collecting data on the actual "experience," the team (management) can evaluate performance, customer satisfaction, and potential alternatives that increase efficiency and effectiveness.

1. Conducting an observational study or a "dry run" by selecting 5–10 samples to "experience" the product or service in action, while carefully monitoring the results

2. Designing and testing using a more efficient experimental approach to evaluate all components of the product or service "experience"
3. Simulating the process to evaluate its capacity and its ability to perform

Designing and planning for such an evaluation is an entire topic on its own. Contact us at IPS for further assistance in conducting such a test.

In concert with testing and evaluation, revisit and rethink, the strategy employed to implement this new application. Management and leadership must reexamine the outcomes and application to determine an overall fit to the business plan (strategy) and alignment with core competencies. This final decision-making phase permits an overall review of how the outcomes align with and support strategic goals and vision. It is opportunity to judge the project's worth and overall contribution. It is also time to communicate and prepare the workplace for this new application. This permits leadership the time to examine the real value for the organization and begin the mechanism needed to communicate and support such an effort.

Now the verification process begins. Create an execution plan that details each action that is required for final approval (revisit the IOP and Project Charter templates with updates). Consider plan elements that verify:

1. Objectives
2. Benefits (profits/ROI)
3. Costs (fixed and variable)
4. Performance (compared to a set of norms)
5. Resources
6. Personnel/Communications
7. Competitive response

Begin the final evaluation process. Use a variety of methods to collect and validate the data. Use various techniques described in this book combined with techniques that capture perceptions, beliefs, and attitudes (Interviews and Surveys).

Test and evaluate success and performance criteria, using empirical tools. Balance these with attitudinal studies (focus groups and perceptual surveys) that capture the intent and meaning customers will attribute to your product or service. Determine if differences exist and how best to evaluate these differences. If the results meet criteria, and test to be satisfactory, then operationalize the project. If not, conduct "5 Why" sessions (asking "Why" numerous times until a specific set or single reason or cause [could be more than 1] is identified). This is the time to address and fix problems, rather than after launch. If a project reaches this stage, the chance of disapproval should be slim. Regardless of outcome, document your activities and file for future reference in case the innovation opportunity decision is not favorable or the project delayed.

EXERCISE 5.9

Describe the rationale for validating a project. What value does verification bring to the decision-making process? How does data provide an unbiased set of results that assists in the decision-making process?

Step 5: New Applications

In step 5, full operationalization is in progress. Alignment refers to the process of "getting everyone on the same page" to rollout the innovation. For this innovation type, alignment focuses on:

1. Communications (the message)—both externally and internally
2. The effect on internal operations (including space allocation, resources/materials, facilitation, process, planning, etc.)
3. Policy and strategy concerns

Communications are the fulcrum for success. Communicating how the application meets an unsatisfied need, how it adds value, and how it outperforms similar products, services, and technology that are all critical from both an innovation and sustained success perspective. You want your customers or users to readily appreciate its innovative capabilities, identify how it exceeds their expectations, and how it will drive them to purchase (Figure 5.8).

**EXERCISE 5.10: PRODUCT, PROCESS, OR
SERVICE MARKETING MESSAGE**

Design a message that will inform customers of a new application-oriented type of innovation. Pick an existing product or one you are familiar with and determine its appeal to customers and users.

Finally, there is the message that must reach the consumer (user). The message must be unambiguous (clear), accurate, and timely. The message is more than advertising, more than media, more than word-of-mouth; it is direct and uncomplicated—meeting an unsatisfied need (requirement) with value to the customer. To deliver the message requires a marketing approach that highlights the value and benefit the innovation will deliver; it most appeals to the consumer segment most interested in this product, service, or technology.

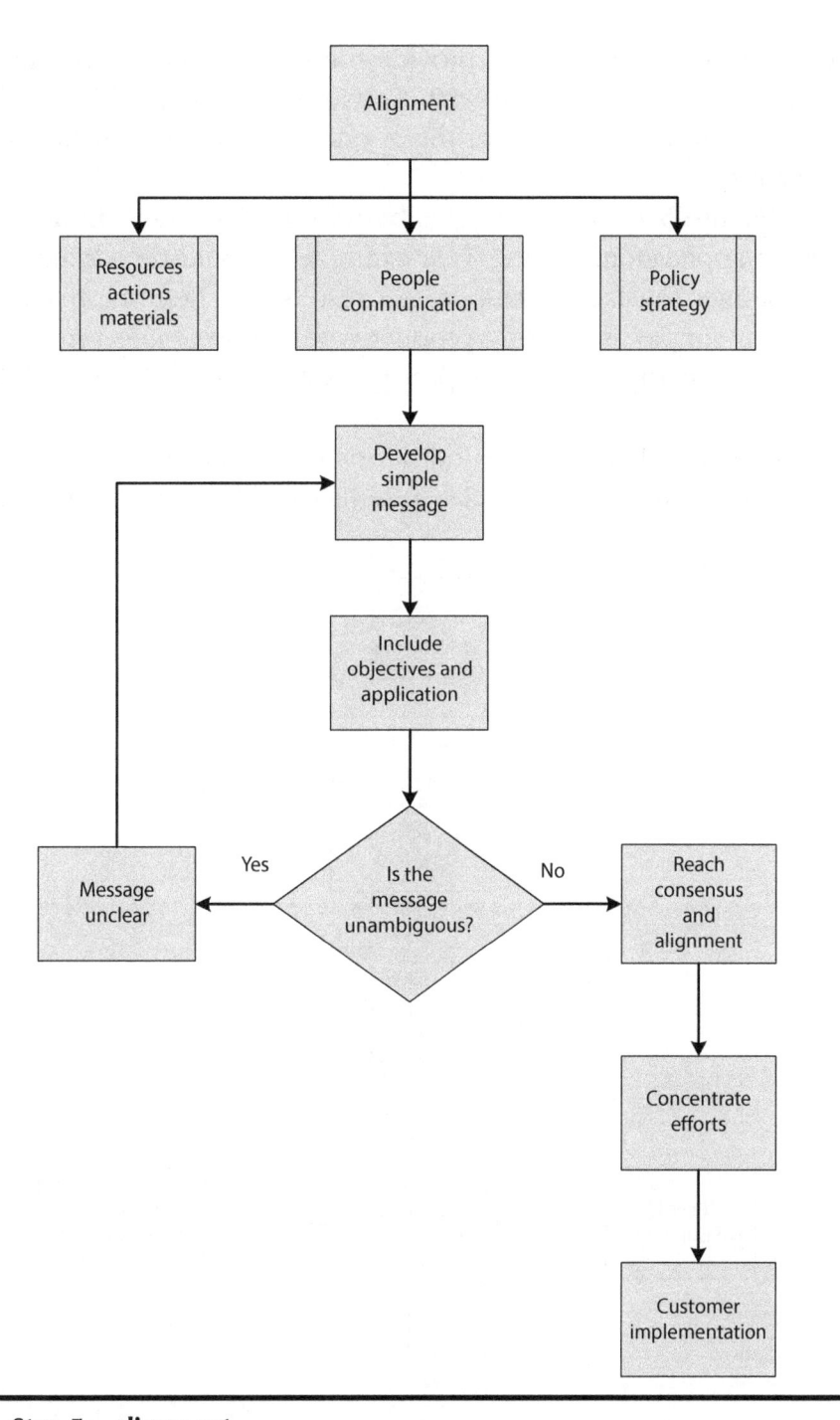

Figure 5.8   Step 5—alignment.

Step 6: Tracking

This process is reminiscent of our previous Step 6 suggestions. It may seem redundant to continue discussing tracking and monitoring various performance and financial metrics, yet this is a topic that ranks lower in importance, given the need to market or implement the application. A functioning measurement system is both real time and forward-looking. It is sustainable, repeatable, and can judge the existing process and provide information on trends and developing patterns. The process (Figure 5.9) provides the empirical feedback and actionable information necessary for the appropriate decision makers to make critical decisions.

This step (Figure 5.9—Step 6) begins by refining (or establishing) tracking metrics for the application. For the Tide example, it could be additional sales, improved customer satisfaction ratings, test results, etc. Refining these measures may be as simple as tracking product types by sales and preferences. The key takeaway is to examine the present system and look for additional opportunities.

These metrics (Key Performance Indicators) must link to the companies or organizations accounting and financial systems capable of tracking the new

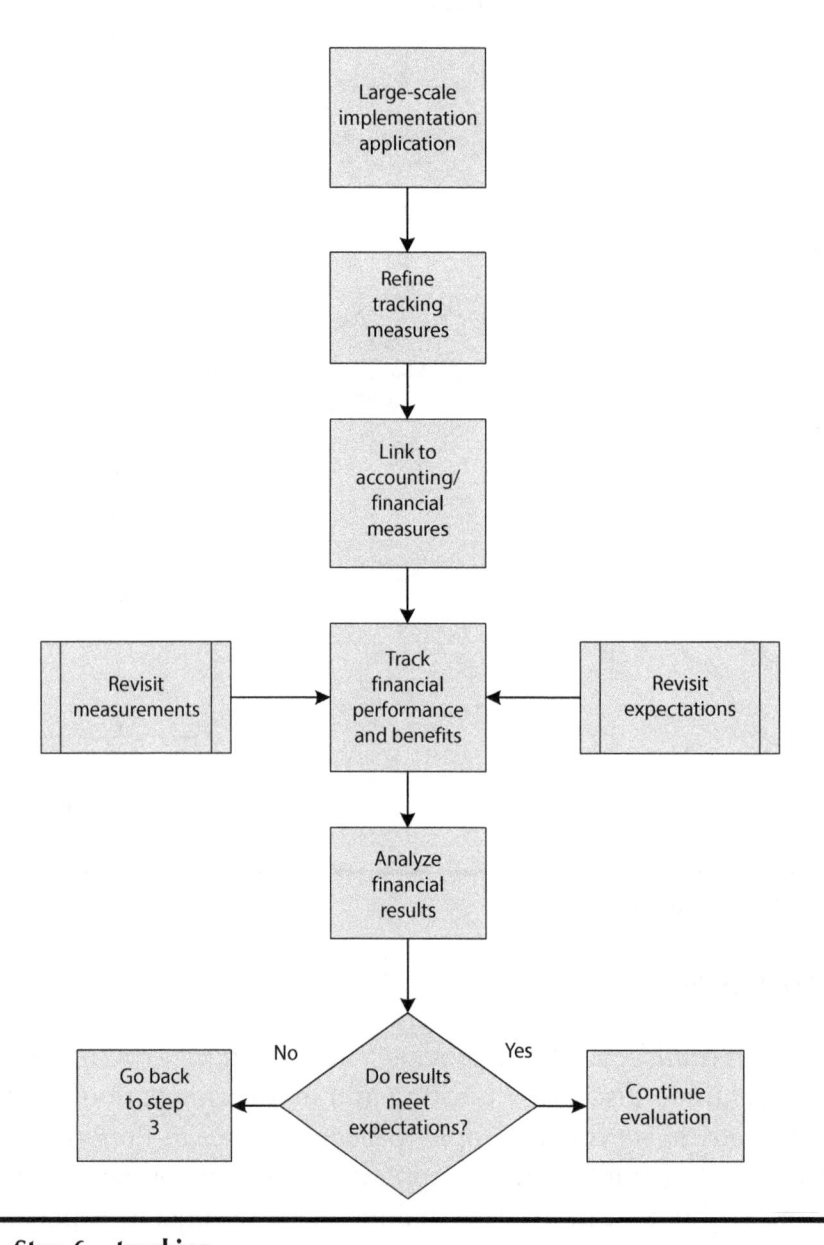

Figure 5.9   Step 6—tracking.

product, service, or technology. Antiquated systems may provide only "after the fact" or less detailed information required to accurately measure the innovation implementation. At this stage, during the evaluation, consider the quality of the metrics and their ability to provide accurate and reliable information. Perform the same review on expectations and perceptions of profit and performance. Determine if there is a gap between what is expected (promised) and the reality of what is possible given the marketplace and existing conditions. Gaps here indicate potential problems when results do not meet expectations.

The more the organization tracks performance the easier it will be to address problems (identified quicker) and provide a solution to these problems. Combined with Step 5, after testing and evaluating the service, it should be obvious if the product or service will meet or exceeds its stated outcomes.

Chapter 6 provides a more detailed explanation as the "new" types of innovation share these last two steps.

Step 7: Release

Finally, the remaining step is consistent throughout all project implementations. The purpose is to evaluate and monitor (see Figure 5.10). Items such as tolerances, specifications, guidelines, and directives are defined and refined. The emphasis now is control and reaction. Control is required when the process

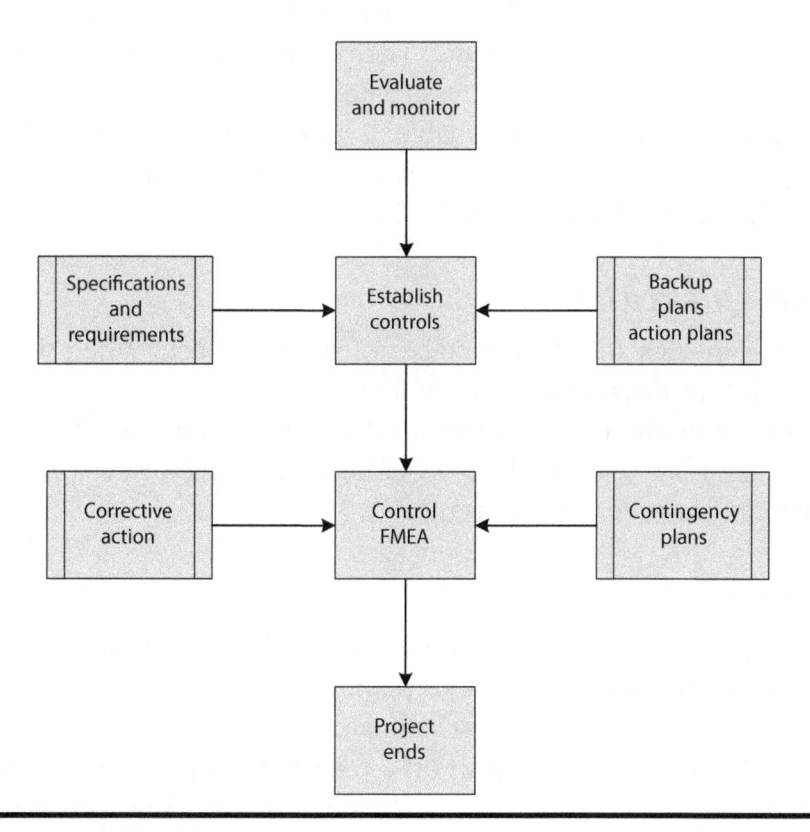

Figure 5.10   New application—step 7.

varies or drops below expected values; reaction when you need to bring the process back to acceptable performance levels. This will include back-up plans, and contingency plans to handle developing problems so as not to disturb longer-term sales patterns. This monitoring should also provide valuable information on process changes that could lead to product, service, or technology reevaluation.

Releasing the process opens the portal for more innovation as micro projects can improve elements of the process on a daily, weekly, or monthly basis. Use this step to monitor and adjust the "experience" as needed.

In summary, this step is critical for sustaining and maintaining long-term performance. Because of its long-term perspective, it is common for management and leadership to overlook the importance of this step (particularly when developing a new product or service application) or undervalue its necessity. We recommend that managers or leaders be required updating their skills. As a reminder, applying sufficient time and resources will ensure the viability of this step. Capable managers enable the organization to react to circumstances that could derail the application of cause and lead to its early demise.

Summary

This chapter describes the process of introducing a "new" application that meets the criteria of being innovative. New applications (uses) provide a business or organization strategy that keeps that business at the forefront of innovation, providing ample competitive advantage. The process to create, develop, and implement is much shorter than that associated with a new discovery or invention. Although a reduction in it is possible, a more likely scenario is that profits and ROI may greatly exceed expectations. Developing this strategy is a key to remaining both competitive and a leader in the field.

DISCUSSION QUESTIONS

1. List the advantages and disadvantages of this approach. When would consumers reject innovation as a desirable trait?
2. Which outcome (the innovativeness, value, performance, etc.) would you expect that customers would want before purchasing a new application? List the outcomes in order of importance.

ASSIGNMENTS

1. Propose a new application for an existing product, service, or technology. Use the seven steps to outline your plan. Estimate a general timeline for completion (based on best guess estimates).
2. Perform a "reality check" (Step 2) on a recent or proposed new application. Would the application pass this test? Identify any missing components and propose a method to address these.

References

Brainstorm Rules (Hasso Platner Insitute of Design Stamford University. http://e145.stanford.edu/upload/handouts/brainstorming.pdf March 31, 2015.

Guidelines for Conducting a Focus Group Eliot and Associates. 2005. https://assessment.trinity.duke.edu/documents/How_to_Conduct_a_Focus_Group.pdf March 30, 2015.

The Tide Story: Storytelling to Reinforce Market Leadership, Omar Kattan | November 10, 2012 | Brand Stories | No Comments, http://www.brandstories.net/2012/11/10/the-tide-story-storytelling-to-reinforce-market-leadership/ March 30, 2015.

Chapter 6

A New Approach

Introduction

The last of the three "new" types of innovation types is that of creating a "new approach." A new approach uses existing resources (technology, products, processes, and personnel) to offer an alternative to what presently exists. Stated differently, "a new approach is one where the new aspect is a new approach for an item within the scope of existing technology" (McLaughlin and Caraballo, 2013a, p. 41). Developing a new approach is similar to extending the life cycle of the existing item through incremental innovation opportunities. The new approach "breathes life" into the product, service, or technology. "This new approach could have a very short life cycle before duplication or superseded by existing competition" (McLaughlin and Caraballo, 2013a, p. 41). Typical new "approaches" include:

- New features
- New "feel" or "look" (emotional response—any of the five senses)
- New process (offered in a different way)
- New outcomes

This method provides a new element or approach without cost or time delays. A new approach or new feature might open up avenues of opportunity for an existing item, process, or service. For example, many banks are beginning to move from full service to limited services (few, if any tellers) with the introduction of new, more automated service offices. This is definitely, a new approach, but at what cost to their older customers, who do not want to participate in the technology. Therefore, for one demographic group the approach represents a positive, for another a negative.

As with any innovation opportunity, a need (requirement) must be satisfied before the consumer perceives it as innovative. Therefore, the new approach must first seek to meet an unsatisfied need. In addition, the fact that competition can easily replicate or duplicate these efforts limits the overall effectiveness of this particular type of innovation opportunity. The business or organization must use a wide swath of information related to perceptions and attitudes (all necessary elements of customer purchase behavior). When advertising or marketing this concept, its unique or new approach message must reach the customer. "In simple terms, communicate to the user what is new, what needs are or will be satisfied, and how the item performs better than its predecessors do" (McLaughlin and Caraballo, 2013b, p. 42). Consumers will comprehend the benefits especially those influenced by the aspect of new, as innovative.

Clearly specify this new approach with its requirements in detail. What distinguishes this new element from existing items is that it fills unsatisfied needs or capability gaps. Therefore, rather than focusing on design and development, the focus transitions to perception and attitude. Realizing that the consumer may be confused trying to determine what constitutes a new approach, communicating the message takes precedence. In this innovation opportunity, articulating the differentiation is the key to success. Rather than stressing only the new approach, stress the improved performance, value-added (benefits), and/or specific needs satisfied. Consider the example of a large pharmacy chain that decided to offer greater than 30-day prescription refills. Perhaps for economic or convenience reasons, the need arose since patients did not want to make such frequent trips to the pharmacy. Subsequently, the pharmacy in cooperation with the care provider decided to offer 60- and 90-day prescriptions for some classes of prescription drugs not controlled or monitored closely by the Drug Enforcement Agency (DEA) and the Food and Drug Administration (FDA). To "sell" this feature requires precise, specific communications and compliance with FDA and DEA guidance and law. This met an unsatisfied need, it was innovative, and it fits the category of a new approach. The bulk of the money spent will be on the process of marketing or advertising the new approach.

The difficulty arises in convincing consumers/users that the new approach is innovative and handling the reality that not all drug prescriptions would qualify for this innovation opportunity. However, businesses can easily adjust components, packaging, or service settings. Consider the ordinary "mixer" used for baking. Simply by adding a new attachment, the machine can now knead dough and with that attachment, this innovation becomes a new approach. The manufacturer does not need to change their production schedule, resources, or equipment; they need only to add a new attachment or perhaps change their production and manufacturing process in the area of packaging. Of course, there is a time required to develop, design, and test such an attachment, but consider the extended life cycle and the ability to advertise such a new product. Now, by adding a shredding device, the mixer has further extended its life cycle and usefulness. As previously discussed, differentiation is again a key variable so that communicating that innovation or increased capability to prospective buyers is all part of this new approach.

A New Approach—Seven Steps

As with all ENOVALE™- and N²OVATE™-derived processes, there are seven steps to complete from development through implementation (operationalization). Figure 6.1 details the seven (high-level) steps.

The process begins by reviewing and evaluating the new approach, then moves to validation and alignment and finally to operationalization. The final three stages are comparable to those steps described in Chapter 4. This chapter elaborates on these three steps in detail.

The letters associated for this new type of innovation opportunity are:

- **R**— Review existing approaches
- **P**— Propose new approaches
- **O**—Objective development
- **V**—Verify/validate
- **A**—Adapt/align
- **T**— Track performance
- **E**— Evaluate and monitor

The focus is on creating approaches based on the experience and knowledge gained previously (step 1, review existing approaches). After establishing a foothold, ideas for new approaches have a mechanism for evaluation and review (step 2). Moving ahead from step 2, the team can then decide upon one or more objectives that will serve as project outcomes (step 3). Steps 4 through 7 are similar to that described in Chapter 4. This chapter details steps 5 through 7, also applicable for those steps in Chapter 4.

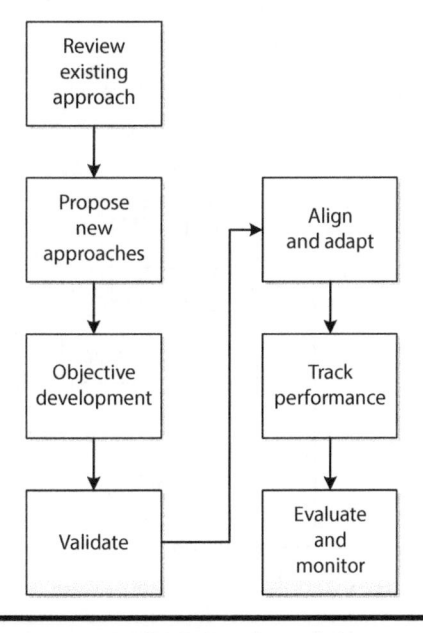

Figure 6.1   New approach seven steps (high-level model).

Step 1: Reviewing Existing Approaches

The decision to begin by reviewing existing approaches originates from the fact that creating a new approach is similar to activities used to extend the life cycle of a product or service (Figure 6.2). The major difference is that innovation begins with a need. Evaluate each new approach based on the criteria listed in Table 6.1. Consider each "new" addition or modification as an "element."

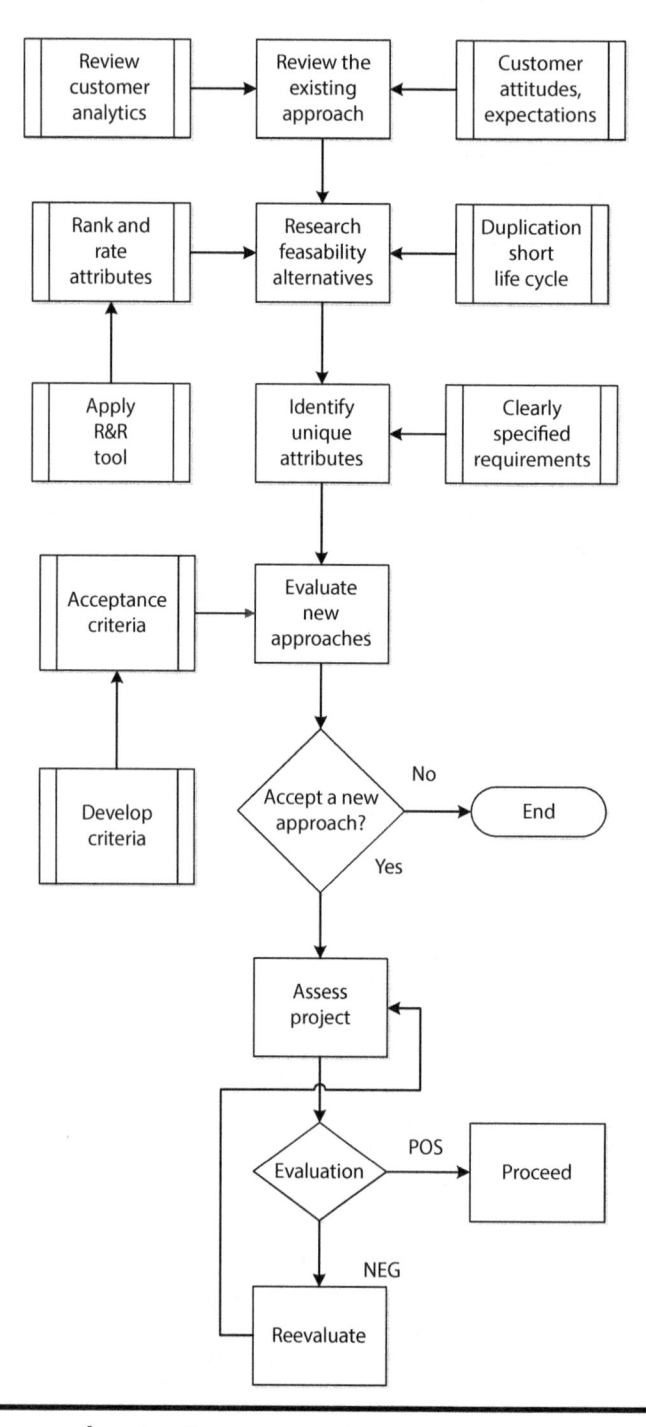

Figure 6.2   New approach—step 2.

Table 6.1 Review of an Existing Approach

Element	Expectations	Experience	Knowledge	Attitudes	Empirical Evaluation	Decision

Begin the process by reviewing existing or proposed approaches. Use a set of criteria that examines customers or user's perceptions, attitude, knowledge, and experience (Table 6.1). Consider a unique aspect or dimension of a new approach. Each new approach has potentially many elements that defines its unique character. An element refers to each unique characteristic of a new approach. Rate each element, using five criteria, as a means of evaluating the new approach.

Expectations: What the customer (user) would want or desire?
Experience: What were customers experiences using the product, service, or technology?
Knowledge: What is their level of understanding with the element?
Attitudes: Prevailing feelings and beliefs about the element
Empirical evidence: The results of specific and focused data collection
Decision: (Not a criteria) A determination of whether to continue to explore, refine, or end the opportunity

Before using this tool, review the scoring guide for each of the five criteria.

Scoring Guide

Expectations:	None (N); Low (L); Medium (Me); High (H)
Experience/knowledge:	Low (L); Minimal (Mi); Needs Upgrading (U); High (H)
Attitudes:	Nonexistent (N); Poor (P); Good (G); Excellent (E)
Empirical evidence:	Inconclusive (I); Poor (P); Marginal (MG); Compelling (C)
Decision:	No change (NC); Reevaluate (RE); Accept with conditions (AC); Accept w/o conditions (AWC)

Interpretation

This is a simple evaluative technique, easily distributed to team members for their input. It is useful in any environment, especially where the team is virtual. Score each element based on the respondents understanding of the new approach and its unique characteristics. Apply a critical thinking mentality to evaluate each element/criteria pair to help reach a decision on whether to pursue the existing approach opportunities, refine the approach, or search for a new opportunity. Evaluate the number and ratio of positive responses. The number of positive responses should exceed all other responses for a final decision to implement. The alternative is if there are no incidences similar to a new approach; then begin with examining the unsatisfied needs or identified capability gaps.

Example

Consider the simple example of offering a 90-day supply of a prescription as an alternative to a 30-day supply. Consider the following elements of this new approach (Table 6.2).

The result of the exercise is that the offer (communication to the patient) and cost are critical to patient's acceptance. Packaging is not an issue. The decision involves beginning the testing of the concept.

EXERCISE 6.1: REVIEW OF EXISTING APPROACH

Consider a product (service) you are familiar with for this exercise. Develop a new approach for this product. Test and identify which element of the new approach is most critical to the overall decision process. Construct a simple table, using the template from Table 6.1.

The next step is to determine the feasibility of alternatives to the existing approach. Issues such as duplication and shorten-life cycle will always be of concern. Any alternative that can extend the life cycle or provide benefit (value) to the organization and the customer (user) is worth considering. Consider using the AREA (alternative repercussions and evaluation analysis) template approach, described in Chapter 9 (McLaughlin and Kennedy, 2015). An alternative to the more detailed AREA is the use of the rating and ranking (R&R) tool (Table 6.3), which evaluates key attributes (KAs) of the proposed alternative. KAs are characteristics of an approach that influence consumer behavior in terms of recognition of the approach as being innovative. Rate each attribute as either negative, positive, or neutral. A positive rating suggests that the business is executing a KA in a way that positively affects the business.

Table 6.2 Review of an Existing Approach—Example

Element	Expectations	Experience	Knowledge	Attitudes	Empirical Evaluation	Decision
Repackaging	N	N	H	Md	MG	NC
Offer	H	H	H	H	C	AWC
Cost	H	H	H	H	H	AWC

Table 6.3   New Approach Key Attribute Rating and Ranking

Key Attribute	Effectiveness Rating	Rate Importance	Needs Adjustment or Replacement	Ranking

Unlike KAs variables from the IOP (Innovation Opportunity Profile) such as KPP (Key Performance Parameters) and KPIs (Key Performance Indicators), which are known, assume that these KAs achieve performance levels that meet expectations. In most instances, the information regarding KAs is scarce or unknown. Therefore, be prepared to make some assumptions based on both experience and knowledge.

Next, rate the importance of each KA and activity. This will begin to focus the team on what items need the greatest attention. Finally, give a quick summary of what needs adjusting (or in some cases replacement). This simple tool provides a mechanism for discussing alternative approaches, yet incorporates the combined wisdom and experience of the team. This "active" type of data (since it is real time) is always useful for innovation opportunity projects.

This tool examines the KAs of a new approach by examining the effectiveness, importance, and replacement potential. The rating scales for each of these three criteria are as follows.

Effectiveness Rating and Definition

Positive (+): A potential positive to the business or organization
Neutral (N): Potential is limited or the attribute lacks effectiveness
Negative (−): Attribute has a negative effect

Importance Rating and Definition

Major: Major importance, has significant effect on customer (user)
Medium: Importance is limited; has a minimal effect on the customer (use)
Low: Low or nonexistent importance

Replacement Potential Rating and Definition

Yes: Easily replaced with a substitute of equal or greater value
No: Not easily replaced with a substitute of equal or greater value

Next, when a rating is lower than expected, assess whether the KA requires adjustment or replacement. Finally, rank the KAs in terms of the ratings, if there a number of attributes that have similar ratings. Use the ranking column as a way to differentiate attributes that could lead to new approaches or result in innovation opportunities.

Consider the following example. A small medical office wants to grow its nutritional business (healthy foods and nutritional supplements), but lacks the knowledge to market the business. They have been offering this business for the last 10 years and need a new approach to increase traffic into their offices. Table 6.4 lists potential new approaches.

All of these potential activities could lead to a few new approaches. The obvious key is the message, which would take first priority and the presentation of the message as the second priority.

EXERCISE 6.2: RATING AND RANKING (R&R) TOOL

Consider a new approach. Describe the unique attributes of this new approach. Use the attribute rating and ranking tool to evaluate each attribute. Assign a ranking scale to determine the effectiveness of the attribute. Use Table 6.3.

Once a potential unique approach is identified, consider the specific requirements (assumptions and limitations) needed to make this approach a reality. For the example, an improved message (regarding the nutritional business), includes the following characteristics: a description of content, clarity, depth, length,

Table 6.4   Rating and Ranking (R&R) Tool—Example

Activity or Attributes	Effectiveness Rating	Rate Importance	Potential Replacement	Ranking
Improve Web Site Design	+	Medium	No	4
Improve Web Site "Message"	+	Major	No	1
Change Brochure "Appearance"	N	Medium	Yes	5
Change Brochure "Message"	+	Major	Yes	2
Free Advertising	+	Medium	No	7
Social Media approach	+	Medium	No	6
Social Media "Message"	+	Major	No	3
Social Media Audience	+	Major	Yes	No ranking

intended audience, wording, and action-orientation wording. A unique approach may seem appropriate but its associated requirements (limitations and assumptions) may be difficult to implement. For example, there is a need to revise the web site for this small medical firm, but with no one to do the web site revision; it may not be a viable or a workable solution. Use this step to identify these unique approaches, however, temper your judgment by the reality of its requirements, limitations, and/or assumptions.

This next step is to evaluate the performance of the key or unique attributes (and approaches). Use any of the evaluative techniques already discussed in this handbook to determine efficacy. Decision criteria should be based upon: empirical evidence (data analysis—internal and external), critical thinking, collaborate tools, experience, knowledge, and past performance. One method is to use the acceptance criteria, discussed in the next paragraph, as information needed for an informed decision. Hasty, ill-informed decisions lead to waste and inefficiencies.

Now, it is time to establish or revisit the acceptance criteria. Acceptance criteria are those performance measurements, that when met, judge whether the new approach is successful. These measures provide a standard from which to judge an outcome and whether it will or will not offer benefit. Coaching is important here since the client often wants to achieve goals that may be unrealistic without changes in philosophy or culture. Focus on establishing criteria (and acceptable limits or ranges) jointly. A surprise this early in the process can be devastating. Estimate as well as you can since no one is omniscient. Acceptance criteria and critical success factors (CSF) provide a method of framing success. Acceptance criteria provide a quick and simple review of planned activities and enable the team to judge whether an activity is worth the expenditure of money, time, and talent. Consider the small medical facility that wants to expand its nutritional business. The criteria in Table 6.5 represent a "best guess" estimate and these provide a set of criteria in which each of the attributes of a new approach

Table 6.5 Acceptance Criteria

Measurement	Minimum	Maximum
Implementation time	3 months	6 months
Overall costs	< $1000	< $3000
Advertising costs	$500	$1000
Marketing costs	$200	$400
Video costs	$300	$600
Number of patients	10	30
Office disruption	0	1 h
Patient satisfaction	Moderate	Exceptional

must meet. Failure to meet these criteria may cause the removal of a particular (unique) attribute from consideration.

> **EXERCISE 6.3: CONSTRUCT A SET OF ACCEPTANCE CRITERIA**
>
> Using a blank version of Table 6.5, determine those measurements that define success. Which KAs do you think meet or operate outside of the criteria?

The final step will determine whether the different KAs of the approach meet the acceptance criteria or need further revision. A decision to operationalize ends this step.

Step 2: Proposing New Approaches

When it is clear what needs accomplishing, then examine alternative approaches to achieving an existing outcome(s). The complexity tends to increase with the number of outcomes. Each component of an alternative is essentially a solution. Proposing new approaches (Figure 6.3) is more than brainstorming a list of ideas; it requires an understanding of the expected outcome (acceptance criteria), its contribution (the benefits and value it generates), and its ability to satisfy the need (designated as a "success"). It may seem simplistic, but the thinking required is three-dimensional (company, customer, and components). The components are elements of the approach. The Approach Benefits Influence Analysis (ABIA) tool is one that

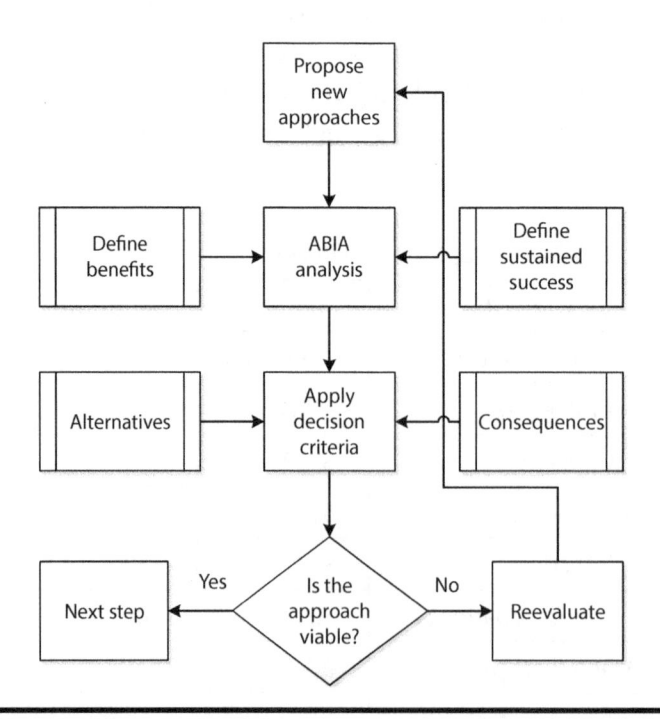

Figure 6.3   New approaches—step 2.

encourages critical thinking about potential approaches. Based on the principle surrounding the Failure Modes and Effects Analysis (FMEA), the tool, used in a team setting, integrates thoughts, experiences, and ideas into a cohesive response.

To use the tool, complete the ABIA worksheet (Figure 6.3). Consider each new component of an approach as a proposed solution. Brainstorm those elements worth implementing. Determine the benefit, its influence (the approach element) and its effect on sustained success. Then, determine what could cause this element and benefit to loose influence (or even fail). What preventative controls (actions) could essentially alleviate the loss of influence, thus leading to sustained success. To begin, the team needs to define the benefit and its overall influence on sustained success. Use the worksheet (Figure 6.4) to develop the basic information.

1. Identify the unique element(s) of the new approach
2. What benefit(s) does it bring (the needs that are satisfied, or improved performance, etc.)
3. Assess the influence of the benefit on sustained success
4. Potential cause or reasons why the element (and resulting benefit) could lose influence
5. Actions needed to sustain the benefit

Approach Benefit Influence Analysis (ABIA) Worksheet

New Approach	Potential Benefit Mode	Potential Influence	Potential Causes	Current Actions/ Controls
Specifically define the components of the new approach	Define the benefit	What is the influence on performance?	What could cause the new approach element (component) to underperform?	What actions are needed for this improvement to be sustained?

Figure 6.4 Approach benefits influence analysis worksheet.

Approach Benefit Influence Analysis (ABIA) Worksheet

New Approach	Potential Benefit Mode	Potential Influence	Potential Causes	Current Actions/ Controls
Specifically define the components of the new approach	Define the benefit	What is the influence on the benefit	What could cause the new approach element (component) to loose influence?	What actions are needed to sustain the benefit?
Increase exposure to social media	Increased number of patients	Space, logistics, time with patients	Lack of updates, incorrect information	Webmaster, responsibility assigned
	Greater billable hours	Increased support, better technology	Unprepared staff, loss of "hands on"	Training, using technology to orient
	Recognition			
	Helping more patients			

Figure 6.5   Approach benefits influence analysis worksheet—medical firm example.

For example, consider the small medical firm that wants to increase their nutritional business, how could the ABIA worksheet help in determining which new approach to implement (Figure 6.5).

Once the worksheet is complete, the team can transfer the information to the full template. The full template (Figure 6.6) also assigns probability to the occurrence of certain events. There are three probabilities (IP, OP, SS) estimated:

1. Influence probability (IP)—the influence the element has on the benefit.
2. Frequency of occurrence (OP)—how often does a negative effect influence the benefit?
3. Chance of sustained success as an estimate of success (SS).
4. Success priority number (SPN)—A calculated value, the greater the value, the better the element, or component delivers on success (makes the new approach successful).

Take the information from ABIA worksheet and transfer this into the full tool, then apply the probability values (obtained from Figure 6.7) to the table to calculate the SPN. A small portion of small medical firm's ABIA is presented. Figure 6.8 presents some preliminary results. The SPN scores assist in determining the elements of a new approach that can provide sustained success, while preventing the element from losing influence and providing less benefit.

Use Figure 6.7 to determine the risk score involved with each approach, the excel worksheet will calculate the SPN. The greater the SPN, the more critical the element to implement. Consider low success priority numbers as an indicator of an alternative.

New Approach	Potential Benefit	Potential Performance	I P	Potential Causes	N E P	Current Actions or Controls	S U S	S P N	Actions Recommended
Approach Benefit Influence Analysis						Prepared by:			Page ____ of ____
Team:						APSA Date (Orig) _____ (Rev) _____			
Specifically define the components of the new approach	Define the benefit	What is the effect on performance?	Impact (influence) probability	What could cause the component to underperform?	How frequently would a negative effect occur?	What actions (controls) are needed for this new approach to be sustained?	How well can the element continue to perform?	Success priority number	What are the actions required for maintaining improved performance?
			0		0		0	0	
			0		0		0	0	
			0		0		0	0	
			0		0		0	0	
			0		0		0	0	

Figure 6.6   Approach benefits influence analysis template.

	Approach Benefit Influence Analysis					Prepared by:			Page ___ of ___
Team:						ABIA Date (Orig) _____ (Rev) _____			
New Approach	**Potential Benefit**	**Potential Performance**	**I P**	**Potential Causes**	**N E P**	**Current Actions or Controls**	**S U S**	**S P N**	**Actions Recommended**
Specifically define the components of the new approach	Define the benefit	What is the influence on?	Impact probability	What could cause the component to underperform?	How frequently would a negative effect occur?	What actions (controls) are needed to sustain the benefit	Sustained success probability	Success priority number	What are the actions required for maintaining improved performance?
Increase exposure to social media	Increased number of patients	Space, logistics, time with patients	9	Lack of updates, incorrect information	7	Webmaster, responsibility assigned	9	567	Monitor progress bi-monthly
	Greater billable hours	Increased support, better technology	9	Unprepared staff, loss of "hands on"	5	Training, using technology to orient	7	315	Monitor progress quarterly
	Recognition							0	
	Helping more patients							0	

Figure 6.7 Approach benefits influence analysis scale for risk analysis.

ABIA Risk Scale

Score	Impact Probability	Score	Negative Effect on Influence (Performance)
10	The AC always or nearly always impacts the B	1	The cause will always influence the P
9	The AC impacts the B more than 85% of the time	2	The cause will influence the P nearly always
8	The AC impacts the B more than 75% of the time	3	The cause will influence the P frequently
7	The AC impacts the B more than 60% of the time	4	The cause will influence the P often
6	The AC impacts the B slightly more than 50% of the time	5	The cause will influence the P more than 50% of the time
5	The AC impacts the B about 50% of the time	6	The cause will influence the P occurs about 50% of the time
4	The AC impacts the B less than 50% of the time	7	The cause will influence the P occurs less than 50% of the time
3	The AC has some impact on the benefit	8	The cause rarely influence performance
2	The AC has little impact on the benefit	9	The cause very rarely influence performance
1	The AC has no impact on the benefit	10	The cause will not influence performance

Score	Sustainability	
10	Sustains B all of the time	**AC - Alternative Element/Component**
9	Sustains B nearly all of the time	**B - Benefit, P- Performance**
8	Sustains B most of the time of the AC	
7	Sustains B about 2/3 of the time	
6	Sustains B more than 50% of the time	**Note:**
5	Sustains B about 50% of the time	If you cannot sustain performance, then the "new
4	Sustains B slightly less than 50% of the time	approach" may not be worthwhile
3	Rarely sustains benefit	
2	Very rarely sustains benefit	
1	Never sustains benefit	

Figure 6.8   Small medical firm example.

To validate, collect empirical evidence (both active and passive) data, examine for patterns and trends, and determine if variation (inconsistency) decreased. Sustained (success) is a key for innovation. *Note*: AC = Alternative element/component; B = Benefit; P = Performance.

EXERCISE 6.4: CONSTRUCT ABIA WORKSHEET FOR A NEW APPROACH

Transfer the worksheet information to the ABIA template and complete the analysis. List the findings and describe the results.

The remaining portion of this step is in validating the results of the ABIA tool and deciding how to proceed. The decision rests with the results of the ABIA and acquisition of confirmatory information. This could come in the form of

1. Empirical evidence (experimentation and simulation are great methods to estimate benefits and life cycle maturity)
2. Past experiences (including those of competitors) that proved highly successful
3. Specific customer/consumer needs collected either through interviewing/ focus groups or analytics to determine needs, wants, or desires
4. The creative minds of employees, partners (suppliers, stakeholders), and management

To evaluate the new approach, consider alternatives and related consequences. Think of alternatives and consequences as the simplest law of Newtonian physics—for every action there is a reaction; for every alternative, there are consequences (and benefits). This process moves critical thinking to a higher dimension

Table 6.6 Alternative/Consequence Evaluation

Key Attribute Component	Alternative	Consequence	Severity	Benefit

(4-C) (company, customer, component [attribute], and consequences). There are consequences with any choice, the goal is to minimize these consequences and deliver increased benefit or value. If a choice is to select a new approach, then what are the consequences (these can be negative, neutral, or positive)? This requires combining the 4-C approach with time (to determine severity). List the components (KAs) that constitute the new approach. Brainstorm a list of alternative approaches and related benefits. Indicate the type and value of the benefit and define the measurement. To determine how the alternative(s) will change the outcome of sustained success, use the 4-D thinking (customer, company, component, and consequence). When developing Table 6.6, use the 4-D thinking (Figure 6.9) to influence your thinking. Next, evaluate the consequence as to its severity. (Note: Consequences with a small or negligible severity are an optimal state. You weigh severity with benefit to make a final decision.)

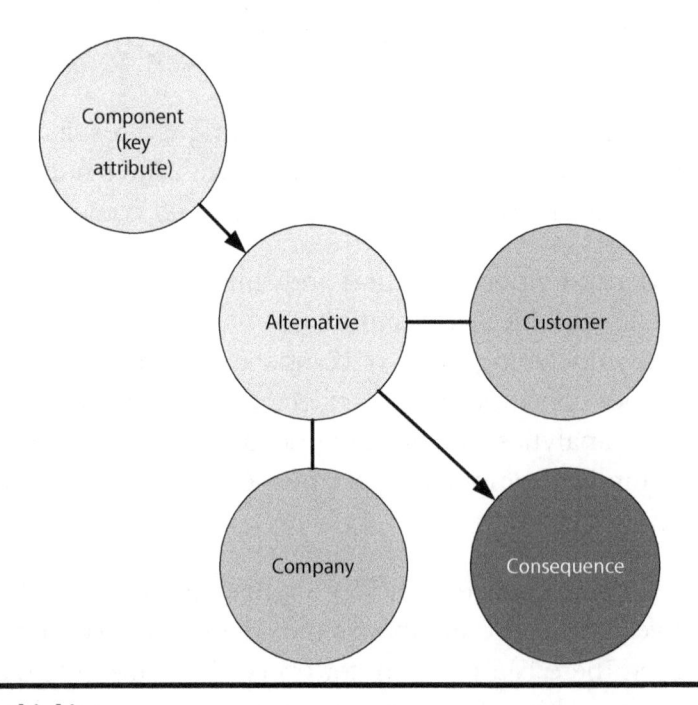

Figure 6.9 4-D thinking.

List the consequences of each alternatives (remember, the consequence can range from positive to negative). This exercise may expose a new alternative or you may consider a different alternative due to the consequences, severity, and benefit. Table 6.6 summarizes the information derived from the 4-D thinking process.

Consequence Scale

- Positive— Adds to or creates a new benefit
- Neutral— Does not add discernible benefit
- Negative—There is no benefit or a negative effect is present

Now rate the severity of the consequence, based on long-term success of the benefit.

Severity Scale

The influence exerted by the consequence requires consideration. If the team chooses an alternative, for example, to save cost (benefit), what are the long-term consequences and can these reduce, eliminate, or create a negative effect on the benefit?

- Major influence—   (positive, negative effects)
- Marginal influence— (limited positive and negative effects)
- Minimal influence— Neutral response—consequence does little to change benefit
- No influence—   Benefit consequence pair is inconsequential

Benefit Scale

- Major benefit
- Marginal benefit
- Minimal benefit
- No influence

Consequences have a major time dependency as well. Consequences may hide or have little effect in early stages of the product or service design but reveal its effect in the future. Choosing an alternative based on traditional thought processes, rather than 4-D thinking, may significantly shorten the life cycle of a new approach. The warning here is to be cognizant of the consequences and develop contingencies to address identified consequences. In summary, choosing an alternative approach may seem simple, yet in reality, the choice may have compound effects that can ripple through the organization long after adopting the new approach as a standard practice.

> **EXERCISE 6.5: COMPLETE AN ALTERNATIVE/CONSEQUENCE EVALUATION**
>
> You can choose either a work or personal example of time when you decided to choose the alternative rather than your initial choice.

Finally, the team should have enough information to judge viability and decide which new innovation opportunity or approach to implement. Because new approaches do not require infrastructure changes or modifications, the approach requires far less time to implement. The evaluations will quicken when a new thought process takes charge. Innovation is just not about the latest gadget or technology; it requires a change of mindset at the organizational level. When the benefit is sustainable over a period and the consequences determined minimal, the implementation occurs rapidly, and the approach perceived as innovative.

Step 3: Developing Objectives

After completing the decision to move on the new approach, the next step is to synchronize objectives. The development of preliminary objectives occurs during the innovation opportunity or project selection phase. If not completed during this phase, then objectives must be set for the new approach. Figure 6.10 details the flow assuming some preliminary objectives exist. The main purpose of this step is to reconcile the objectives, based on the latest version of the new approach.

Convert the benefits from the previous step to outcomes for this step. The outcomes become objectives when the item is properly staged (benefits, requirements, assumptions, and limitations). Remember to apply the SMART criteria when building any objectives. Objectives need a defined time line and must link to some existing performance (generally financial) measure.

Compare those objectives created during the project selection phase with the acceptance criteria developed during this process. Use the reconciliation tool to examine differences and apply modifications. Typical success measures include:

- The customer's perception of innovation and appetite for new approaches
- Acceptance criteria developed to measure performance and success
- Cost and overall appeal
- Profitability, based on present costs and availability of resources

These high-level success measures are criteria to measure objective effectiveness. It is possible that objectives generated at the project selection phase can convert to innovation project objectives as the project progresses. Project objectives must transform into a set of more realistic objectives used to track and monitor (performance) success. Use the reconciliation tool (Table 6.7), to revise and modify project objectives to longer-term performance metrics, used to judge success.

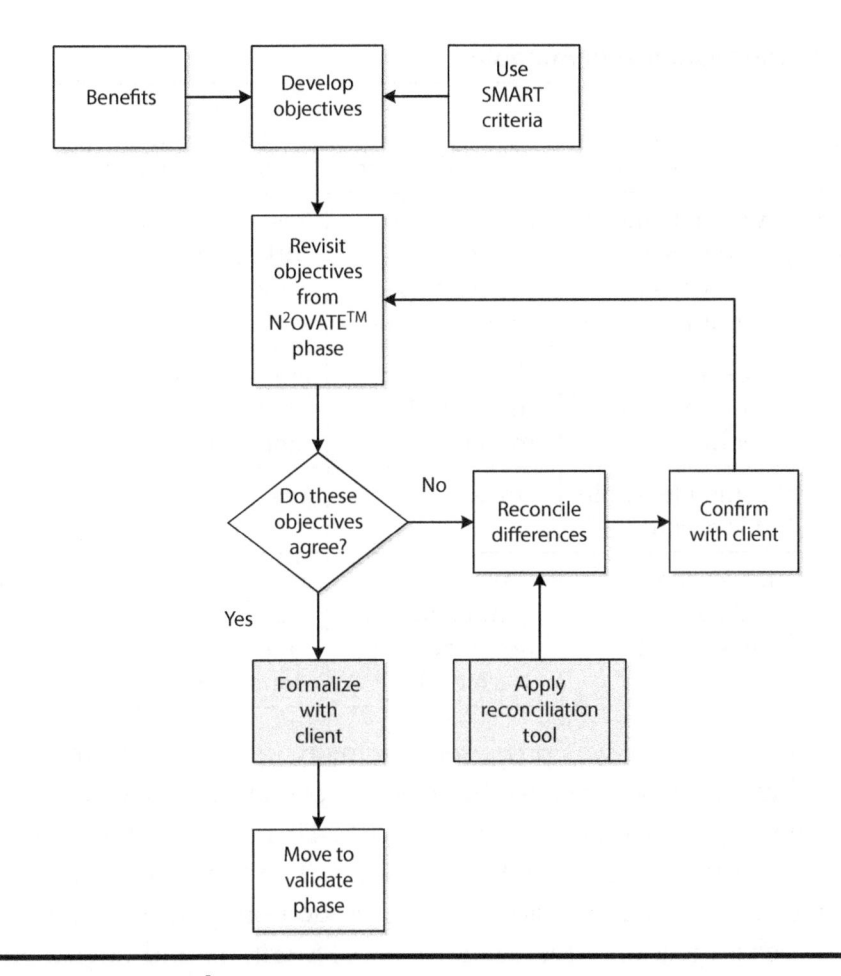

Figure 6.10   New approach—step 3.

This is a simple tool to reconcile any differences or modify an objective using the most recent information. Consider the following example: Small medical firm (with two offices) trying to diversify outside of their traditional chiropractic practice. Table 6.8 details the example.

Table 6.7   Reconciliation Tool

New Approach Element	*Existing Objective*	*New Objective*	*Does It Meet Success Criteria?*	*Does It Add Value?*

Table 6.8   Reconciliation Tool Example

New Approach Element	Existing Objective	New Objective	Does It Meet Success Criteria?	Does It Add Value?
Nutritional guidance	Add-on to more traditional services—2 months	More holistic approach: separate space/ office, 3 months	Yes, focuses each office, more effective use	Yes
Social media	Face book presence—1 month	Hire web manager, 1 month	No, but required to manage message and "hits"	Unknown
New brochure	Complete within 1–2 months	Similar	Yes	Yes
New message	Review and validate message, 2–3 weeks	New message combined with new marketing, 1–2 months	Yes, convince customers new approach is innovative	Yes

Only the new brochure was proposed originally in its same form. Items, such as social media exposure and the message content underwent an objective change, adding time to accomplish the task. This is a useful tool for alignment, especially if the team has not met recently. The tool demonstrates the fluid aspect of objective creation and adjustment. In addition, it asks a simple set of questions—does it meet the organization's success criteria and does it add value. These two criteria grow in importance as the project continues. As the third step ends, management and the team reach consensus on the objectives. As the project evolves, objectives will change. This tool assures that the objectives meet the success criteria and adds value.

> **EXERCISE 6.6: RECONCILIATION TOOL**
>
> Create and use a Reconciliation Tool, check again a set of objectives created in the past. How does time affect the objective?

Step 4: Validation

Figure 6.11 documents the validation stage for a new approach. Obviously, planning such an event is a huge undertaking. It is important to mention that planning takes different forms throughout the N²OVATE™ process. Planning at step 1 focused on evaluation and review; planning at this stage involves testing and verification. Identifying the test and data needed begins the process. Important to note, the results of the data analysis at this stage must support the objective and meet the acceptance criteria. We recommend that the team consider both quantitative data (numbers) and descriptive data (perceptions, feelings, likes/dislikes,

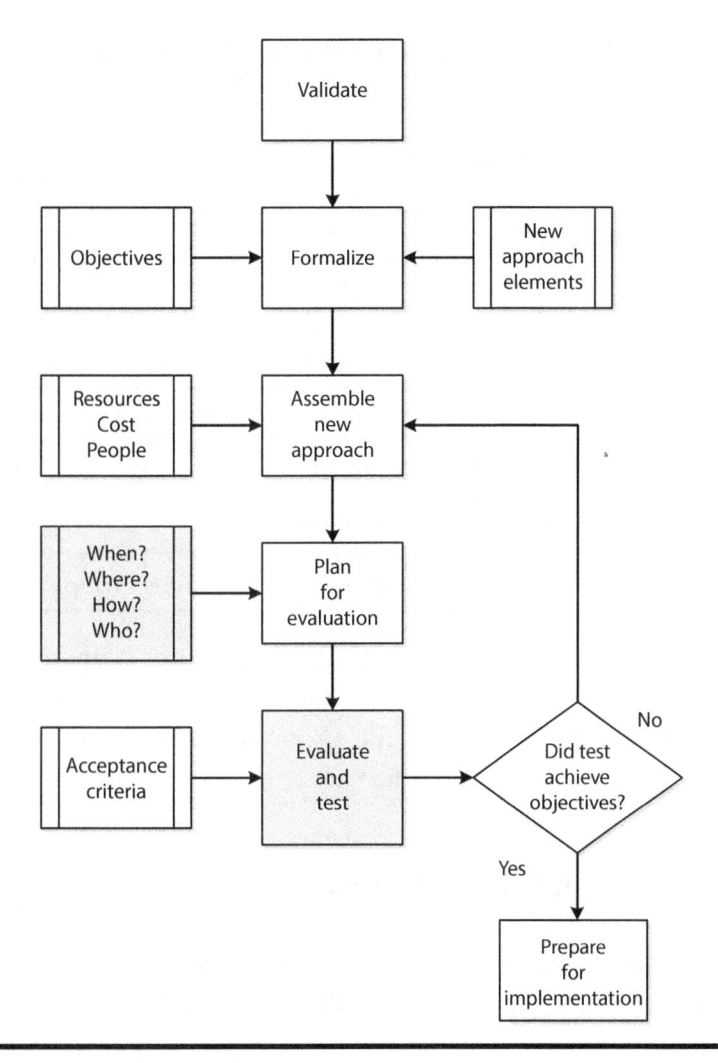

Figure 6.11　New approach—step 4.

etc.). Consider that quantitative data can come from numerous sources (especially since the product remains the same). Descriptive data (preferably that of active data—data collected through the interaction of receiver and provider) provide real-time analysis for decision making. (Note: Passive data are a lagging variable with time dependencies, for example, quarterly financial data.)

Determining the data permits an evaluation or test for verification. Using the small medical firm described previously, examine the data collection description and possible tools that could be used to support test and evaluation. Based on their acceptance criteria (copied from Table 6.8), the team assigned a description of the data needed to evaluate the new approach. Table 6.9 also includes a tool or tools that analyze the data, permitting a verification of the process.

EXERCISE 6.7: ACCEPTANCE CRITERIA AND TOOL SELECTION

From the acceptance criteria table developed previously, describe the data and try to determine a tool you might use to evaluate the measure.

Table 6.9 Data Description and Tool Selection for Verification

Acceptance Criteria	Data Description	Possible Tool
Implementation time	Counts—Passive	Simulation
Overall costs	Accounting—Passive	Forecasting/risk analysis
Advertising costs	Accounting—Passive	Forecasting/ risk analysis
Marketing costs	Accounting—Passive	Forecasting/ risk analysis
Video costs	Accounting—Passive	Forecasting/ risk analysis
Number of patients	Counts—Passive	Simulation/forecast
Office disruption	Descriptive (active) perceptual	Surveys, interviews
Patient satisfaction	Descriptive (active/ passive) perceptual	Surveys, interviews, focus groups

Although presented at this phase, it would be far more beneficial to complete at step 1 (for future projects), given a fuller understanding of the process, using this information to evaluate and verify the progression from initialization to full implementation. This then concludes step 4.

Step 5: Alignment and Adaptation

Step 5 has two unique elements, one for adaptation (Figure 6.12), and other for alignment (Figure 6.13), the process of acclimating to the new process and set of outcomes.

Adaptation involves elements of performance, human expectations, and acceptance. Performance is not restricted to a traditional definition but here defines the ability to accept and acclimate. One such measure is adaptation time that measures initiation to full implementation. Adaptation time permits employees to adjust and modify their behaviors to the new reality. Other measures of performance at this stage:

- Adoption time—Time from full implementation to full committal (stakeholder buy-in)
- Adoption cost—Total cost to full committal
- Achievement time—Time to achieve (meet) objectives (financial, process, quality)
- Achievement cost—Total additional costs incurred to meet objectives
- Effectiveness time—Time to reach and maintain a stable state (process operates without frequent adjustment or monitoring—output is consistent)
- Effectiveness cost—Additional costs required to achieve steady state

Next step is to determine whether performance measures meet expectations. Often, planners do not consider time and cost expenditures to reach full capacity as

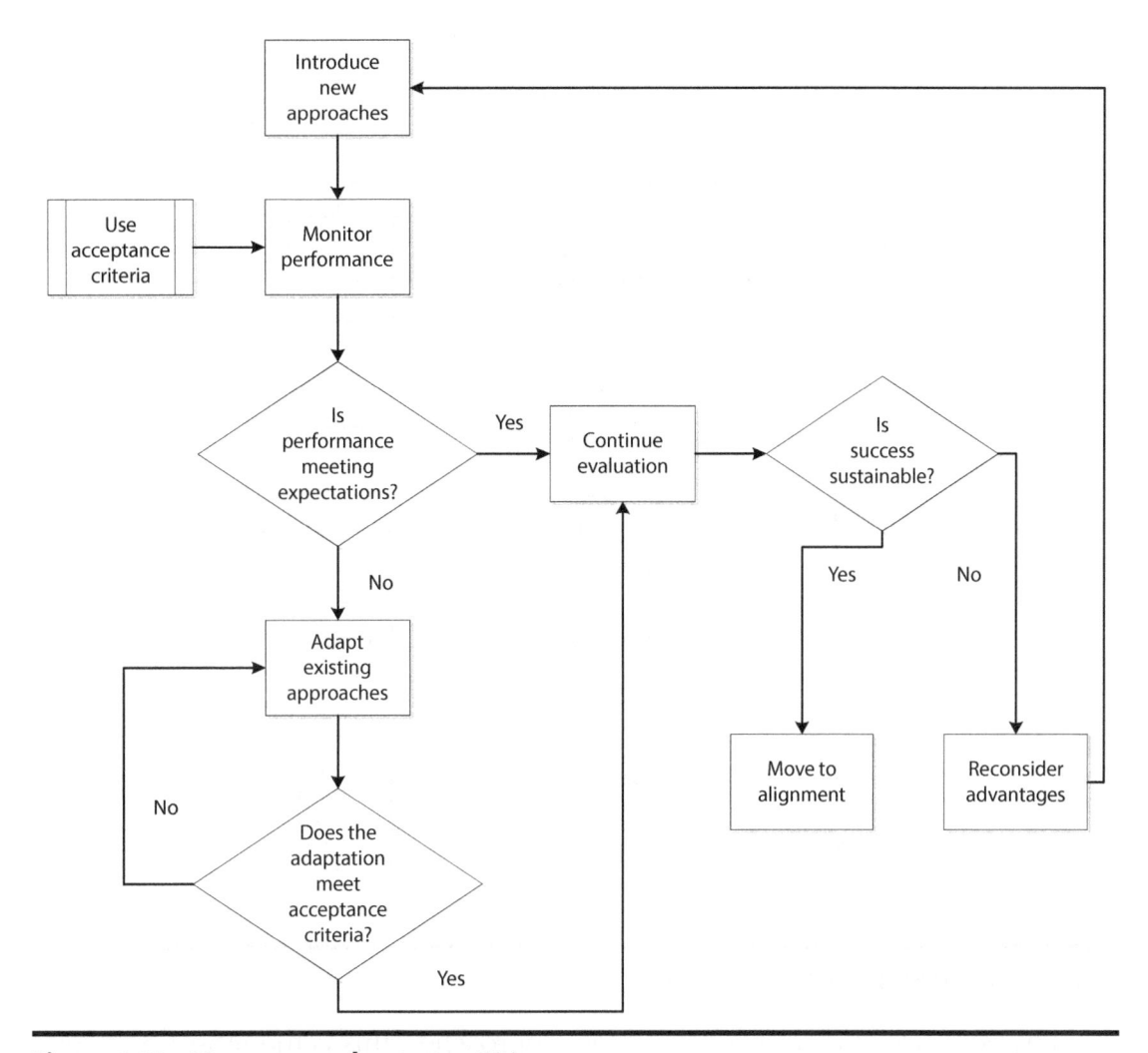

Figure 6.12 New approaches—step 5(a).

a legitimate expense and the project suffers as it struggles to meet established expectations. Careful planning will alleviate this concern. When reality meets expectations, this step is nearly complete. Consider adaptation as the nonhuman component; alignment is the unique process of accepting and internalizing the change.

EXERCISE 6.8

Complete a cursory review of a project alignment performance measures. Is the expenditure of time and cost above or below your expectations? Explain.

Figure 6.12 details the alignment phase. Its focus is on people as they adjust to a new reality. Achieving alignment requires that all inputs (resources, materials, etc.) match up with all human actions, promoted strategies, and outputs (outcomes). The most tangible portion of the alignment phase is the message that is distributed. Customers need to believe (and accept) that their needs are satisfied and the product, service, or technology is innovative. Therefore, develop a simple message that includes objectives and expected outcomes that must be

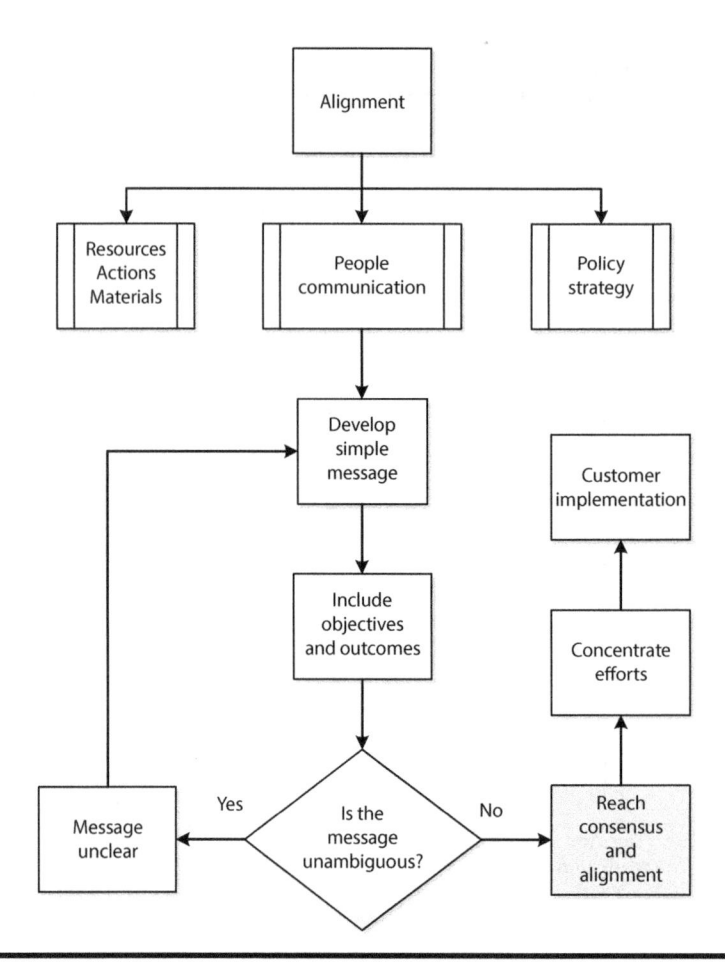

Figure 6.13 New approach—step 5(b).

unambiguous, clear, and sincere. For new approaches, this is the most powerful mechanism to get the item into the hands of those who want to understand it as innovative. Do not tell your customers it is innovative; rather show them how your organization has satisfied the need while maintaining a fair price (excellent value). Enable the customers (users) to want the item!

EXERCISE 6.9

Consider a product, service, or technology that has successfully introduced a "new approach." Create a message that would attract prospective buyers to the product and identify who might want the item.

Step 6: Tracking Performance

Performance measures will vary from one organization to the next. Identify measures of performance into two categories: tangible and intangible. For an organization that produces products and technology, the number of tangible measures will exceed the number of intangible items. For those organizations that provide services the opposite will be true.

For many, innovation remains only within the realm of technology development. These types of innovation are easy to track and generally easy to measure improvement. Services, on the other hand, are difficult to measures and yet easy to determine if successful. This is due to a large number of intangible measures that are difficult to measure, but simple to observe. Service innovations are generally quicker to implement and are also easier to copy and replace. Therefore, those in service businesses may choose a new approach as their most frequent innovation type. This then would require service providers to rely on intangible performance measures as a critical source of feedback. Service performance measures such KPPs and KPIs that would more often be combinations of both tangible and intangible measures.

Defining and classifying service performance requires categorizing by internal and external measures as well as categorization into tangible and intangible metrics. For innovation, the focus is on the external as the human customer is the judge of innovation. This judgment will include both tangible and intangible measures to evaluate product, service, or technology performance. The key takeaway is that you need to measure both tangible and intangible measures, especially when dealing with service innovation.

The list (Table 6.10) provided is only a place to start given the differences within each organization. Some measures are "universal" for businesses (i.e., these measures apply to Service (S), Product (P), or Technology (T) offerings). Process measures are unique to each business or organization. Who benefits from the measure depends upon whether it is internal (Organization/Business, O/B) or external (Customer/User, C/U).

For external measures: For the CSFs, KPP, and KPI measures, establish specifications or expected levels of performance. Usually accomplished at the project selection phase (of the N²OVATE™ process); performance tracking can also occur at this phase as well. Avoiding the project selection phase would cause this information to be finalized at this stage.

Now if an organization misreads or improperly identifies the needs of the customer/user, they risk the customer or user not recognizing the product or service as innovative. This happens all the time—consider the accident avoidance devices on high-price luxury cars which have become commonplace just as air-conditioning did 40–50 years ago. The accessory has gone from being innovative to now routine (expected). The manufacturers need to introduce innovative improvements just to keep the interest of the customer/user.

The most difficult challenge is keep introducing new and "better" innovations that keep the consumer wanting more. A reduction in costs and increases in profit are measures of performance, but if the customer/user never experiences these benefits, they may not judge the item as innovative. The customer measures performance based on their use and the resulting experiences they encounter. This measure of use has a tangible and intangible component. There are a number of caveats, though. Small innovative projects do not require the attention to measure that large innovative projects demand. This is why innovation is not an everyday

Table 6.10 External Evaluative Measures

Product/Service Technology	Beneficiary	Measure of Performance	External Tangible	External Intangible
S/P/T	O/B, C/U	Costs	X	
S/P/T	O/B	Market share	X	
S/P/T	O/B	Profit	X	
S/P/T	O/B, C/U	New business	X	
S/P/T	O/B, C/U	Growth rate	X	
S/P/T	O/B, C/U	ROI	X	
S/P/T	O/B, C/U	Image		X
S/P/T	O/B, C/U	Reputation		X
S/P/T	O/B, C/U	Satisfaction		X
S/P/T	O/B	Company—CSR		X
S/P/T	O/B, C/U	Meeting needs		X
S/P/T	O/B, C/U	Processing time	X	
S	O/B, C/U	Delivery time	X	
S/P	O/B, C/U	Wait time	X	
S/P/T	O/B, C/U	Functionality[a]	X	X
S/P/T	O/B, C/U	Reliability	X	X
S/P/T	O/B, C/U	Dependability	X	X

[a] These include all measures of usage and expected performance.

business or operation. Business and organization need innovation—but not all the time. To capture these human measures, consider the following list (Table 6.11).

Many businesses or organizations consider the intangible costs, as the cost of doing business. If these costs were small and had little impact, then this would be a reasonable assumption. However, most businesses and organizations consider these "annoyance measures" and either do not measure these effectively or estimate these measures far below their actual importance. Consider a restaurant. It offers both product (food) and services (serving the customer). One can easily measure the cost of food, employee salaries and benefits, rent, utilities, etc. How does the establishment measure customer satisfaction? Poor service kills a restaurant as quick as poor food or presentation. These measures are equally important. Focusing on one and not the other is "suicide" for the business. It happens, unfortunately, all the time with service businesses.

Customer complaints frequently beset cable companies. Customers leave for a "better deal" with another provider, only to lave again for the next best deal. The amount of profit (and goodwill) lost by the cable companies is enormous. It

Table 6.11 Human Measures

Product/Service Technology	Beneficiary	Measure of Performance	Internal	
			Tangible	Intangible
S/P/T	O/B	Job satisfaction	X	
S/P/T	O/B	Stress	X	X
S/P/T	O/B	Motivation	X	X
S/P/T	O/B	Productive hours[b]	X	X
S/P/T	O/B	Time to finish task[b]	X	
S/P/T	O/B	Task accomplishment	X	X
S/P/T	O/B	Wait time[b]	X	X
S/P/T	O/B	Functionality[a]	X	X
S/P/T	O/B	Performance	X	X
S/P/T	O/B	Honesty		X

[a] Meets all functional requirements.
[b] Effectiveness—communications, decision making, follow-through, etc.

seems to be a management mindset that this is a normal behavior. Not measuring or addressing the intangibles can lead to a great loss of potential profit. If you do not measure this loss, you will never know your company's profit potential.

With innovation, leadership is looking for both tangible and intangible benefits. More often, the tangible benefits are the deciding factor for innovation projects. This can be effective for products and technology but indecisive for services. Nonetheless, there is a need for establishing the return on investment (ROI) of any innovation project.

One of the provocative questions focuses on how a business or organization truly measures project ROI? That is, if a business invests $50,000 in innovation training and project support, what can they expect in return? A simple ROI calculation is, ROI = (Gains from investment Costs of investment)/Costs of investment. This is the definition usually specified in the finance community. A less-used ROI calculation uses net present value, which appears better suited for service applications. There are pros and cons in using annual nominal dollars versus current (NPV) dollars. Using NPV typically results in more conservative and less optimistic ROIs. In the opinion of the authors, NPV calculation is best. Avoiding this approach could lead to an incorrect ROI and could result in a bad investment decision, especially when longer-term benefits are increasing over a longer-time horizon.

This would result in the ROI equation (Thanks to Joe O'Donnell in a personal e-mail, dated June 22, 2015):

$$ROI = (NPV \text{ of benefits} - NPV \text{ of costs})/NPV \text{ of costs}$$

Expect both tangible and intangible benefits (be sure that both are measured and analyzed) as both contribute to the bottom-line. Consider a value-added ROI approach, applying value to the intangible components.

Figure 6.14 provides the framework for analyzing (tracking) performance measures.

All innovation projects must deliver benefit to the customer and to the organization. Using the above measures, the most natural measures are revenue, cost reduction, market share plus a variety of intangible measures (this depends upon the classification type—product, service, or technology).

Begin with an appropriate ROI (say 10%). The difficulty is in assessing intangible benefits—what is a happy customer worth? Most businesses truly never address these measures in detail. For services, this is a key measure requiring some form of evaluation and estimation. Another difficulty is assessing overall market share improvement. Is this increased product or services sales? On the other hand, is there a longer-term component to market share. What about competitive advantage—is this market share?

Much of the intangible information comes from interacting with the customer or user. The key is measuring this with your customers. Every X percent of customer satisfaction is equal to Y percent increase in sales. Remember, though, that

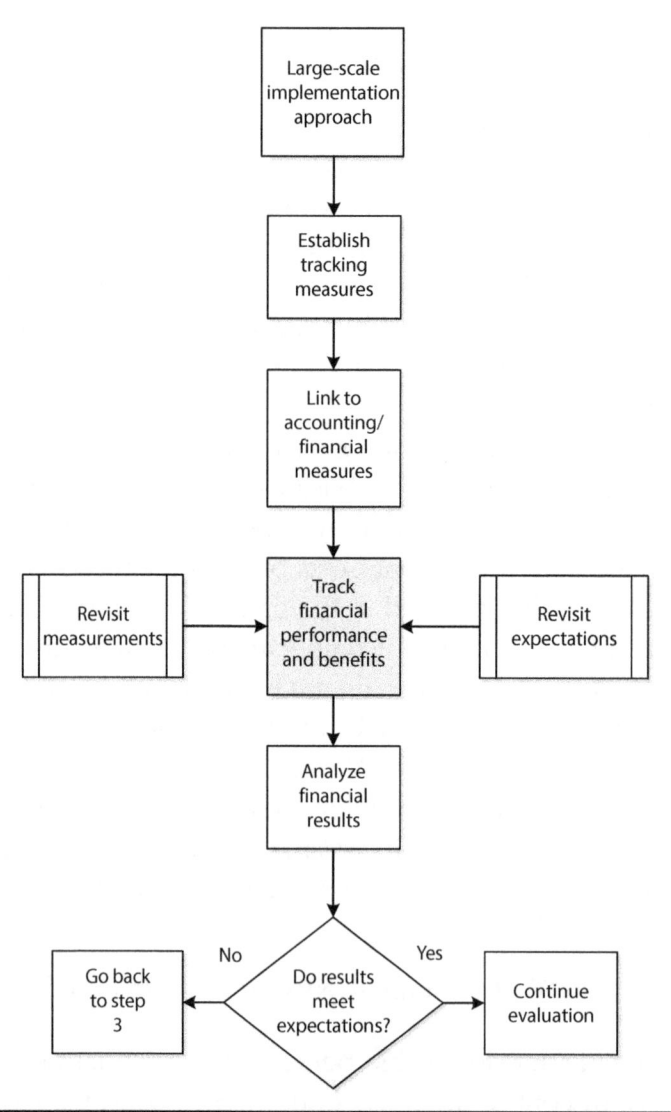

Figure 6.14   New approaches—step 6.

innovation meets some needs that have previously been ignored (or abandoned) and this should be worth a Y percent increase in sales/profit/market share, as well. As with any customer, there is also "the hassle" effect. Meeting a specific, unfulfilled need may greatly reduce the "hassle effect" (repeated customer complaints (e-mails, paperwork, etc.), problem solving, lost time, and productivity). What is this worth to the company? For some customers, reducing their complaints (inquiries) is worth a 10% or more improvement in efficiency and productivity.

Many of these intangible measures come from a survey (or focus groups) and are estimates. These surveys are useful for assessing needs as well. Never underestimate the information gained from this approach, nor undervalue its information content.

CEOs want to see bottom-line improvements (which is understandable) but it may not be possible if the cost accounting systems (cost improvements mixed in with losses) cannot account for the intangibles and provides only lagging rather than leading information.

We recommend the following:

1. Evaluate internal accounting systems to determine if all costs have a direct impact on profits. Remember tangible costs are only one measure of performance and not the entire domain.
2. Determine the appropriateness of intangible measures—what is their cumulative effect on overall costs and profits?
3. Use a survey (telephone, e-mail, or secure link) or interview (focus group) to collect information on customer needs, what satisfies the customer and make that customer recommend the business.
4. Create a scale of success (profitability). Rank the top intangible measures. Determine (estimate) how the intangible measure increases (decreases) sales, improves market share and competitive advantage. This is an estimate, but a critical measure of success. If you do not ask, you will not truly know! Consider an intangible such as customer satisfaction.
   a. Create a scale for customer satisfaction (with 1 = small improvement, 5 = large improvement), for example:

Scale	Sales Improvement (%)	Profit (Bottom-Line)
0	0	$0
1	1–3	(Depends on the business)
2	4–6	
3	7–8	
4	9–10	
5	Over 10	

   b. Create a similar scale for market share/competitive advantage, etc.

5. Identify tangible costs (training/development, resource costs, project costs, wages and benefits, lost time, etc.) + Intangible costs (lost opportunity, waste, inefficiencies, ineffectiveness, etc., of present process).
6. Identify benefits (customer satisfaction, increased sales and market share, efficiency improvements, effectiveness, productivity improvements, employee satisfaction).
7. ROI = ($ Benefits − $ Costs). This will be an estimate (any time intangibles exceed tangible measures).

EXERCISE 6.10

Create a scale that links an intangible measure to a success measure. Estimate how much an increase or decrease will affect the measure of success.

Innovation benefits should easily exceed costs for a project to be profitable. Relying on just tangible measures will inaccurately identify opportunities and increase failure (due to lost opportunities).

Developing and implementing these measures is beyond the scope and intent of this handbook. It is a developing topic, given the rise of analytics and big data. These intangible features contribute much to the success of an item. Avoiding these will result in lost opportunity.

Step 7: Monitor and Control

The final step is initiating a monitor and control mechanism. This will be similar for step 7 in Chapter 5. The purpose is to create a mechanism for monitoring and control, which also serves to highlight problems before these cause significant damage. This process is critical for maintaining the success level achieved during early stages in the development cycle. Figure 6.15 details this monitor and control phase. However, this step requires a new set of analytical techniques, developed specifically for evaluation and monitoring purposes. This flowchart is identical to that described in Chapter 5 so no further discussion is necessary. Rather, we present a description of the use of control charts as a control mechanism.

Analyzing Data

The key is to analyze the data, look for warning signals, react when there is a signal, and leave the process alone when there is not signal. This is true for any type of continuous (the data exist across a continuum) data, such as financial data, processing speeds, temperatures, etc. Discrete data are a snapshot of the process, very useful for intangible data. Discrete data require a standard or requirement from which to judge the data. Errors are discrete data, collected over time. For something to be in error, there must be a standard from which to judge the item.

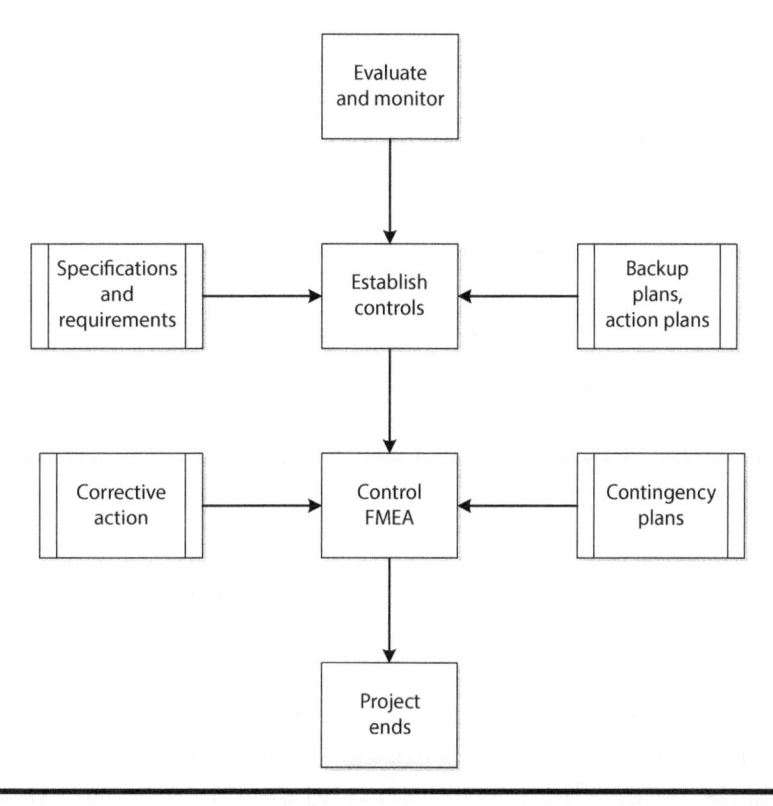

Figure 6.15   New approach—step 7. (Excerpt taken from McLaughlin, G. and Kennedy, W.R. (2015). *A Guide to Innovation Processes and Solutions for Government.* **Productivity Press, Boca Raton, FL. ISBN: 978-1-4987-2157-8.)**

Identify the critical measures (CSFs, KPIs, and KPPs) to evaluate. For tangible measures, use run charts or control charts. Find a description of run charts in the *ENOVALE: unlocking sustained innovation project success* (McLaughlin and Caraballo, 2013b). In contrast, control charts (Figure 6.16) provide a unique opportunity to control long- and short-term variation (volatility) and may help to define pattern, trends and cycles as well as explain expected long-term behavior. Control charts explain common and special cause variation. Common cause variation is random, everyday variation (consistency or volatility); special variation is unpredictable, due to one or more specific causes. Control charts identify special from common cause variation. You can only predict or forecast when common cause variation is present. Common cause variation is generally that variation between the upper (UCL) and lower (LCL) control limits. Common variation is innate to the process.

Special cause (you could call this disruptive) variation results in a process change and is present when a data point is "out-of-control." An out-of-control condition exists when any point is:

1. Outside of the control limits (control limits are based on actual process data) follow the assumption that the process is normally distributed.
2. There is a distinguishing pattern to the data set, exhibited in the chart.
3. There are cycles or trends in the data, exhibited in the chart.

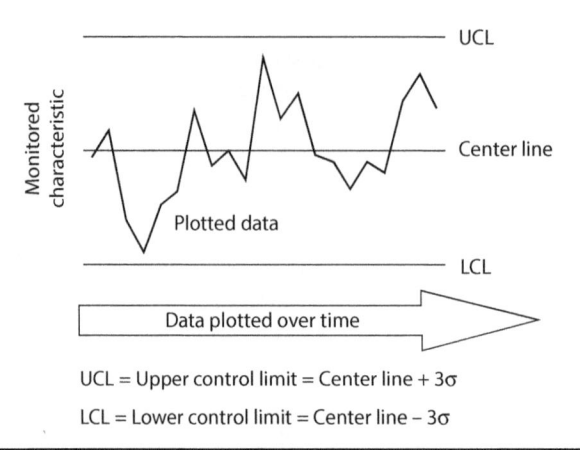

Figure 6.16   Control chart.

An out of control process means the entire process is shifting and is unpredictable. Control charts use either individual points or statistics (small group averages (medians), ranges, or standard deviations) to track a process shift. Control charts use ranges (max–min data point) or moving ranges (ranges based on present and past data) to track process consistency (volatility).

Control charts exist for both continuous and discrete data. Our discussion focuses only on continuous data, using only the most common control charts.

Figure 6.17 details a flowchart to assist in choosing the best control chart for the available data.

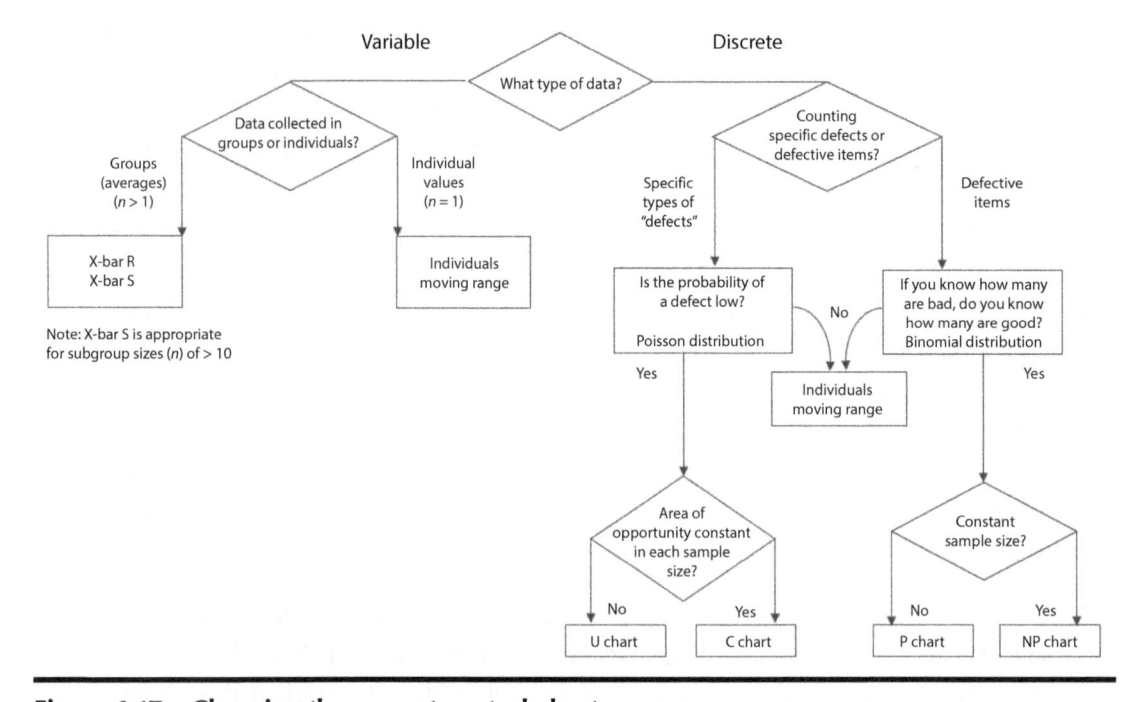

Figure 6.17   Choosing the correct control chart.

Control Chart Types and Examples

Individual control charts (Figure 6.18) are the most frequently used control charts. Some characteristics are:

1. Present information in time order, using consecutive individual data points
2. This chart assesses the stability and predictability of the process average (often used to predict future behavior)
3. Moving range chart (Figure 6.18) describes short-term variation in the process, assessing long-term process volatility
4. The moving range is the difference between consecutive data points

The interpretation of this control chart consists of:

1. The process has not changed; however, repeat visits can vary from 11 to 70 per month.
2. The moving range (measures day to day) is as high as 36 visits and as low as 0 visits. Each return visit, costs on average, $500.00.
3. This process could use improvement. Note: Apply innovative techniques to "in-control" processes.

For control purposes, the process is stable (in control), it needs only monitoring. Yet, the technique could be helpful for determining why the number of repeat visits is so large.

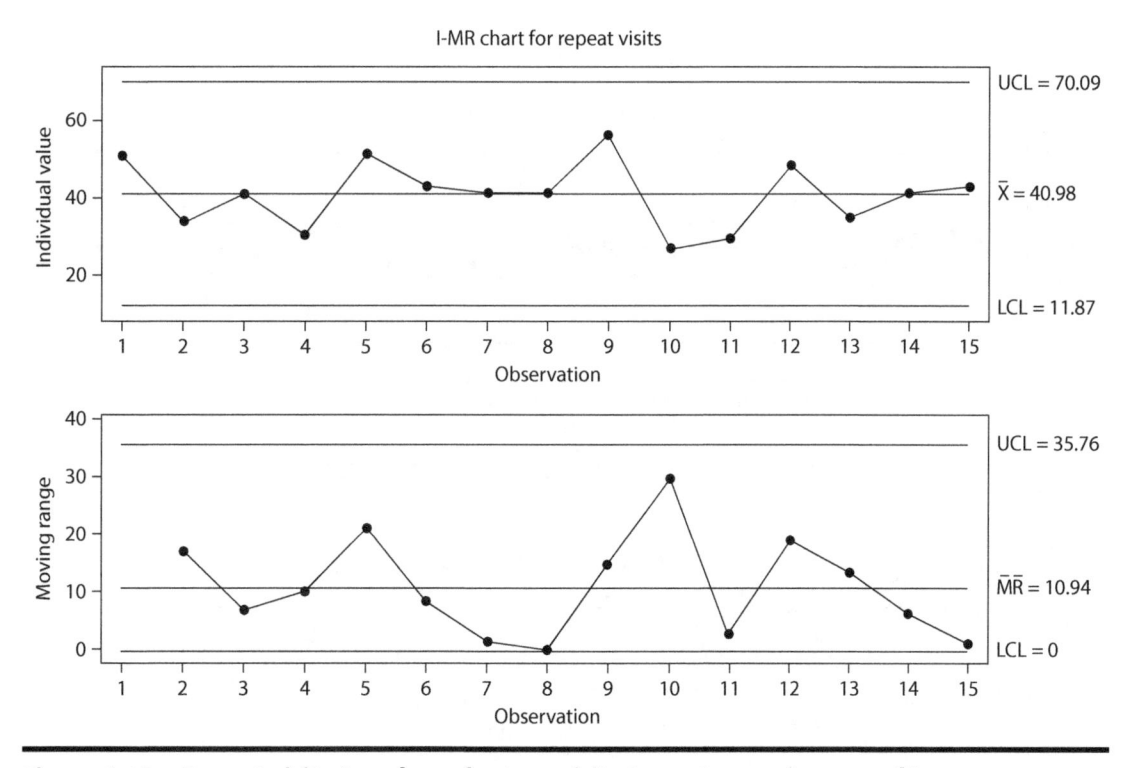

Figure 6.18   Repeat visits (number of return visits to customers in a month).

Calculation (formulas) of control limits and "out of control" situations are detailed in "Understanding Statistical Process Control" (2010, 3rd edition, SPC Press) by Don Wheeler.

For data that can be collected in small numbers, an average and a range (maximum value–minimum value) is the best choice. Each small group (2–10 samples) is a rational subgroup. If a business samples within the span of time of 1 lot, 1 day, 1 h, then the sample can examine volatility on a much smaller scale.

Average and Range Charts

Averages and ranges of samples are plotted on the chart. Control limits reflect expected variation in averages and ranges of size n.

- Average of subgroup averages
- Average of subgroup ranges

Each point on the X-bar chart (Figure 6.19) is based on the average (X-bar) of a rational subgroup of data points.

A *rational subgroup* is a subset of data defined by a stratifying factor or time. The purpose of rational subgrouping (average and range control charts) is to identify and separate special cause variation (within group variation) from common cause (between group variations).

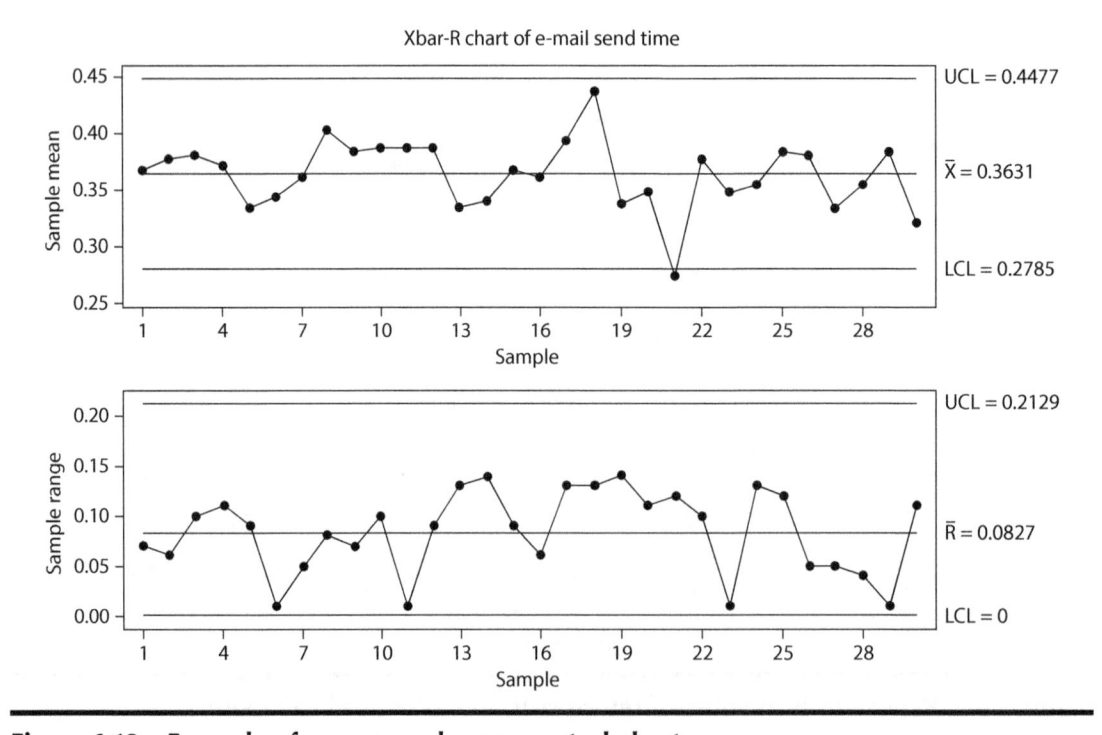

Figure 6.19 Example of average and range control chart.

The range chart exhibits variation from 0 to 20 s. The average chart shows an out-of-control point at sample average point 21. This suggests a special cause took place. On the positive side, these charts clearly demonstrate that the process improvement is possible. If this was used for control purposes, the business would want to examine what occurred at point 21. The formula for this chart is located in Appendix.

Control charts enable both process evaluation (monitoring) and control, but serve a purpose for real-time analysis. After plotting the data, the interpretations are made, and the team can then go on to evaluate the FMEA control phase (described in Chapter 5). Using what is described in Chapters 5 and 6, we have the two greatest control tools that permit a fixing a problem identified.

Summary

This completes the third chapter on new types of innovation. Rather than just focus on the extraordinary new types of innovation projects, this chapter focuses on everyday issues that still can meet the criteria of be new without the development costs. Consumers are often attracted to new products, services, or technology because of both its unique and special characteristics and the capability of participating in a product or service's evolution. Although the new approach may have the shortest life cycle, it promises to meet or exceed expectations when encountered by the public.

DISCUSSION QUESTIONS

1. Discuss strategies it would require to accept the concept of selling a new approach.
2. Discuss how a reality check in your organization would work. Can you identify simple opportunities outside the existing scope of your business today?
3. Identify and discuss personal new approaches in your job that you can implement today without a massive research effort.

ASSIGNMENTS

1. Consider a new approach for a product, service, or technology within your company or organization. This could be as simple as something you would do differently or a new approach to an existing process that you know needs innovation. Develop an approach, using steps 1 and 2.
2. How would you "sell" an idea on a new approach to your business associates? What triggers would it take to capture their interest and support?
3. Choose an element of a new approach and apply the control FMEA. Can you assure that this element will never sway off target again?

References

McLaughlin, G. and Caraballo, E. 2013a. *Chance or Choice: Unlocking Innovation Process.* Productivity Press, Boca Raton, FL. ISBN: 9781466581869.

McLaughlin, G. and Caraballo, E. 2013b. *ENOVALE: How to Unlock Sustained Innovation Project Success.* Productivity Press, Boca Raton, FL.

McLaughlin, G. and Kennedy, W.R. 2015. *A Guide to Innovation Processes and Solutions for Government.* Productivity Press, Boca Raton, FL. ISBN: 978-1-4987-2157-8.

Wheeler, D.J. and Chambers, D.S. 2010. *Understanding Statistical Process Control,* 3rd edition. SPC Press, Knoxville, TN.

Chapter 7

Incremental Innovation: Performance below Expectations

Introduction

Perhaps one of the most prominent and familiar meanings people tend to associate with an innovation is the improvement on a particular product, process, or service. In this chapter, we focus on the necessary steps to implement a project focused on improvement. Once you receive approval for your project to implement, the steps and examples presented in this discussion are crucial for your innovation team. One precursor for your team to understand is that with any innovation project, conditions, and situations may change as you proceed through the steps either prior to or during the implementation process. Subsequently, be open to change and flexible to the evolving nature of innovation. It may require periodic and recurring negotiations and evaluations as you move from concept to reality.

In this chapter, we introduce how the seven steps of the N²OVATE™ process is applied to an incremental innovation situation focused on improving performance in the manufacturing and production environment. Most specifically, we introduce steps associated with:

1. Nominating and negotiating an innovation opportunity focused on improving performance
2. Identifying reasons and requirements for achieving that improved performance
3. Operationalizing the outcome of the innovation solution
4. Verifying and validating the innovation solution
5. Adapting and aligning your organization and stakeholders, shareholders, and customers successfully implement the innovative solution
6. Tracking and tying the innovation to performance
7. Establishing the necessary controls to maintain and sustain that desired performance

The case study scenario and examples in this discussion will focus on incremental improvements in the manufacturing and production industry, most specifically, the manufacturing of corrugated boxes, which are representative of one of the more stable packaging segments within the United States.

Scenario 1: Incremental Improvement in Manufacturing and Production

Although a significant amount of manufacturing and production have been outsourced or transferred to other countries primarily to reduce the cost and increase profit margin, this has not always resulted in a positive outcome for some companies. In essence, off-shoring or near-shoring efforts have sometimes resulted in a reduction in quality, increased defect rates, public scrutiny on adherence to increasing demands for corporate social responsibility (CSR). That said, some companies have experienced a "win–win" scenario where these companies have achieved their financial objectives, improved the quality of their product, and effectively led the way in introducing CSR initiatives in other countries that directly improved the quality of life in other companies and served as models for CSR.

In regard to defining characteristic or critical element associated with innovation, an incremental improvement is performance. If the performance is substandard, then the innovation team's purpose will focus on raising performance to the levels that exceed expected objectives. Further, if performance currently meets the expected objectives but leadership's desire is to add more value by increasing production or improve efficiency, we would also contend this qualifies as an incremental improvement. In the case of manufacturing and production of packaging products, if a Flexoprinter and Folder Gluer machine center (hereafter referred to as "Flexo") has an advertised capacity to run some 5000 sheets per hour (objective or expectation) and it is only running 4200 sheets per hour (actual realized performance), there is an opportunity for incremental improvement. For this example case study, the performance is not meeting standards at present by some 16% from the objective. For this example, we offer the following modification to our N²OVATE™ process which involves the following steps for the innovation team's consideration:

1. **N**: Nominate and negotiate
2. **R**: Reasons and requirements (needs)
3. **O**: Operationalize the outcome
4. **V**: Verify and validate
5. **A**: Adapt and align
6. **T**: Track and tie to performance
7. **E**: Establish controls

To best illustrate the use of the NROVATE process, we will offer an example scenario of an actual incremental innovation improvement project from the manufacturing and production industry. Please keep in mind, the term "process" in this discussion can also be synonymous with product or service performance improvements.

Scenario and Machine Center (Equipment) Background

To help set the stage for our example scenario, the segment of the manufacturing and production industry we use to illustrate the incremental improvement process of NROVATE will be in the corrugated packaging segment. More specifically, our discussion focuses on the Flexo. We assume the equipment configuration for our Flexo has the following:

- A three-color printing capability (blue, green, and red)
- A feeder unit and conveyor capability (where stacks of precut sheets from a corrugator are loaded to feed the Flexo)
- Stacker (stacks the finished products)
- Strapper or bundler (applies strapping tape around the bundles for loading on a pallet for shipping) that feeds the conveyor system thoughout the plant

The machine is capable of running single and double wall-corrugated wallboard in B, E, C, and EB flute configurations with a maximum capacity or format of 650×1500 mm and a maximum of 650×2100 mm.

The typical shift staffing for the Flexo is two operators (one fully trained lead operator and one temporary operator). The lead operator handles the programming specifics (i.e., graphics and printing requirements, size and parameters of the product, color selection, recurring product quality checks, safety and compliance, data collection and entry of production numbers throughout the shift, and supervision of the temporary employee). The temporary employee, typically a term employee, is usually sourced from a temporary job agency and has minimal knowledge of the equipment. Their focus is to ensure sheets are stacked properly at the feeder section and check the bundles are properly stacked on the pallets for transportation to the shipping and receiving point.

The Flexo is scheduled to operate three 8-hour shifts a day, 5 days a week (Monday through Friday) to meet the current customer demands. Further, working Saturday and Sunday requires overtime pay for both the maintenance and operations departments, which if pursued would significantly impact the profit margin per unit produced. The plant sales staff and customer service department are in the final stages of securing a new client who requires the Flexo to produce a minimum of 600 additional units (boxes) per hour to meet the new customer demand and the expectation of the Director of Operations.

Currently, the availability rate of the Flexo over the past 12 months has averaged 90% (available to run corrugated sheets and produce box products) and the 10% is downtime attributed to unscheduled maintenance (6% due to unplanned equipment faults breakdowns and scheduled or preventive maintenance activities and 4% due to replacement of high wear parts and required alignments/operator cleaning requirements). The average uptime rate over the past 12 months has averaged to 64% (the machine is actually producing boxes). Further, the terms "company" and "plant" are used interchangeably but equate to the same organization.

Step 1: Nominating and Negotiating

In the first step, Figure 7.1, we suggest a team lead is assigned and begins with identifying members for the innovation team. The team lead should complete an initial assessment of the expected outcome and determine the start developing the preliminary list of resources required while drafting initial expectations (objectives) defined my leadership and management. This initial gauge will help guide the team selection process. In actuality, these activities should set the stage for the steps identified in step 1, Nominate and Negotiate, and occur prior to the start of implementation. Keep in mind, as you progress through the steps identified in this stage, negotiations with management will continue to refine objectives, requirements, and success factors.

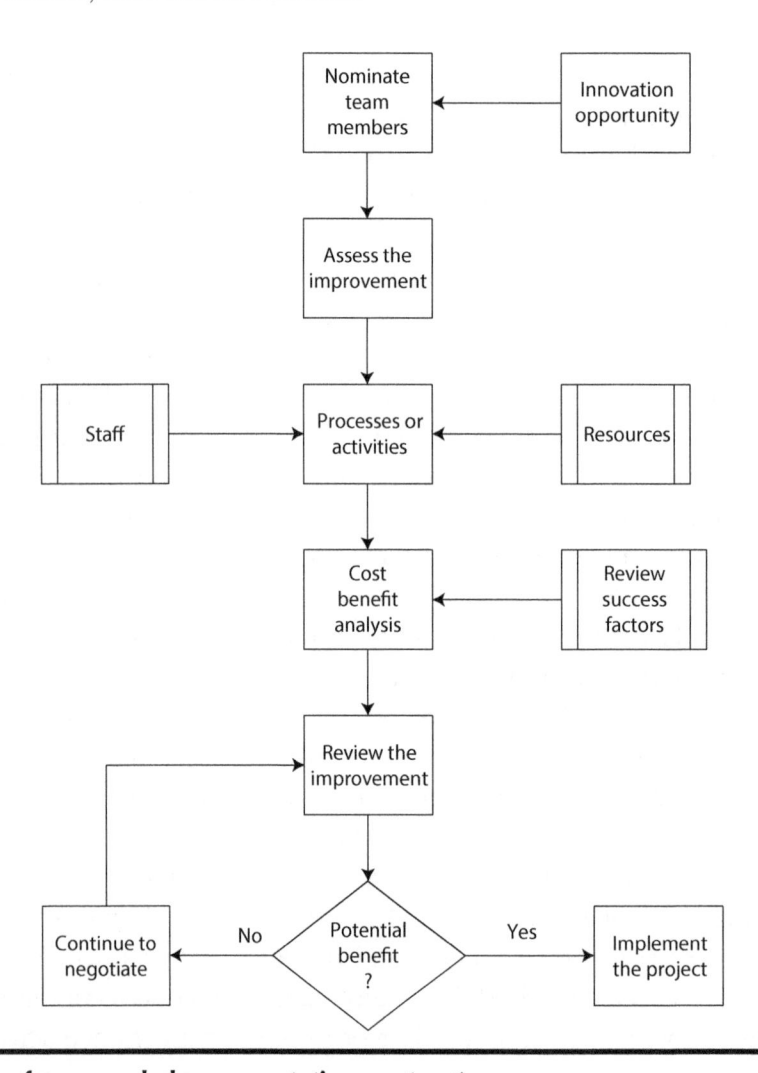

Figure 7.1 Performance below expectations—step 1.

Nominating the right complement of team members can be one of the most complicated steps a team leader will face in this process. Often times the resources you feel will be the best fit for your project are not available or are already over-tasked with their primary responsibilities. Request senior leadership's full support and cooperation as competing interests will truly have a significant impact on your ability to achieve the very objectives you seek to achieve. Be prepared to have a backup or alternative list of resources in case your primary choice is not available. Some primary considerations in selecting team members for this example scenario are knowledge of the equipment (Flexo), standard operating procedures, training, qualifications for running the equipment, maintenance concepts, preventive main-tenance (quality) and recurring cleaning requirements, production scheduling or orders, and daily performance and data collection requirements for starters.

After identifying your team requirements and securing the support of senior leadership and management, ensure your team and management understands the schedule meetings and time requirements you will require from each member on the team. Publish an initial schedule that you, as the team lead, will need to share with the team and management. Keep in mind that your initial schedule will be evolutionary in nature with changes shared at all levels within your plant or facility as you move through the steps of your innovation project. Nominating and selecting your team will be a challenge. In our example scenario for this discussion, you will need to consider representation from the following departments (at a minimum):

- Operations
- Maintenance (in-house or the contractor representative if your equipment is maintained under warranty or contract support)
- Quality assurance and safety
- Customer service (and possibly accounting)
- Scheduling
- Shipping and receiving
- Facility manager
- On-site contractor support and key suppliers (partners) involved with the machine, process, or service your project focuses on

If you have a reliability manager or an engineer on staff, they might also be a consideration since they typically are your process improvement leads and have an enterprise-level perspective on your facility's operations. Once you have narrowed your list of potential team members down, review all the steps in the NROVATE process with the goal of assigning when each of the areas identified above are required in your process flow. This will help you better estimate the time requirements and specific tasking's your team will need to project the worth in pursuing the project after assessment. Depending on the initial assessment of the complexity and value added that your project can provide in achieving performance improvements in the Flexo production capability, you may want to perform an initial personality compatibility assessment.

The next step is to make your team member selection. Although acquiring valuable information and inputs from all the aforementioned players (departments) is important in achieving buy-in and surfacing potential negative impacts on the anticipated outcome(s) from an innovation project objective or purpose, the innovation leader must remain cognizant of the ultimate goal or objective. In this case, resolving the performance disconnect between the advertised or expected capability of the Flex and the Director of Operations desire to improve that level of performance to support the new clients requirements.

Selecting team members can be a challenge. You want to avoid assigning members to your core team based on:

■ Position or title
■ Past successes (which don't directly translate to the project objective)
■ Known competing interests and hidden agendas
■ The simple desire to be part of the project for personal recognition or gain

For an innovation project, the goal is not to assemble a diverse group of representatives from every department or that hold different views on innovation. The goal is to assemble a team of "like-minded" individuals who understand, define, or see innovation through the same lens. Consider the results of the innovation comprehension survey (from Chapter 2), if the need is for incremental innovation improvement, then choose team members who best understand this type of innovation. Consider the results of the values and work environment surveys (Chapter 2) as a guide for selecting team members.

Many might argue that the traditional business philosophy would dictate that building a team of different minded professionals with varying views on innovation would provide the best opportunity for success. This is not the approach we advocate. One thing to keep in mind from our perspective is that the objective is to identify core members of the team as previously stated and identify potential "consultants" with diverse views within your organization that can be called upon at various stages in the project when their expertise, views, and inputs can add value to the project's success.

Further, like-minded core team members stand a better chance to handle attend all meetings and accept all responsibilities for ongoing tasks and deliverables throughout the NROVATE process. Consultants provide support that is specific and timely in support of the core member's assigned responsibilities. Once you have nominated and secured your core innovation team members, it is time to introduce your team to your initial assessment of the project and the objective of what you hope to accomplish. You should schedule your first meeting with the following goals in mind:

■ Ensure a member of the senior leadership team or management is present to share their thoughts and emphasize their support for your project
■ Introduce yourself and have your core team share their specific skill sets and thoughts on innovation

- Outline the rules of engagement and initial meeting schedules and assignments
- Conduct a team building to help secure buy-in from all team members
- Present your initial assessment of the objective(s) and expectations set and approved by management:
  - Key areas you want to focus on are the staff, processes, and activities, and the current and required resources
- Gather initial inputs from the team on your initial assessment
- Share contact information for each of the team members
- Assign someone (not typically the team lead) to take minutes and publish those minutes in a timely manner
- Determine the best day and time for follow-on and recurring core team meetings

Once the team leader has the core team members selected, assigning responsibilities, accountability, support networks, communications requirements, and touch points are required. We recommend the innovation team lead and members then build a charter to assist in developing buy-in and support from the organization's leadership, management and decision makers. A basic example of a charter follows in Figure 7.1. Beyond the development of the team charter for the innovation project, coupled with the organizational chart with contact information, a useful tool for this step is the RACI or RASCI model. In essence, this essential step outlines:

- **R**esponsibility—Who will own the activities, problems, or goals associated with the innovation project?
- **A**ccountability—Who is the decision maker or approval authority for the work at each level building up to the final implementation of the innovation?
- **S**upport network—Who can provide the necessary support throughout the stages of the project and ultimately the success of the innovation implementation?
- **C**onsultant support—Who has the knowledge and information necessary to support your project throughout the steps toward implementation?
- **I**nformation requirements—Who in the chain of command or leadership hierarchy is notified at agreed when inch and milestone as the project moves through the NROVATE process steps?

EXERCISE 7.1: RESPONSIBILITY, ACCOUNTABILITY, SUPPORT, AND INFORMATION (RACI) MODEL EXERCISE

In this exercise, build a table with headings of responsibility, accountability, support, and information like the completed example given in Table 7.1. Please keep in mind that your goal is to capture as much fidelity as possible in the initial version of your RACI matrix.

Once you have completed Exercise 7.1, please keep in mind that your goal is to capture as much fidelity as possible. However, the RACI table is also

Table 7.1   RACI Model Table (Project Example)

Responsibility	Accountability	Support Network	Information	Current Status/Date
Identify team lead and team members	• Jim Smith (General Manager) • Joe Johnson (Operations Manager)	• Jim Smith (General Manager) • Joe Johnson (Operations Manager) • Innovation Team Members' names and position • Department leaders	• Joe Johnson (Operations Manager) • Jaime Diaz (Plant Superintendent) • Department leaders; Innovation Team Member names and positions	Closed 15 Aug 2015
Develop project plan: Identify project deliverables; identify risks and develop risk management plan; direct the project resources (team members); scope control and change management; oversee quality assurance of the project management process; maintain all documentation including the project plan; report and forecast project status; resolve conflicts within the project or between cross-functional teams; ensure that the project's product meets the business objectives; and communicate project status to stakeholders. Note: Each task above can be tracked individually on the RACI matrix (i.e., identify project deliverables).	• Jan Smith (Team Lead)	• Jim Smith (General Manager) • Joe Johnson (Operations Manager) • Innovation Team Members, department player names, and positions	• Joe Johnson (Operations Manager) • Jaime Garcia (Plant Superintendent)	Open 7 Sep 2015

(Continued)

Table 7.1 (*Continued*)   RACI Model Table (Project Example)

Responsibility	Accountability	Support Network	Information	Current Status/Date
Identify project deliverables (specific goals and objectives)	• Jan Smith (Team Lead)	• Jim Smith (General Manager) • Joe Johnson (Operations Manager), Innovation Team Members; department key player names and positions)	• Joe Johnson (Operations Manager) • Jaime Garcia (Plant Superintendent)	Open 12 Sep 2015
Identify subject matter experts (SME) that will provide advice and information support during the certain phases of the innovation project. SMEs provide expertise on a specific subject. Responsibilities include: Maintain up-to-date experience and knowledge on the subject matter; and provide advice on what is critical to the performance of a project task and what is nice to know.	• Jan Smith (Team Lead)—Jim Smith (General Manager) • Joe Johnson (Operations Manager)	• Jan Smith (Team Lead)—Jim Smith (General Manager) • Joe Johnson (Operations Manager) • Innovation Team Members (by name)	• Joe Johnson (Operations Manager) • Jaime Garcia (Plant Superintendent) • Owning department leaders; SME names	Open 15 Aug 15

Flexographic (Flexo) Printer Performance Improvement Innovation Project—Project # 031-2015.

evolutionary as new tasks and responsibilities develop and these will compile as you move through each stage of the NROVATE steps. Version control is extremely important so maintaining an accurate status is normally an innovation team leader's responsibility. Version control typically logs by date and version (i.e., "Version 1" or "V1" for short). Most corporations place version control in the footnotes section, while the project title (name and project number) is identified in the header section. We recommend placing this information on your company intranet and Internet for ease of updating and access.

While creating your RACI model matrix, create your innovation team project team charter (Figure 7.2). The charter is a seminal instrument that helps set the stage for a successful innovation project. The project team charter is your initial declaration of the sponsor and key players; the project's description, objectives, identified assumptions and limitations, the perceived impact and benefits statement, business plan and operational impact, roles and responsibilities, required resources, risks, and measurements of success. You can append additional topics to the charter but remember to include those topics addressed in Figure 7.3.

> **EXERCISE 7.2: INNOVATION TEAM PROJECT CHARTER EXERCISE**
>
> Utilizing the RACI model matrix you created in Exercise 7.1 and using Figure 7.2 as a guide, develop your team's draft charter for your project.

In the innovation team project charter (Exercise 7.2), utilize the RACI model matrix you built in the previous exercise to help populate the areas in your draft charter. Note, examples and descriptions of the content for each area identified in the charter are provided (by section) in each section of the example provided in Figure 7.2 for your reference. When building your initial draft charter, incorporate the inputs of your organization's resources (shareholders, stakeholders, and customers). Seek key player buy-in prior to presenting your final draft to the sponsor for consideration and approval. Remember, the charter remains in draft form until signed and approved by the sponsor.

Innovation Team Task Assignment Tool

In a fast moving or complex incremental innovation project, tracking team member responsibilities, accountability, assignments, and reporting requirements can be a challenge. A simple and effective tool to track task assignments is the (Figure 7.3) innovation team task assignment tool. Place a task assignment list with appropriate categories you want to track on a common access drive within your intranet or accessible through a handheld device like a mobile phone or tablet as the optimal way to proceed if your organization's IT supports this capability. However, there are organizations where some members involved in your project's success have minimal or one-time roles or do not have access to IT resources on a regular basis. In our Flexo scenario, shift work is common in the manufacturing

Innovation Team Project Charter (Tracking #: _____)

I. General Information

Project Title	Short title of the incremental innovation project				
Project Description	Short description of the incremental innovation you wish to achieve.				
Prepared By	Team leader name				
Date	DD/MMM/YY	Version	1	Expected Completion Date	DD/MMM/YY

II. Project Objective

Detailed description of the innovation project objective.

III. Assumptions and Limitations

Identify known assumptions and limitations. Update as required.

IV. Project Scope

Identify the focus, objectives and time line in as much detail as possible. Include the boundaries of the innovation project.

V. Project Milestones

Identify inch stones and milestones that are critical in achieving your objective(s).

VI. Impact Statement

Potential Impact	Affected Domains (Departments, Activities, etc.), Processes, Machine Centers, etc.
Identify potential initial perceived benefits and add others as the project proceeds through each of the steps.	Identify areas that will be affected by your innovation project. For example, all departments, activities, and machine centers.

VII. Roles and Responsibilities

Sponsor (Decision maker) **Name and Position**	Provides overall direction on the project. Responsibilities include: approve the project charter and plan; secure resources for the project; confirm the project's goals and objectives; keep abreast of major project activities; make decisions on escalated issues; and assist in the resolution of roadblocks.
Innovation Team Lead (Project Manager)	Leads in the planning and development of the project; manages the project to scope. Responsibilities include: develop the project plan; identify project deliverables; identify risks and develop risk management plan; direct the project resources (team members); scope control and change management; oversee quality assurance of the project management process; maintain all documentation including the project plan; report and forecast project status; resolve conflicts within the project or between cross-functional teams; ensure that the project's product meets the business objectives; and communicate project status to stakeholders.
Team Member(s) - Others have requested to be added but approval from their respective department head is required.	Works toward the deliverables of the project. Responsibilities include: understand the work to be completed; complete research, data gathering, analysis, and documentation as outlined in the project plan; inform the project manager of issues, scope changes, and risk and quality concerns; proactively communicate status; and manage expectations.
Subject Matter Expert(s)	Provides expertise on a specific subject. Responsibilities include: maintain up-to-date experience and knowledge on the subject matter; and provide advice on what is critical to the performance of a project task and what is nice-to-know.

VIII. Resources, Project Risks, and Success Measurements. These areas will be captured in the next version of this plan.

Figure 7.2 Innovation team project charter (basic).

Task Assignment   Innovation Team Member Task #2015 - _____

| Primary Designee: | Alternate Designee: | Date Assigned: |
| | | Due Date: |

Task:

Deliverable (What I would like to see please):

Additional Comments:

Figure 7.3 Innovation team task assignment tool.

and production environment. Personal contact is not always given and you may go a week or more without achieving contact with an employee who has been assigned a specific task and associated "complete by" date.

> ### EXERCISE 7.3: INNOVATION TEAM TASK ASSIGNMENT TOOL
>
> Using Figure 7.3 below, design your own task assignment tool for use by your innovation team.

This may appear like a primitive form of communication, but it has proven effective when teams encounter difficulties in getting timely and actionable information from employees within the organization. The task assignment tool can also serve as visual reminder to this employee that you require their input by a set date and its importance to the success of the project. There is no exercise for this tool due to its simplicity. We suggest you have these preprinted and available for meetings to help track assignments as well. We also recommend you accomplish these in duplicate so you can file them in a folder (by date).

Returning to our discussion on the innovation team project charter, we feel it is important to reiterate—the charter also sets in motion a deeper dive into the benefits your project will provide and the overall contribution (value added) it will make to the agency or organization. Updating the charter at this point might also be worth considering at this point. We term this next phase in step 1 as assessing the "cost-to-benefit ratio." This will focus on gauging the initial return on investment (ROI) measured by a review of the success factors identified by the plant or company's senior leadership team (shareholders, stakeholders, and customers). This is considered a critical review focused on evaluating not only the cost and benefits in light of the success factors but most specifically, a review of the anticipated improvements (in this case, an increase of at least 600 sheets per hour).

This process also includes negotiation if the projected ROI and assessed improvement do not lead to a clear potential benefit that would trigger the next step or project implementation. Once the team determines the cost-to-benefit ratio is favorable and the potential benefit deemed positive, it is time to move to Figure 7.4. Please note that it is common for the team to arrive at

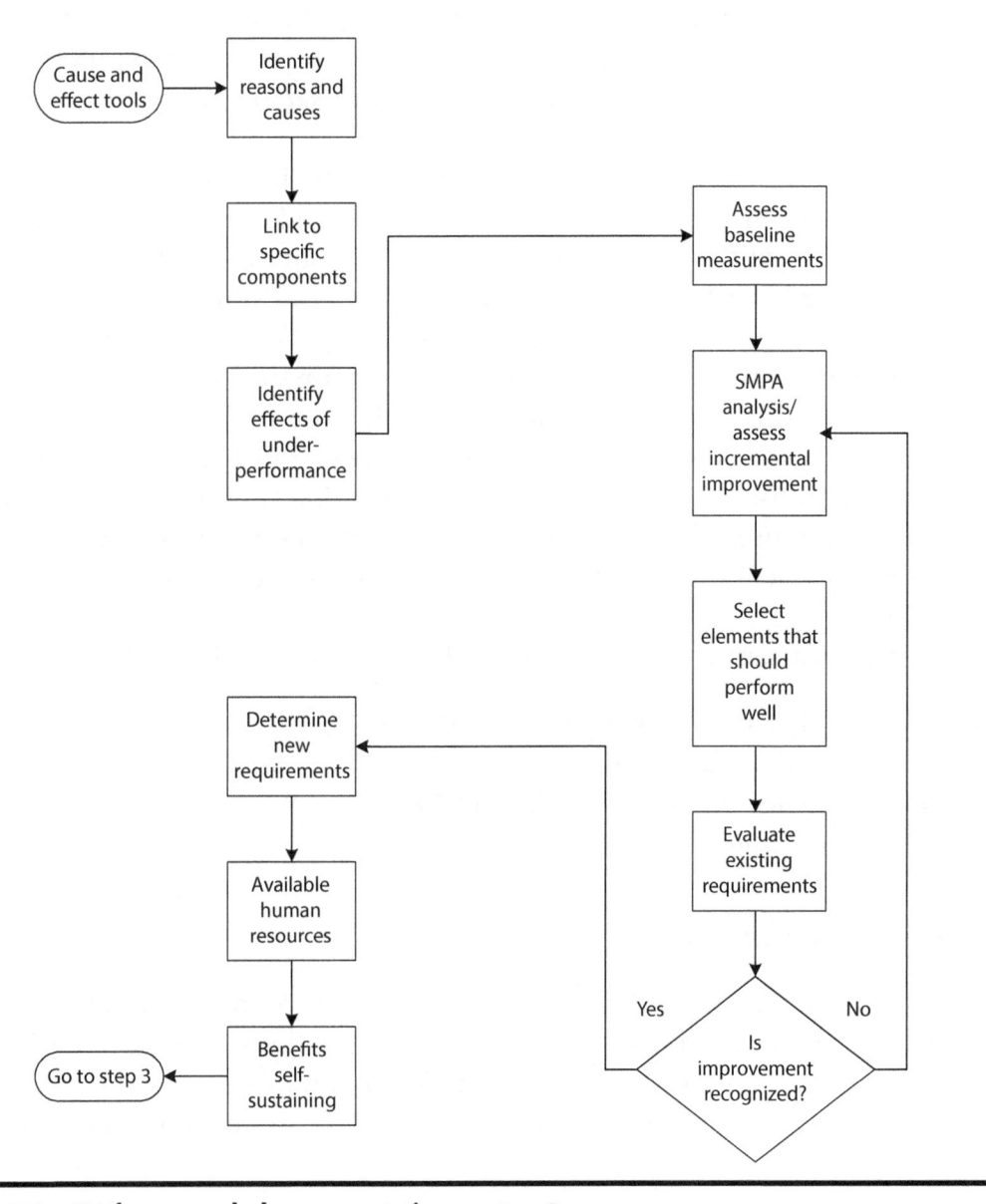

Figure 7.4   Performance below expectations—step 2.

some immediate reasons why the performance of the Flexo is not meeting the manufacturer's advertised capability. Ensure you capture these thoughts the innovation team initial meeting notes, as you will be revisiting them in the next step.

Step 2: Reasons and Requirements

In the next step of the NROVATE process (reasons and requirements), the innovation team will determine reasons and causes for the lack of performance, allocating resources, and determining overall requirements. We have developed and provided several existing tools (success modes and performance analysis [SMPA], run and control charts, failure mode and effect analysis [FMEA], Ishikawa or fishbone diagram, root cause analysis [RCA], process and value stream mapping, etc.) for use in this stage and they are described in great detail in our text, *ENOVALE: How to Unlock Sustained Innovation Project Success* (McLaughlin and Caraballo, 2013).*

This is a lengthy stage, given all the components that must come together to understand the causes, effects, and reasons for underperformance (current performance at the plant of 4200 sheets per hour versus the manufacturer's advertised capability of 5000 sheets per hour). Even though the team may have identified some possible solutions in step 1, it is now time to revisit these initial thoughts on reasons why performance is lacking. Further, the results from this step may result in modifying the project's objective(s) and expectations, based on the empirical evidence your team will collect and diagnose in this stage. In incremental innovation (improvement), underperformance requires a more thorough understanding of the process. This requires a great deal of active versus passive data collection, analysis, and interpretation.

This step uses several tools with examples and associated exercises.

- Process (value stream) mapping tool (Figure 7.5)
- Cause and effect diagrams (Figures 7.6 and 7.7)
- Cause and effect (C&E) matrix (Figure 7.8)
- SMPA tool (Figure 7.9)

Value Stream Mapping

Value stream mapping provides a great opportunity to identify current process performance by means of systematically investigating the waste, value, or benefits opportunities in each step (functional block) of a process to add value to the customer. The real value is in reducing the waste (i.e., unnecessary transport of

---

* A revision of this text is due for publication by CRC Press by the end of 2015.

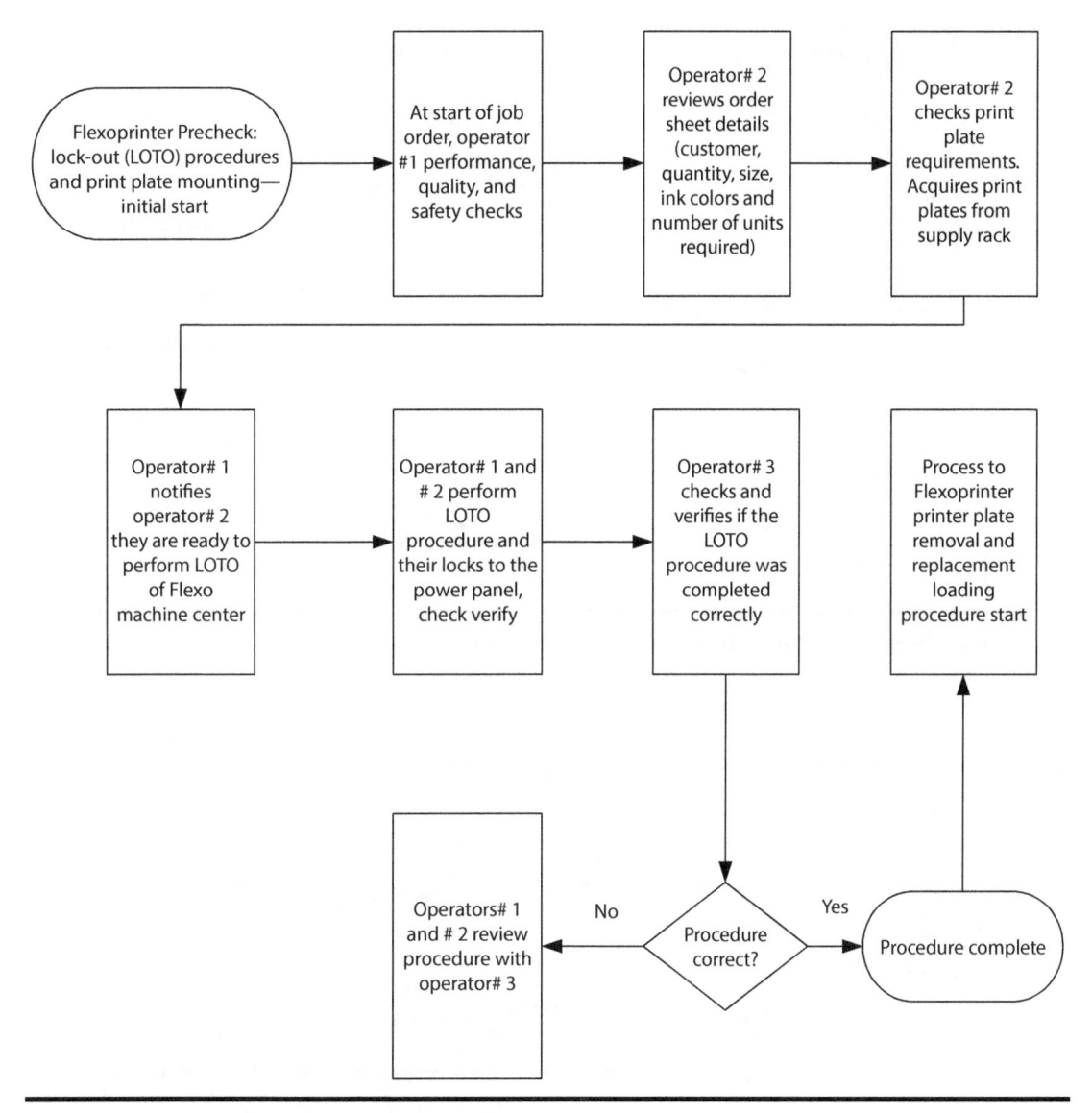

Figure 7.5   Value stream mapping—basic.

materials, overproduction, wasted time, excess inventory, defect, and unnecessary movement) in our manufacturing and production scenario. The primary focus is on underperformance, we see potential value in incorporating this tool into this particular incremental innovation project. Again, we are not advocating you should use all the tools presented in this handbook for every innovation project. We provide the tools for your innovation tool bag so that you can achieve a successful outcome.

In Figure 7.5, we have provided an example of what an initial process map might look like as it relates to our Flexo underperformance scenario for the reader's consideration. When considered in its entirety, the associated processes would take volumes and chapters to cover. Our intent here is to introduce the reader to the concept and run a basic exercise. If accomplished correctly, this can be a time consuming but valuable tool not only for innovation teams involved

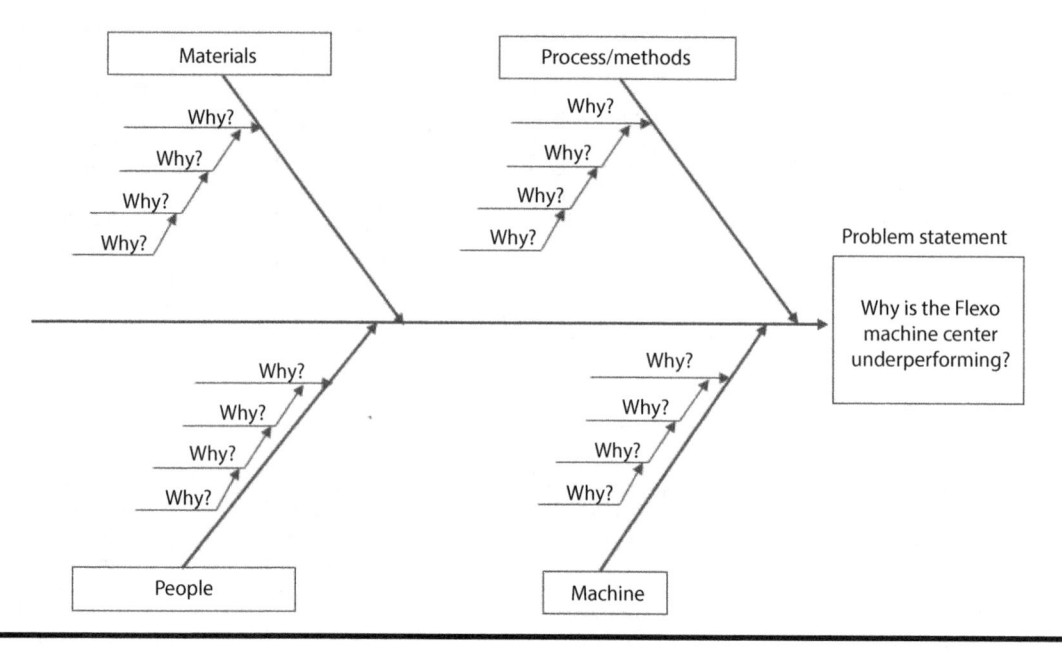

Figure 7.6   Basic fishbone diagram (QI Macros 2015).

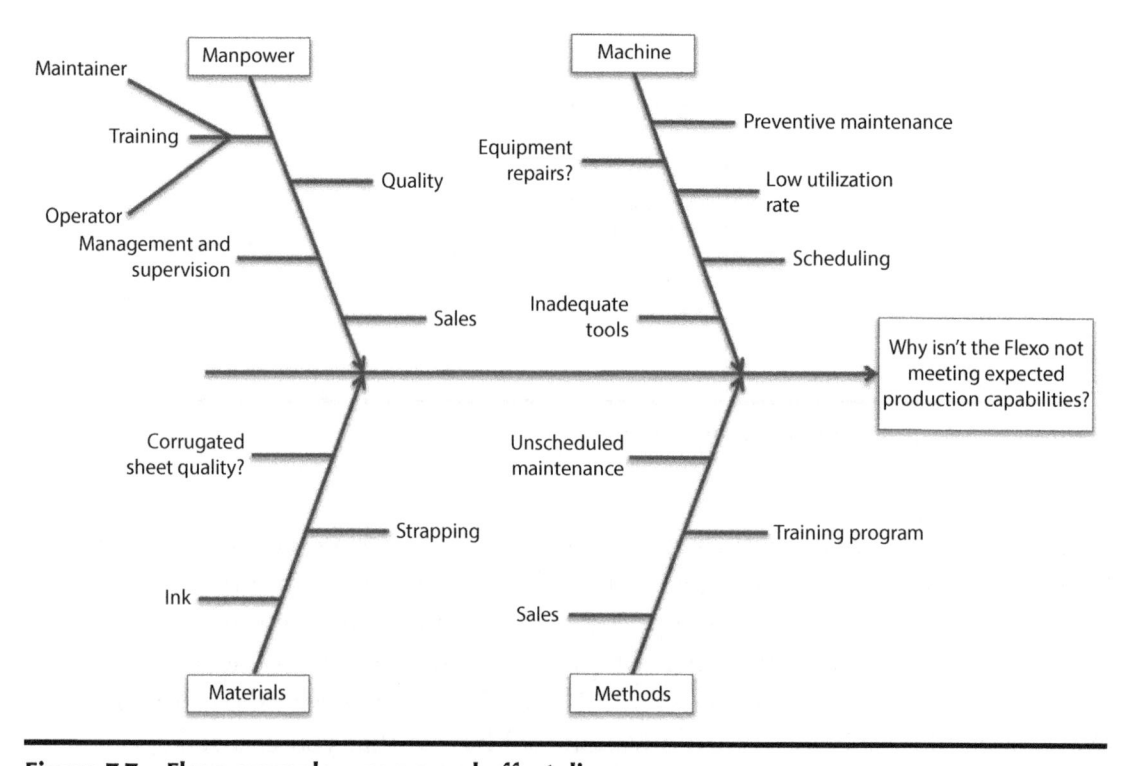

Figure 7.7   Flexo example—cause and effect diagram.

in an innovation project, as it can also support continuous process improvement projects that do fly under the radar or are simply outside the scope of incremental innovation.

The three major steps in process (value mapping) are investigation, analysis, and identifying improvement opportunities.

EXERCISE 7.4: VALUE STREAM MAPPING TOOL EXERCISE

Using the process in the previous section and example value stream map provided in Figure 7.5, select a short process you are very familiar with and run the sequence of steps and diagram those steps in the format provided in Figure 7.5. With an eye on the seven common waste sources (unnecessary transport of materials, overproduction, wasted time, excess inventory, defect, and unnecessary movement), build your own inventories for each step (start to finish or process output) in the process you have selected.

In Exercise 7.4, we suggest you revisit the Flexo scenario provided earlier in this chapter. Using the process in the previous section and example value stream map provided in Figure 7.5, select a short process you are very familiar with and run the sequence of steps and diagram those steps in the format provided in Figure 7.5. With an eye on the seven common waste sources (unnecessary transport of materials, overproduction, wasted time, excess inventory, defect, and unnecessary movement), build your own inventories for each step (start to finish or process output) in the process you have selected. Investigate the process for a lack of flow or excessive waste. These are opportunities for improvement and change, which can generate value while reducing waste. This is not an exercise in reducing the number of steps. Adding steps where there is a lack of flow might add value to your process. Concentrate on the value each step in the process provides. Once you have mapped out the process and built your inventory lists for each step, share what you have found with a peer and get their input on your results.

Cause and Effect (C&E) Diagram

In this discussion, the terms C&E, "fishbone," or "Ishikawa" diagram are used interchangeably and indicate the same tool. Based on its resemblance to a fish's skeleton, the C&E diagram, is referred to as the fishbone diagram. Another name is the Ishikawa diagram, after the name of its creator, Professor Kaoru Ishikawa, for the main purpose of continuous quality standard improvements. The diagram is a powerful tool for gaining common understanding across the organization and concentrating on ferreting out the root cause or the potential cause(s) for a given event or problem. This tool is essential in RCA and resulting action plan development (identifying the "who, what, when, and how" to get the performance back on track) to get the performance back in line with the key performance indicators (KPI). For example, in our Flexo scenario, we are focused on finding the root cause for underperformance of the Flexo machine center output (number of units produced per hour).

The steps of completing the diagram are straightforward. The first step is to draw the fishbone diagram. There are several ways to accomplish this with your team. If you have access to a large erasable whiteboard in your conference room, draw the base diagram with the problem or issue you want to determine the root cause at the head of the diagram (refer to Figure 7.6). Identify each major category at the end of each line (i.e., 4Ss, 4Ms, 4Ps, 5Ms, etc.). Major categories that are popular across multiple industries are

- 4Ss—Suppliers, surroundings, skills, and systems
- 4Ps—People, policies, procedure, and place
- 5Ms—Machines, material, measurement, methods, and management

Choose your major categories as the problem or challenge you wish to resolve dictates. Next, provide each member with ample number of sticky note pads for their thoughts or ideas. Team members can use these note pads to identify causes (inputs) for the fishbone diagram. An option for geographically separated team members is to accomplish this online (electronically), as there are multiple software capabilities available on the Internet that have user-friendly fishbone templates already built.

Your next step is to populate the diagram with the thoughts and ideas of the team under each category to produce subfactors. The primary focus is to ask the group, "why is this happening?" In our example, we are repeatedly asking, "what is causing the Flexo machine center to produce less units per hour than it is capable of performing (underperforming)?" Label additional segments under each specific factor (these are essentially, "subfactors"). Continue the same line of question (why?) until the team can no longer provide value-added or useful inputs (information).

The next step is to cycle through each note placed under each category and combine the duplicate comments and ideas in the same category from your team (e.g., simply place one sticky note over the other if you are using this approach). Note: it is common to have duplicate inputs in multiple categories, so do not remove or combine these unless the team is in full agreement. Once that is accomplished, assess all the inputs with the overarching question and thought of, "why do we see happening?" At this point, the team will analyze the results of the fishbone after they all are in agreement there is an adequate amount of fidelity (detail) provided under each category. Now that you have consensus, it is time to start looking for those items appearing more frequently in more than one major category (or subcategory). View those that occur more frequently as the initial list of "most likely" candidates for causation (i.e., the causes of why the Flexo is underperforming in our scenario). As a team, prioritize the most likely causes and label the highest priority by team consensus as the "most probable" cause. The final step—often forgotten—document the team's actions, decisions, and the resulting fishbone diagram. If there are any team members with differing views, which does occur, ensure to capture, and document those views.

EXERCISE 7.5: C&E DIAGRAM EXERCISE

Using the Ishakawa or fishbone diagram (Figure 7.6), gather your team and use a large erasable white board and draw out a fishbone using any of the major category approaches or headings you feel best fit your objective (the defined problem or issue statement you are trying to resolve). As a reminder, the most common major categories across multiple industries are 4Ss—suppliers, surroundings, skills, and systems; 4Ps—people, policies, procedure, and place; or 5Ms—machines, material, measurement, methods, and management.

In summary, when using the C&E tool (Figure 7.6), focus on identifying the potential reasons and causes for why the Flexo is not performing at the manufacturer's advertised capability. We have selected this tool to introduce the reader to others tools presented in the text associated with this handbook. For Exercise 7.5, your team's goal is to provide potential or contributing causes that fall under any of the four to five components that team members feel could be possible contributing factors as to why the Flexo is underperforming. Follow the steps provided in the discussion above on the C&E diagram.

We have provided some example contributing factors (by component) the innovation team might find useful as they complete this exercise (Figure 7.7).

People (Manpower)

- Paper machine operators
- Corrugator operators
- Converting operators
- Forklift drivers
- Field assembly
- Field drivers
- Storage handlers
- Over packing

Machine

- Paper machine—Toledo
- Corrugator
- Converting
- Forklifts
- Bagger
- Cascader
- Hydrocooler
- Squeeze
- Forklift

Methodology (Process)

- Cooling time
- Cooling
- Trucking
- Cutting dies
- Print plates
- Bagging/wrapping
- Dunnage
- Product packing
- Field palletizing
- Squeeze handling

Materials

- Paper
- Pallets
- Ink
- Starch formulas or type (used for bonding)
- Wax cascade
- Recycled content

Areas for Investigation

- Paper mill data (source of paper for corrugated sheets)
- Adhesive
- Resin
- Corrugator setup (production machine center for the source sheets)
- Converting setup (how Flexo is set up and programmed?)
- Pallets, palletizing, and wrapping
- Climate and conditions throughout system (and plant)
- Trucking (shipping, receiving, and transportation of product to customer)
- Field assembly, packing, and palletizing
- Field hauling
- Hydrocooling and cooler

There are many approaches to completing the fishbone exercise, but some of the most popular are having your team members write directly on the white board or providing them a stack if sticky notes to write on and then post in the associated component or designated area on a whiteboard. Using the sticky notes will facilitate the grouping of like terms as you seek to narrow down the top three general causes that are most popular with your team during this first exercise. After logically grouping the causes, take a picture of the completed fishbone diagram and include it in your final minutes for the session. You may also want to use specialized software to transfer this information for storage electronically.

Cause and Effect (C&E) Matrix

Another value-added tool for rating the C&E to customer needs or project objectives in the C&E matrix (Figure 7.8). The C&E matrix sets the stage for the FMEA process and can help innovation teams prioritize the requirements when

Cause and Effect Matrix																	
Rating of Importance to Customer (needs) or Requirements (Y)																	
			1	2	3	4	5	6	7	8	9	10	11	12	13	14	15	
	Identify a Process Step (X)	Identify a Causal Element (X)	Need/Requirement	Need/Requirement	Need/Requirement	Need/Requirement	Need/Requirement	Need/Requirement	Need/Requirement	Need/Requirement	Need/Requirement	Need/Requirement	Need/Requirement	Need/Requirement	Need/Requirement	Need/Requirement	Need/Requirement	Total
	Process Step	Causal Element																
1																		0
2																		0
3																		0
4																		0
5																		0
6																		0
7																		0
8																		0
9																		0
10																		0
11																		0
12																		0
13																		0
14																		0
15																		0
16																		0
17																		0
18																		0
19																		0
20																		0
																		0
																		0
Total			0	0	0	0	0	0	0	0	0	0	0	0	0	0	0	

1. List the key Needs or Requirements (type each of these in a separate Needs/Requirements cell). There are the Y's.
2. Rate each variable on a 1–10 scale to importance to Innovation Performance, or sustained value, competitive Advantage)—Choose only one and be consistent
3. List Key Process Step or Causes identified with the Fishbone Diagram. (Choose either the process steps or causes). These are the X's.
4. Rate each Process Step or Cause in relationship to a particular need/requirement. Align the need/requirement (Y) with each X to evaluate the relationship between the process step/cause and the need requirement. Use a rating scale of: 0 - no relationship; 1 - minimal relationship, 3- marginal relationship, 9- strong relationship.
5. Using the Excel template, it will rate the strongest relationship between the X's and Y's. The strongest relationships contribute most to innovation success. These KPI and KPP's (CSF) will become the basis of the improvement efforts.
6. The Totals row (at the bottom of the chart) indicates the Importance of (Y)

Figure 7.8   Cause and effect (C&E) matrix template.

competing interests or leadership positions differ on what is the most important need or requirement for the team to focus on. When each of the output variable (project objectives) is not correct, that represents the potential "effects." When each input variable is not correct, that can represent the "failure modes."

Completing the C&E matrix is relatively straightforward:

1. List the key needs or requirements (type each of these in a separate needs/requirements cell). There are the Ys.
2. Rate each variable on a 1–10 scale to importance to innovation performance, or sustained value, competitive advantage—Choose only one and be consistent.
3. List key process steps or causes identified with the fishbone diagram (Choose either the process steps or causes). These are the Xs.
4. Rate each process step or cause in relationship to a particular need/requirement. Align the need/requirement (Y) with each X to evaluate the relationship between the process step/cause and the need requirement. Use a rating scale of 0—no relationship, 1—minimal relationship; 3—marginal relationship; 9—strong relationship.
5. Using the Excel template, it will rate the strongest relationship between the Xs and Ys. The strongest relationships contribute most to innovation success. These KPI and KPPs (CSF) will become the basis of the improvement efforts.
6. The total row (at the bottom of the chart) indicates the importance of (Y).

Using our example with the Flexo performance challenges and example of a completed C&E matrix is provided for reference in Figure 7.9.

The value of the C&E matrix is that it will help you identify true priorities at the completion of the process. In the next step, it is essential you remain objective when assigning (rating) each variable (process step or cause) on a scale of 1–10 as that importance relates to the desired improvement. Next, list the key input process variables for each key step identified in your first step.

EXERCISE 7.6: C&E MATRIX TOOL EXERCISE

Using the example C&E matrix provided in Figure 7.8, complete a C&E matrix for an innovation team project of your choice.

Once you have identified the key potential causes your team feels are logical starting points or causes for underperformance, develop a strategy to establish baseline measurements to further verify and clarify the potential causes. You can now consider using the SMPA tool (Figures 7.10 and 7.11), to help track the results of your measurements and responses. Here you focus on surfacing elements that should perform well and while evaluating those results against existing requirements. The key question here is "are you seeing noticeable improvement(s)?" If not, return to the SMPA phase and rerun the process steps until you see

Cause and Effect Matrix																		
Rating of Importance to Customer (needs) or Requirements (Y)			10	5	1	10	10	10	1	4	1							
			1	2	3	4	5	6	7	8	9	10	11	12	13	14	15	
Identify a Process Step (X)	**Identify a Causal Element (X)**		Meet established MC output	Meet quality standards	Meet MC availability rate	Meet MC utilization rate	Meet training standards	Meet ROI requirements	Meet all MC performance	Meet established safety standards	Meet scheduling requirements							**Total**
	Process Step	**Cause**																
1	Training		3	9	9	9	9	3	9	9	3							342
2	Material		3	3	3	1	1	1	1	1	3							86
3	Maintenance		1	1	9	3	3	3	9	9	3							162
4	Scheduling		3	3	3	9	3	1	9	9	9							232
5	Quality		1	9	1	1	1	9	9	1	3							182
6	Ink		1	1	1	1	3	3	9	9	3							134
7	Management		3	3	3	3	3	3	0	9	3							177
8	Sales		1	9	0	0	0	3	9	1	3							101
9	Operations		9	9	9	9	9	3	9	9	3							402
10																		0
11																		0
12																		0
13																		0
14																		0
15																		0
16																		0
17																		0
18																		0
19																		0
20																		0
																		0
																		0
Total			2	3	4	1	1	2	4	3	33	0	0	0	0	0	0	

1. List the key Needs or Requirements (type each of these in a separate Needs/Requirements cell). There are the Y's.
2. Rate each variable on a 1 to 10 scale to importance to Innovation Performance, or sustained value, competitive Advantage) - Choose only one and be consistent
3. List Key Process Step or Causes identified with the Fishbone Diagram. (Choose either the process steps or causes). These are the X's.
4. Rate each Process Step or Cause in relationship to a particular need/requirement. Align the need/requirement (Y) with each X to evaluate the relationship between the process step/cause and the need requirement. Use a rating scale of: 0 - no relationship; 1 - minimal relationship; 3- marginal relationship, 9- strong relationship.
5. Using the Excel template, it will rate the strongest relationship between the X's and Y's. The strongest relationships contribute most to innovation success. These KPI and KPP's (CSF) will become the basis of the improvement efforts.
6. The totals row (at the bottom of the chart) indicates the Importance of (Y)

Figure 7.9   Cause and effect (C&E) matrix example—Flexographic machine center.

noticeable improvements. Ensure you capture the data points generated with each run through the action loop. Once you achieve noticeable improvement(s), proceed to the next stage, which is determining the new requirements.

Figure 7.10 displays an example of the SMPA template. The need is for improving customer wait time on the telephone (at a call center). Figures 7.11 and 7.12 display the SMPA template and rating scales used for estimating the chance (probability) that a success mode affects performance.

In identifying, the links to the specific components that contribute to the underperformance of the Flexo is central. This information provides a framework to select elements capable of undergoing modification to ensure improved

Success Methods and Performance Analysis
SMPA (Abbreviated)

Process or Product Name:						Prepared by:			Page #	
Responsible:						SMPA Date (Orig)		(Rev)		
Process Step	**Key Process Input**	**Potential Success Modes**	**Potential Performance**	**P R B**	**Potential Causes**	**N E P**	**Current Actions or Controls**	**S U S**	**S P N**	**Actions Recommended**
What is the process step?	What is the component, part or element?	In what ways can the component, part, or element improve?	What is the affect on performance?	Impact Probability - Rate the chance of continued improvement	What could cause the component, part, or element to affect performance negatively?	How frequently would a negative effect occur?	What actions (controls) are needed for this improvement to be sustained?	How well can the improvement sustain increased performance?	Success Priority Number	What are the actions required for maintaining improved performance?
	Customer's Available Time	Less Wait Time	Judged more efficient	10	Problems with routing	6	Modify software	5	300	
	Customer's Available Time	Less Wait Time	Judged more efficient	10	Problems with routing	6	Increase operators	1	60	
	Customer's Available Time	Less Wait Time	Judged more efficient	10	Problems with routing	6	Increase menu options	10	600	Check feasibility of increased menu selection
	Customer's Available Time	Less Wait Time	Judged more efficient	10	Software	8	Purchase or design software	8	640	Check available hardware for purchase
	Customer's Available Time	Less Wait Time	Judged more efficient	10	Human interaction	8	Training, follw-up	6	480	

PRB—Probability of Improvement; NEP—Negative Effect Probability; SUS—Sustainability Unit Score; SPN—Success Priority Number

Figure 7.10   SMPA example.

Success Methods and Performance Analysis
SMPA

Process or Product Name:								Prepared by:			Page ___ of ___					
Responsible:								SMPA Date (Orig)_____ (Rev)_____								
Process Step	Key Process Input	Potential Success Modes	Potential Performance	P R B	Potential Causes	N E P	Current Actions or Controls	S U S	S P N	Actions Recommended	Resp.	Actions Taken	P R B	N E P	S U S	S P N
Process Step	What is the component, part, or element?	In what ways can the component, part, or element improve?	What is the effect on performance?	Impact Probability - Rate the chance of continued improvement	What could cause the component, part, or element to affect performance negatively?	How frequently would a negative effect occur?	What actions (controls) are needed for this improvement to be sustained?	How well can the improvement sustain increased performance?	Success Priority Number	What are the actions required for maintaining improved performance?	Who is responsible for the recommended actions?	What are the completed actions taken? Be sure to include completion month/year.				
									0							0
									0							0
									0							0
									0							0
									0							0
									0							0

Figure 7.11 SMPA template.

Score	Impact Probability	Score	Negative Effect on Performance
10	The SM always or nearly always impacts the PE	1	The cause will always negatively affect the PE
9	The SM impacts the PE more than 85% of the time	2	The cause will negatively affect the PE nearly always
8	The SM impacts the PE more than 75% of the time	3	The cause will negatively affect the PE frequently
7	The SM impacts the PE more than 60% of the time	4	The cause will negatively affect the PE often
6	The SM impacts the PE slightly more than 50% of the time	5	The cause will negatively affect the PE more than 50% of the time
5	The SM impacts the PE about 50% of the time	6	The cause will negatively affect the PE about 50% of the time
4	The SM impacts the PE less than 50% of the time	7	The cause will negatively affect the PE less than 50% of the time
3	The SM has a small impact on the PE	8	The cause rarely affects the PE negatively
2	The SM has little impact on the PE	9	The cause very rarely affects the PE negatively
1	The SM has no impact on the PE	10	The cause will not negatively affect the PE

Score	Sustainability	
10	Sustains PE all of the time	
9	Sustains PE nearly all of the time	SM- Success Mode
8	Sustains PE most of the time of the SM	PE - Performance
7	Sustains PE about 2/3 of the time	
6	Sustains PE more than 50% of the time	Note:
5	Sustains PE about 50% of the time	If you cannot sustain performance, then the innovation
4	Sustains PE slightly less than 50% of the time	may not be worthwhile
3	Rarely sustains PE	
2	Very rarely sustains PE	
1	Never sustains PE	

Figure 7.12   SMPA scale.

performance. The SMPA tool is a method to define successful performance as a function of those elements that sustain that performance over the life of the product, process, service, or technology (Figure 7.11). The example (Figure 7.10) demonstrates how to improve Flexo hourly throughput by examining elements that directly influence this performance measure (i.e., training, machine center alignments and run speeds, etc.).

Two elements that directly affect performance are operating training and machine quality checks. These would require additional actions to prevent a loss of performance. This tool is an excellent brainstorming tool used in a face-to-face environment or completed virtually. This tool can assist in determining the best measures (empirical data) to control the loss of performance. The SMPA tool also involves employees in the problem-solving process. Clients find this tool useful for planning and operational purposes. This contributes to the C&E analysis and subsequent data collection and analysis phase.

EXERCISE 7.7: SMPA TOOL EXERCISE

Using the example SMPA matrix provided in Figures 7.10 through 7.12, complete an SMPA matrix for an innovation team project of your choice.

Finally, identifying the reasons for a lack of performance provides a framework for requirements testing, evaluation, and/or establishing new requirements. With new requirements comes a new round of data collection, baseline measures, and new measurement systems. The idea is to continue the iteration process until performance has exceeded expectations and is operating at a validation and verification (new level of sustained performance). As with all ENOVALE-based methodology, the next step is verification with empirical evidence. Data collection should not be a burden. We recommend you collect only "enough" data to detect a change in the process. Be aware that calculations, such as averages, hide information, and not good measures for detecting variance. Your goal should be to watch and monitor the variation. This statistic best describes the consistency (repeatability) of the process. We define an inconsistent process as one that is impossible to repeat and to forecast.

Finally, when determining new requirements, it is imperative that you ensure you reflect back on the original objective(s) the team was chartered to resolve or achieve. Once you have assessed, quantified, and documented the new requirements, you will need to reassess your staffing requirements and be prepared to report hose changes to the decision makers and senior leadership (as well as your findings to date). Included in this report to the decision maker is your team's determination on whether the findings and benefits you have arrived at are self-sustaining and beneficial to the plant (shareholders, stakeholders, and customers). Once you have briefed the appropriate parties and received support and concurrence to continue, it is time to move on to step 3, Operationalization.

Step 3: Operationalization

In operationalizing the outcome, your first steps are to initiate data collection to determine the effect of influence, prediction versus chaos, and the identification of best practices (often captured in SOPs) across departments within the plant environment (Figure 7.13). Once the innovation team has categorically collected data for each of the three aforementioned areas; the next step is to analyze the data and make an objective assessment on whether the Flexo is still underperforming and if so, how much so in light of the projects objective(s) or expectation(s). If the feedback or results have shown no marked improvement in the current throughput numbers of 4200 sheets per hours, the team adjusts the process and reinitiates data collection efforts to determine the effect of influence, prediction versus chaos, and the identification of best practices. This cycle repeats until reaching an acceptable level of sustainable improvement.

As stated in our previous book, *A Guide to Innovation Processes and Solutions for Government* (McLaughlin and Kennedy, 2015),[*] a common mistake organizations make during incremental improvement projects is to short-change the data collection and analysis steps. This occurs when organizations rush to implement or operationalize an innovation, due to the misconception that it is easier to implement and then confirm performance improvements versus under-

---

[*] *A Guide to Innovation Processes and Solutions in Government* (McLaughlin and Kennedy, 2015).

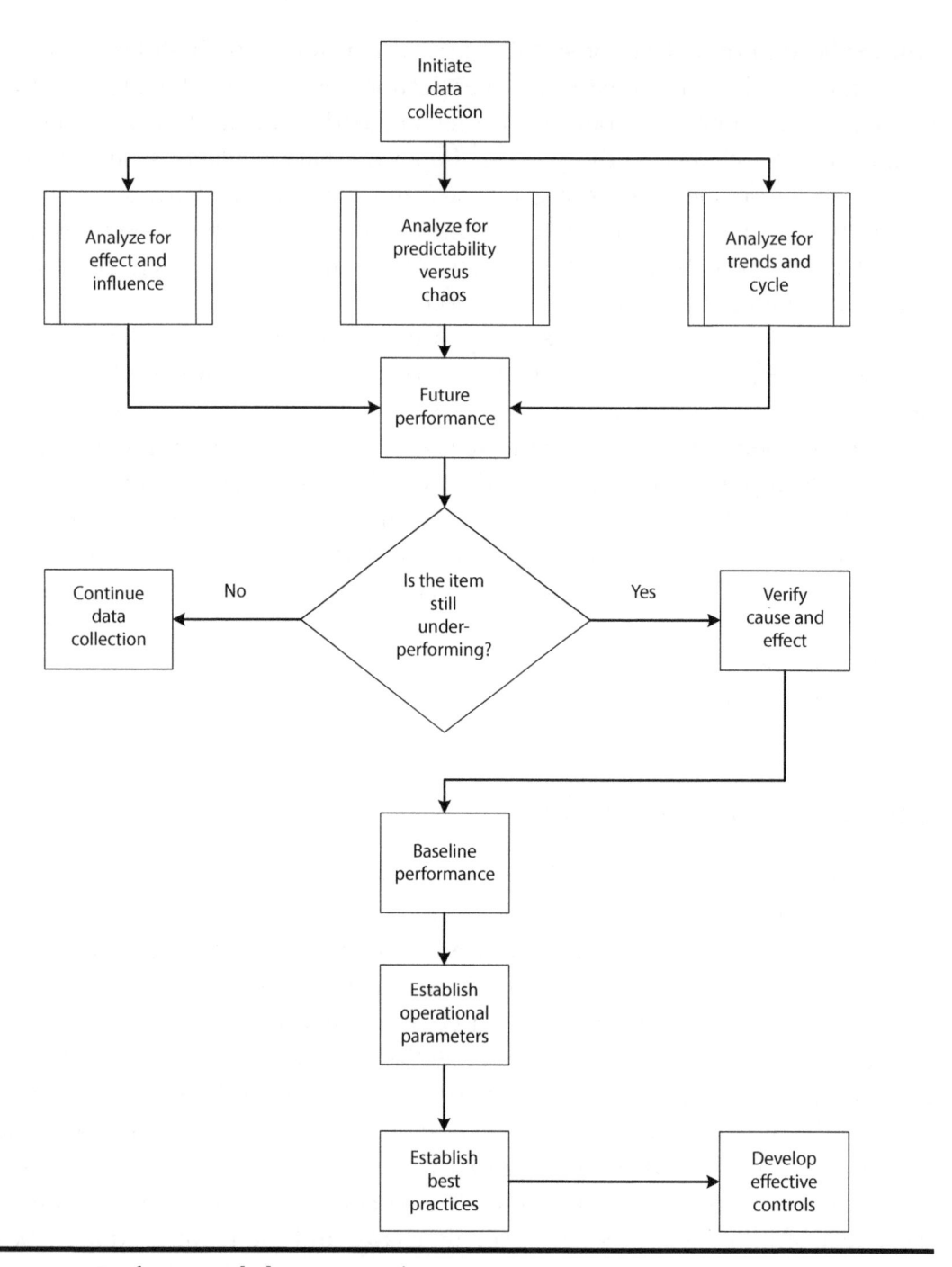

Figure 7.13 Performance below expectations—step 3.

standing those improvements prior to implementation. We contend it only takes a short amount of time and a small amount of data to help verify operational parameters if they are functional and descriptive.

We cannot emphasize enough that pursuing nonfunctional operating limits will cause frequent adjustment, slowdowns, and increased losses. Even for processes that are human focused, the innovation team must be intimately knowledgeable of the parameters (guidelines and requirements) in which they must operate. Ensure you estimate, document, and then verify these operational limits (boundaries). Innovation team leaders should anticipate that this step will take time and should not be rushed or overlooked as inconsequential. If executed improperly, it will not only elevate the risk factors associated with success but induce inherent difficulties in convincing senior leadership and management (the decision makers) of its importance. More specifically, taking short cuts will increase the risk of failure due to vague operating (requirements) which can limit results by inducing frequent adjustments (attention), repairs, and increased maintenance costs. Determining operating limits (and specifications) is both a science and an art. To summarize, consider these items as necessary:

1. Processes normally operate within a range, so do people.
2. The range needs to define the process operating limits while remaining with the requirements (limits and specifications) nearly 100% of the time.
3. Specification limits are customer or user driven.
4. Limits are set based on empirical evidence.
5. Process can run (operate) outside of limits (for a short time) but with increased risk of failure.
6. There should be a one-to-one relationship between operating limits and user or specification limits—operating limits must ensure that the product, service, or technology meets specifications 99.7% or better.

Once an acceptable level of achievement is realized, the team will need to verify and document the resulting C&E, baseline the performance parameters, and establish and publish the new operational parameters. It is important to include these documents in your project file. Establishing and publishing the new operational parameters should be recorded and reported (in our scenario an increased production capability of at least 600 units [sheets] per hour under normal operations and the scheduled work week of three 8-h shifts per day, 5 days a week). For example, if a potential contributing factor this should have been accomplished already or underway while your innovation team moves into the final phase of step 3, analyzing the data collected during your test runs.

> ### EXERCISE 7.8: OPERATIONALIZE THE OUTCOME EXERCISE
>
> Using the operationalization (step 3) process map in Figure 7.13, walk through each step and anticipate potential key tasks associated with each step using the discussion in this section as a starting point. List your thoughts under each step.

As a general note, processes and services are not different. Generally, operating limits are not part of the conversation when developing incremental improvements to services. However, when applied, these ensure nearly flawless execution. The provided flowcharts work well for product (manufacturing and production in the packaging industry) or services improvements. That said, for services, incremental innovation requires a change in mindset and recognition that a service is essentially a process by nature. In the past, theorists referred to this mindset as systems thinking (today, we also consider this as "critical thinking"). There are three basic elements of critical thinking—"function, structure, and process" (Ing, 2013, p. 528). In common terms, systems thinking is "the outcome, the inputs and components, and the sequence of activities" (Ing, 2013, p. 528). In services industries, for example, they contain all three of these elements and therefore can be designed (and developed) to exceed expected performance. Much like services, our example in the manufacturing and production of corrugated boxes with the Flexo apply these same criteria to develop more efficient and effective operations while providing an environment for incremental innovation.

Step 4: Validation and Verification

The next step (Figure 7.14) is one of verification and validation (a central theme). The first stage in step 4 is data analysis. When performing analysis on the data your team has collected during the innovation project, we suggest you approach this effort by keeping it simple statistically (the KISS principle). Visible representations, such as charts and graphs (some mentioned in step 2, Reasons and Requirements), will go a long way in readily providing decisions makers with the right information at the right time to make timely decisions. They can also serve as status checks for the entire team and condense difficult messages and concepts you are trying to share with others. Keep in mind, there are a host of other automated tools widely available in today's business community and we recommend you leverage these capabilities to augment our process and to help interpret the data your team has collected.

Validation is the verification of key operational parameters previously identified and documented in step 3, Operationalization. Using established requirements to verify the documented operational parameters your team has identified or have been provided, prepare your organization and leadership for initiation of your proposed innovation solution. By developing policies and procedures from your validated operating limits, you want to ensure you make a concerted effort to inform, educate, and secure buy-in from your shareholders, stakeholders, and also your customer if the situation warrants their participation.

The next step is one that is often neglected. In this step, the attempt is to focus attention on adapting (aligning) all employees to the innovation improvements. It is time to celebrate but also prepare those responsible for their new duties. Here consensus is key and leadership's role critical. Communication is vital, especially for those with new or additional responsibilities. It may also be

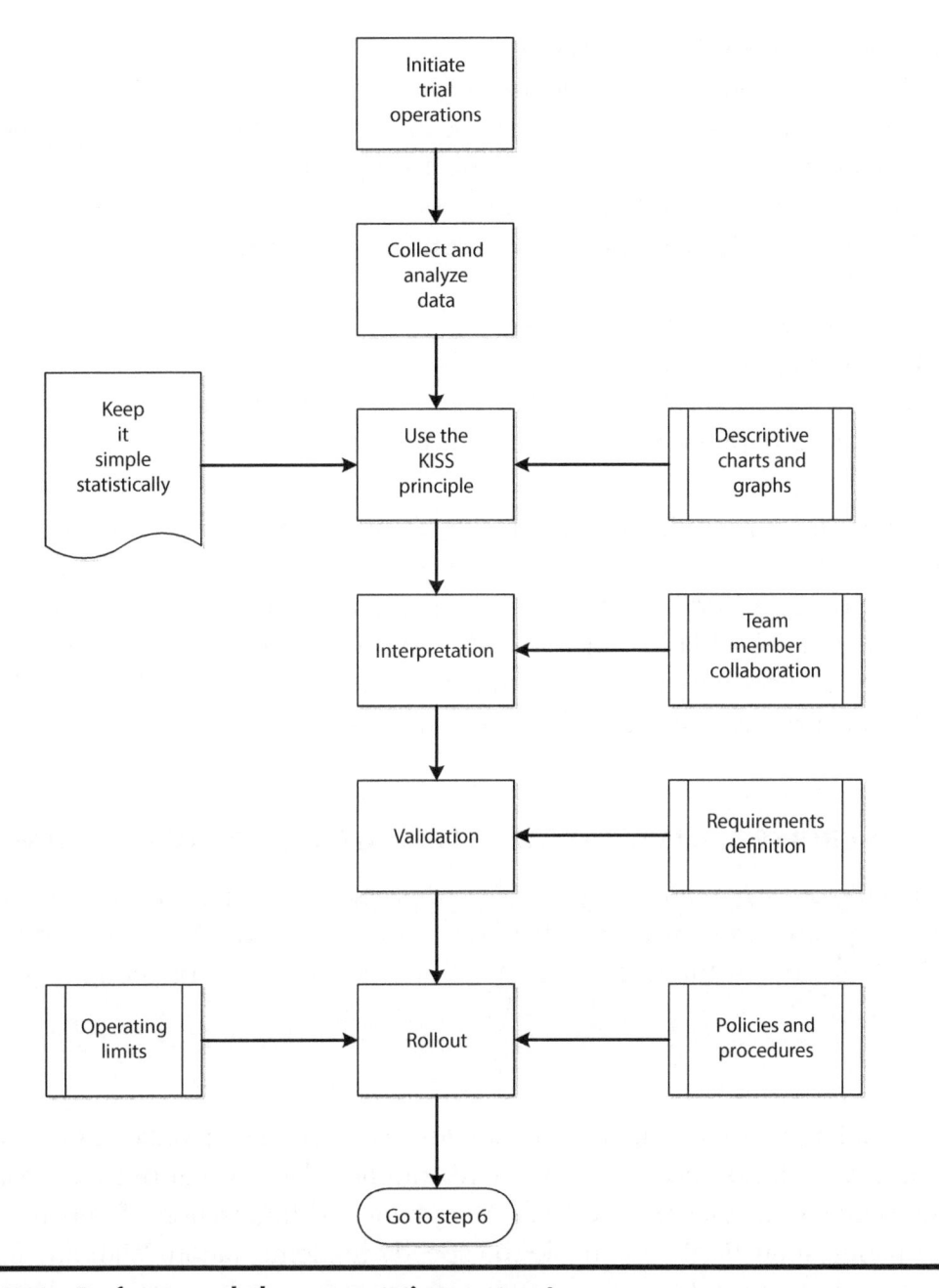

Figure 7.14   Performance below expectations—step 4.

time to communicate with suppliers and users (customers), especially if affected by the improvement. There multiple ways to accomplish achieving buy-in from essential players in your innovation rollout. In our Flexo performance improvement example, this effort expands the pool of key players you will need to inform, educate (train), and gain support and buy-in from include, but are not limited to:

■ Plant general manager
■ Plant director of operations
■ Plant operations superintendent

- Plant and Flexo shift supervisors
- Flexo operations leads and team members
- Maintenance (in-house or the contractor representative if your equipment is maintained under warranty or contract support)
- Quality assurance and safety managers
- Customer service (and possibly accounting) representatives
- Scheduling supervisor
- Shipping and receiving supervisor
- Plant facility manager
- Any on-site contractor support and key suppliers (partners) involved with the machine, process, or service your project focuses on

Further, new or modified requirements are instituted prior to full rollout (implementation). You may recall, in the operationalization step, your team prepared the product, service, or process for implementation. If this step is skipped or diluted, the risk of failure increases due to unplanned or untested conditions. The less you know about a process the greater the chance of errors, mistakes, and miscalculations. Prevention is always the best cure!

EXERCISE 7.9: OPERATIONALIZE THE OUTCOME EXERCISE

Using the operationalization (step 3) process map in Figure 7.14, walk through each step and anticipate potential key tasks associated with each step using the discussion in this section as a starting point. List your thoughts under each step.

In addition, consider aligning the employees to the new realities as crucial for success. As innovations become more commonplace, it will become easier to adapt to new outcomes (Figure 7.14). Alignment and finalization of benefit and cost savings (reduction) will enable the speedy implementation. With any innovation, there is a comfort factor (zone) that needs to be reached with employees, customers (users), and suppliers.

Step 5: Adaptation and Alignment

The next step is your quest for a successful incremental innovation effort to improve performance in adapting and aligning your organization with your new approach (Figure 7.15). As a point of reference, this step is one that is often neglected. The focus in this step should be on adapting (aligning) the plant's or organization's employees (shareholders, stakeholders, and customers) to the improvements which you introduced in step 4 (Validation and Verification), which essentially set the stage for enterprise-wide adoption.

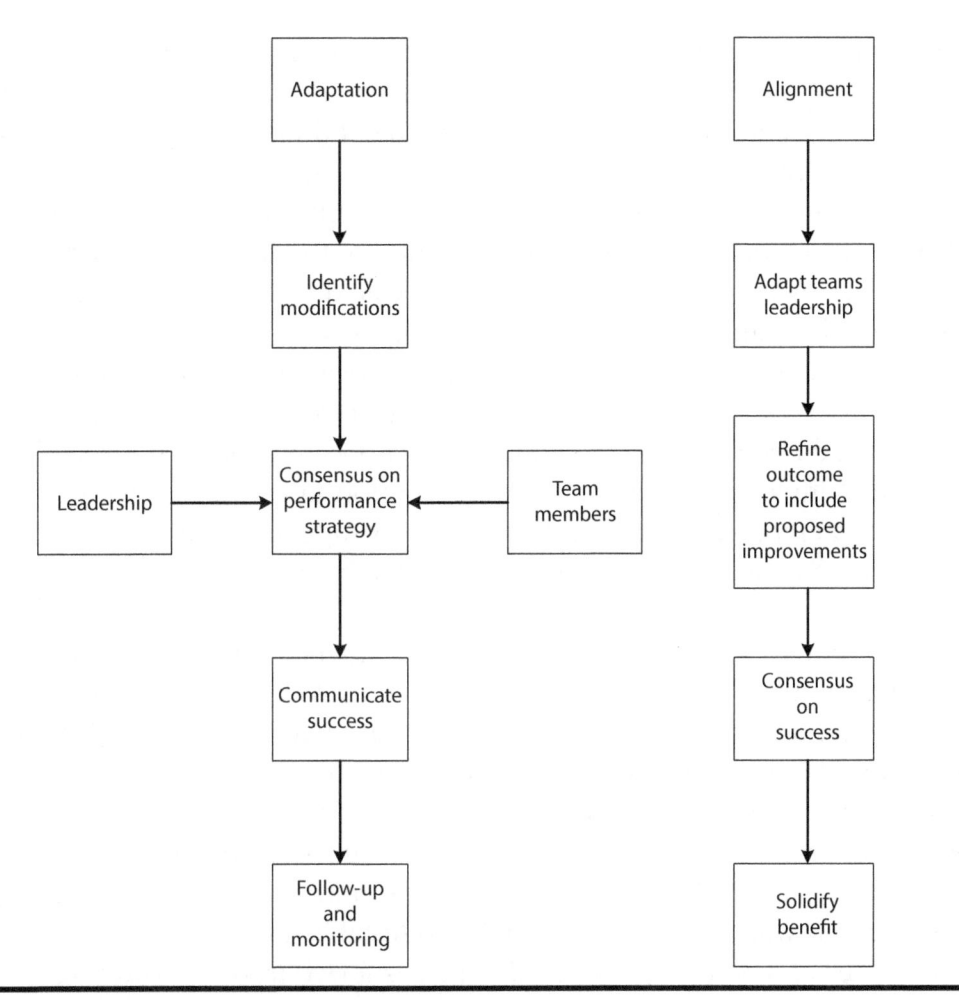

Figure 7.15 Performance below expectations—step 5.

This step also begins by reviewing your proposed incremental innovation process and measures for both relevancy and use. At this step, improvement in overall value is the key. If efficiencies, effectiveness, or cost savings improve there must be an associated value. Once reviewed, determine whether the value measure links directly to associated process measures. A change in value can signal a change in performance. As well, subtle changes in performance can easily indicate movement in value. Although we promote celebrating success in a timely manner, your work is not quite finished as preparing those responsible for their new duties requires a culture-driven approach. Each organization has its own culture, values, and SOPs and the tone of organizational culture is typically set by leadership.

We contend that gaining consensus is paramount in instituting sustained change and that also starts with leadership buy-in and support. Organizational leaders have a seminal and critical role in supporting your team on innovation specialists continue to reinforce the new or additional responsibilities through open and transparent communication, education, and confirmation. Do not forget to include your shareholders, stakeholders, and customers—such as suppliers, embedded contractors, and users, who are affected by the improvement. A comprehensive list of shareholders, stakeholders, and customers should be included in your innovation project charter and a schedule of recurring contacts developed, tracked, and documented for historical reference. We also recommend that these contacts be formalized by having training and knowledge shares documented and confirmed by some means such as a signature by each individual who have had their responsibilities change with your new innovation. This also confirms buy-in and affirms acknowledgment that the individual clearly understands their new responsibilities and the associated performance expectations.

Revisiting key takeaways from this step (Figure 7.15), aligning the employees to the new realities is crucial for success. As innovations become more commonplace, it will become easier to adapt to new outcomes. Alignment and finalization of the realized benefit and cost savings (reduction) will enable the speedy implementation. With any innovation, there is a comfort factor (zone) that needs to be reached with employees, customers (users), and suppliers. Reaching or achieving this comfort zone achieves a level of acceptance, which is critical for sustaining success.

As operations come "online," outcome performance (financial, operational, and strategic) measures must begin functioning as well. These should be shared with the organization as a whole. We recommend you identify a high traffic area where all employees and visitors can readily see the performance improvements metrics your team has collected. Now is the time to start developing tools that support sustainment of your new innovation process or best practice. The storyboard is a useful tool that can share the organization's journey. Although this is something you will share after the final step (establishing controls), you can start the processes of assembling the needed pieces for your storyboard (Figure 7.16).

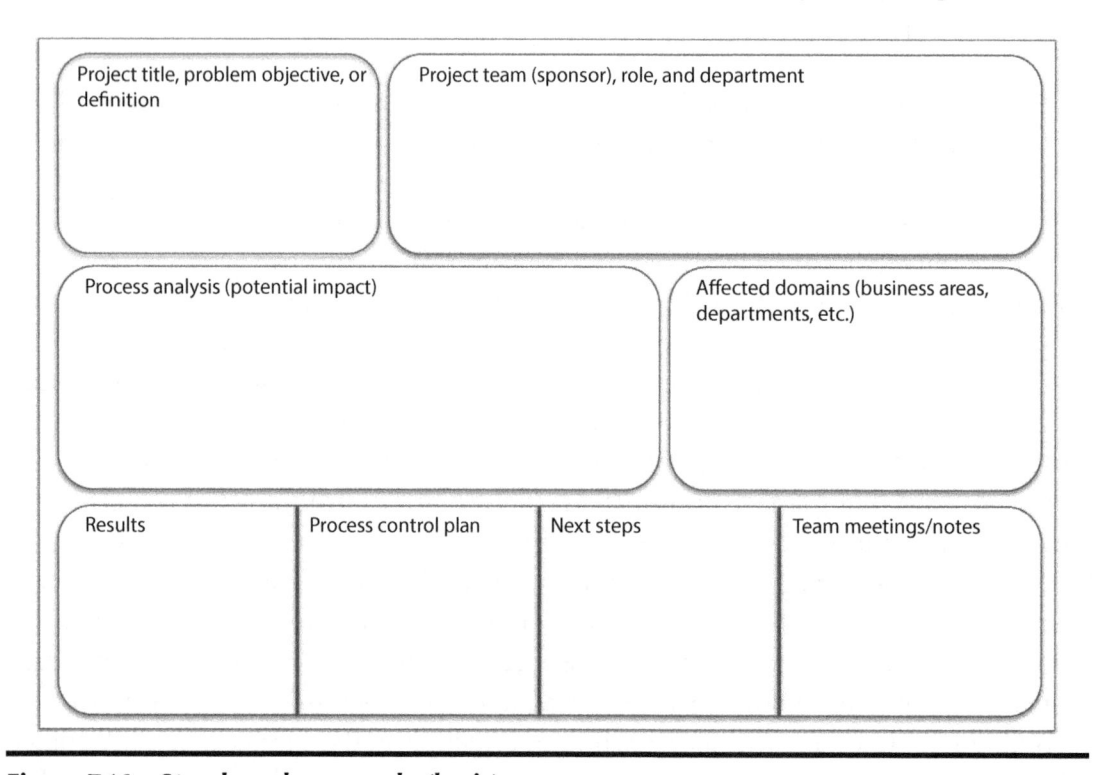

Figure 7.16 Storyboard—example (basic).

Storyboards not only deliver your message, but they can also help promote a culture of continuous innovation and acceptance of change as an organizational cultural norm. When designing your storyboard, we suggest you focus on open and transparent communication in a visual format. Basic components of the storyboard include an introduction (the new process, product or service and its innovative nature, benefits, or cost savings), organizational authority (devoted leadership supports for the innovation project), application and customer benefits (testimony of how the innovation changed or improved employee or customer satisfaction or performance), future vision (outline the opportunities for future incremental innovation projects and performance increases), and a summary (restate the key message you want your organization and customers to take away from your incremental innovation project). Other elements you might add to the storyboard are the plan and problem definition, supporting data and data analysis, actions taken, study results, and actions taken to standardize or adopt the new activity/process.

> **EXERCISE 7.10: STORYBOARD EXERCISE**
>
> Using the example storyboard provided in Figure 7.16, identify key elements for a storyboard your innovation team and organization would find useful in sharing your innovation journey.

We also recommend you do not focus on providing minute details that distract from your message. Also avoid signaling out specific individuals for praise—this is a time for celebrating your success, so we recommend you focus on team contributions, successes, and acknowledgement of the new best practice or performance improvement results. Finally, keep in mind, depending on the robust nature of your organization's IT capability, sharing the storyboard on your intranet or Internet might be a more effective option to complement the posting of the storyboard in company break rooms or high traffic areas. The next step in establishing a sustainable, value-added incremental innovation process, project, or service, is tracking and tying the effort to performance.

Step 6: Track and Tie to Performance

If the project continues to offer, the benefits identified in phase 1 of step 6 (Figure 7.17), then continue to pursue a successful outcome and focus on setting the stage for sustainment. In the first phase, your innovation team will focus on linking your incremental to measurable, validated, and verified value. Measures unique to innovation efforts are new (internal and external), improved (internal and external), and change (internal and external). Since this discussion focuses on improved performance, your team will concentrate on measuring the elements of efficiency and effectiveness, productivity, risk and reward, user acceptance, satisfaction, and ultimately success.

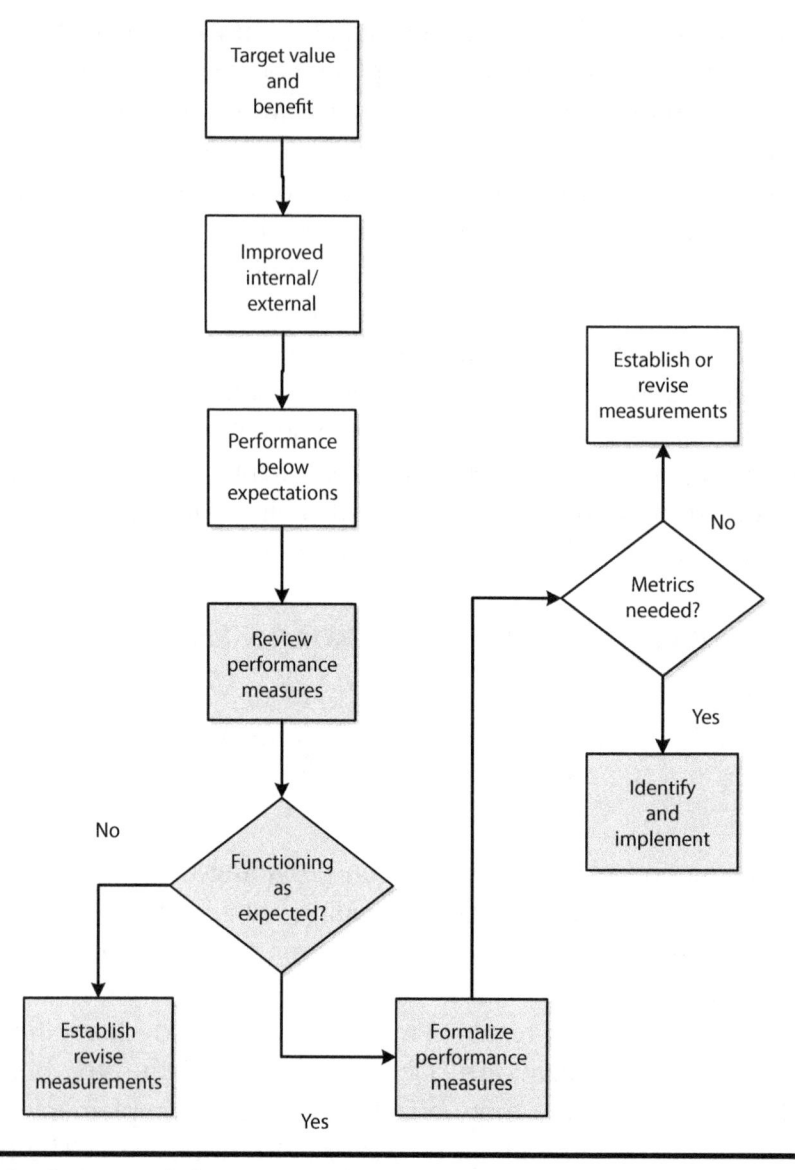

Figure 7.17   Performance below expectations—step 6.

In our example with the Flexo's performance disparities, examples of the measurements that the team may focus on:

■ Efficiency and effectiveness—Improved machine center uptime and availability rates
■ Productivity—Increase in number of units produced per hour
■ Risk and reward—Improved reward (units per hour) at no increased safety risk
■ User acceptance—Decreased number of quality defects cited by customer
■ Satisfaction—Client (customer) feedback
■ Success—Sustained increase in production (units per hour); new best practice/performance standard

EXERCISE 7.11: MEASUREMENTS EXERCISE

Using the example categories cited above (efficiency and effectiveness, productivity, risk and reward, user acceptance, satisfaction, and success), provide examples from one of your innovation team projects for each category. Share them with your team.

Once your team has reviewed the performance measures and methodologies, determine if they are effectively measuring the events you desire and providing useful data points to assess benefit and performance. If your team concurs the measurements and are achieving the level of fidelity (parameters) you have established (documented) in your incremental innovation team project charter, then formalize the performance measurements and decide what metrics you want to collect, analyze, and publish as benchmarks for implementation. If the measurements do not provide the level of fidelity that meet your established requirements, revise, and establish new measurements.

For our Flexo performance improvement example, we are assuming the measurements meet our requirements and the metrics we are collecting to quantify, analyze, and track will verify and validate value-added benefits (measures and indicators). Further, performance improvements can exist at multiple stages in the process implementation. For example, some of the performance factors or measurements for our Flexo scenario might entail measuring, tracking, and analyzing (by hour, shift, day, week, month, or quarter):

- Machine center uptime rates (via run chart)
- Machine center availability rates
- Units produced
- Sheets fed into the prefeeder
- Waste percentage—number of quality or deficient units identified by machine center operators or customer
- Machine center operator feedback
- Customer feedback

As these are an incomplete list on potential measurements, they do represent the common elements that are important to Flexo performance. Not mentioned above but intimately associated in any manufacturing and production environment are safety, reliability, and quality. When increased throughput demands are placed on an inherently human-centric operation, an increase in pressure, stress, and pace often are by-products. When operating heavy equipment and machinery, the risk of injury is present. Always consider safety first whenever implementing any innovations. The reward is simply just not worth the risk!

As critical as safety is to the process, both reliability and quality is key to sustained performance. Reliability is associated with performance as measured by wear, rates of failure, and use. Quality measures performance to requirements. Both elements are part of any process, whether service or manufacturing. Both directly influence the customer's view of innovation.

The final element before establishing controls is to include and fully align your measures to financial and accounting parameters associated with the incremental innovation project charter. Once you complete this phase, the project becomes reality and it is time to establish your system of controls and feedback procedures.

Step 7: Establish Controls

Although the final step in the NROVATE process (Figure 7.18) appears simple and straight forward, it actually requires an innate amount of discipline and rigors. In essence, this step ensures your prior efforts culminate in sustained performance of the new process and plants the seeds for follow-on product, process or service improvement opportunities. Further, at this point, the discussion and process flow is complete.

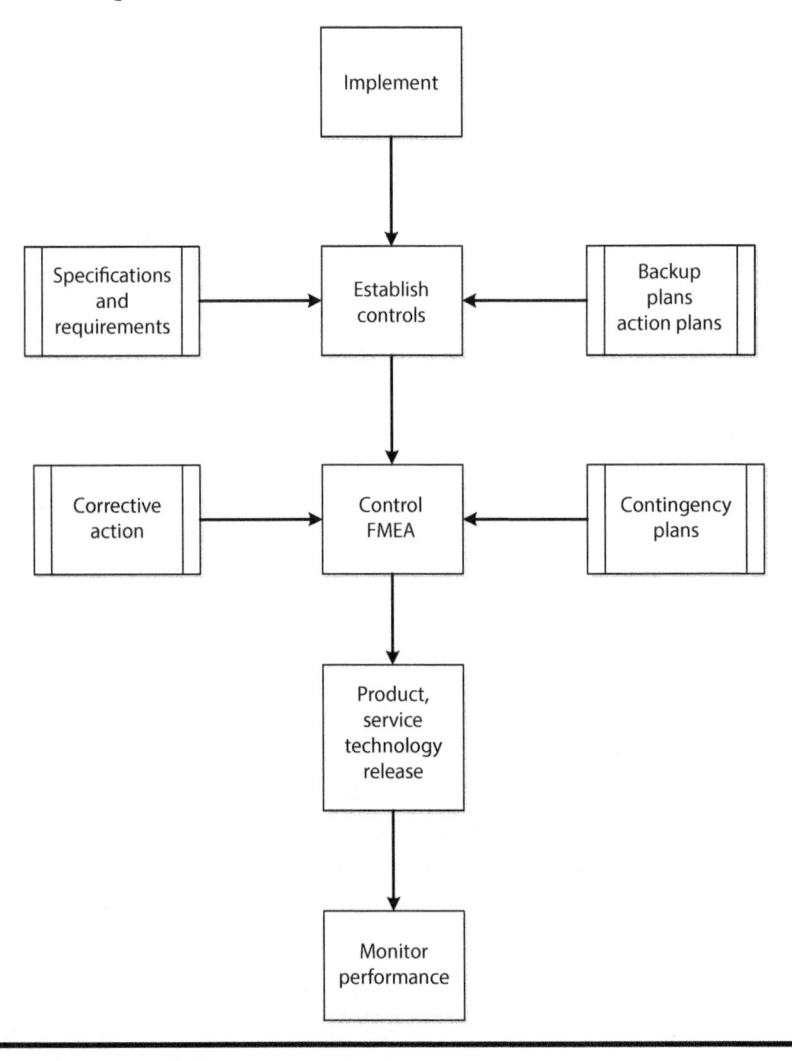

Figure 7.18 Performance below expectations—step 7.

The final phase (Figure 7.18) is similar to that detailed in the previous chapters. The phases in this final step are full implementation of the new process. The critical elements include:

■ The formalization and establishment of the recurring system of controls or pulse checks that will produce the measures and metrics required to monitor variance
■ The tools (i.e., control FMEA) to assess variance if it breaches the established upper control limits and lower control limits established in your plan to monitor performance

As with every process, there are far too many unknowns to have a "one size fits all." Each process is unique, yet fundamental issues remain constant. This process deals with these issues that leaders and executives must manage. Failure to do so increases risk, waste, and the failure.

> **EXERCISE 7.12: ESTABLISHING CONTROLS EXERCISE**
>
> Using the discussion and process map provided in Figure 7.18, walk through each step and identify and list two to three important measurements and/or controls that you feel are tantamount to achieving an effective monitoring process.

Summary

One precursor for your team to understand is that with any innovation project, conditions and situations will likely change with each innovation team project. Subsequently, these processes are guideposts and the example tools provided deployed or implemented as the each situation dictates. In this chapter, we introduced how the seven steps of the NROVATE process applied to an incremental innovation situation focused on improving performance in the manufacturing and production environment. From introducing steps associated with nominating and negotiating an innovation opportunity focused on improving performance to ultimately establishing the necessary controls to maintain and sustain that desired performance, the process is proven and effective when the team remains disciplined, follows the steps without short cuts, and remains focused on stakeholder, shareholder, and customer requirements.

DISCUSSION QUESTIONS

1. After running the process maps and tools provided on one of your organization's incremental innovation projects, gather as a team and discuss the following:
   a. Exercise results. Share your results from each exercise and discuss your answers.
   b. What step in the NROVATE methodology did you find most beneficial to you project or event?

   c. What tools offered in this chapter provided the best value added to your project or event?
2. If you had the opportunity to evolve the NROVATE methodology for incremental improvement when performance was substandard, what area(s) would you recommend changing? Are there any other tools or process steps you feel would add value to an incremental innovation project or event? Were there any tools you found added more value to your project or event? Share your thoughts with your innovation team in open discussion.

ASSIGNMENTS

1. Identify a problem that needs improving. Discuss why performance is below expectations and what are the reason and causes for this problem. Construct a basic fishbone diagram.
2. Select the primary causes and use the C&E matrix to identify which causes have the strongest effect on Y. Select a set of needs and requirements associated with the problem. What does the relationship between the causes and effects suggest about a possible innovation project?
3. Think about a process that you wish could perform better. Use the SMPA to identify which characteristics, if properly modified and controlled could deliver the performance you desire.

References

Ing, D. 2013. Rethinking systems thinking: Learning and coevolving with the world. *Systems Research & Behavioral Science*, 30(5), 527–547. doi:10.1002/sres.2229.

McLaughlin, G. and Caraballo, E. 2013b. *ENOVALE: How to Unlock Sustained Innovation Project Success*. Productivity Press, Boca Raton, FL.

McLaughlin, G. and Kennedy, W.R. 2015. *A Guide to Innovation Processes and Solutions for Government*. Productivity Press, Boca Raton, FL. ISBN: 978-1-4987-2157-8.

Chapter 8

Incremental Innovation: Accelerated Performance

Introduction

A common theme throughout this handbook is that innovation, regardless of its impact or magnitude of impact can be categorized as new, improved, or changed. In this chapter, our goal is to build on our previous work by providing additional tools to compliment those previously provided in our preceding books on the innovation body of knowledge. In considering incremental innovation focused on continuously improving processes, services, or products, we are assuming that readers will have varying levels of experience and understanding of well-known Lean Six Sigma tools that support continuous process improvement (CPI) efforts. The performance acceleration process combines Lean Six Sigma tools with specialized tools (described in this chapter) and additional tools previously described in earlier chapters. Of paramount importance to consider here, the performance acceleration process aligns best with small- to medium-sized projects, including a specific target set (defined goals and objectives).

With minor adjustments throughout the process steps, there are striking similarities between the RNOVATE™ (process acceleration) and the N²OVATE™ methodology and process.

1. **R**: Recognize the opportunity
2. **N**: Normalize the performance
3. **O**: Operationalize
4. **V**: Validate
5. **A**: Adapt
6. **T**: Track to improvement/performance
7. **E**: Evaluate and review

An outline of the RNOVATE performance acceleration process is provided and explained in this chapter along with associated process maps for each step.

Scenario 2: Performance Acceleration: Aircraft Communications

With the complex and dynamic nature of the world's net-centric environment, the increasing demand to be "virtually connected" with both home and business networks 24 hours a day, 7 days a week, 365 days a year, is fertile ground for continuous innovation opportunities across the international business landscape. For this scenario, we are focusing on airborne communications—identifying incremental and game-changing innovation opportunities, where the current capability meets or exceeds identified performance standards.

In regards to defining characteristics or critical elements associated with innovation, the focus is on incremental improvement as it relates to performance. If the performance is substandard, then the innovation team's purpose (goal or objective) would focus on raising performance to the levels that meet or exceed expected objectives. If this is the case, please refer to Chapter 7. If the current performance or capability meets expected objectives and the innovation team's focus is on adding value by increasing capabilities or improving efficiency (effectiveness), the RNOVATE process steps are designed to achieve this goal.

For this example case study, the performance meets established requirements (needs), but the team's objectives are improving or optimizing an airborne communication system's performance through improved scalability (size, weight, and power requirements) while providing improved reliability and efficiency. To illustrate the use of the RNOVATE process, we will offer an example scenario of an actual incremental innovation improvement project from the aviation or airborne communications industry segment. Please keep in mind that the term "process" in this discussion is synonymous with product or service performance improvements. Further, the terms "platform" and "aircraft" are interchangeable terms.

Scenario: Airborne Communications Background

To help set the stage for our example scenario, we have narrowed the airborne communications project to the day-to-day services required of business enterprise communication systems on airborne platforms (voice, video, and data services and capabilities). Since most executives and senior leaders use commercial-derivative small body (7–12 passengers) to medium body (15–25 passengers) size aircraft, we will focus our discussion on small body aircraft in this scenario. Further, while fulfilling the organization's strategic objectives, senior leaders and their staffs seek net-centric capabilities and must have unfettered access to real-time, high-quality, and reliable communications while airborne (or in transit) to address the full range of their organization's assigned responsibilities. These communication requirements often entail seamless (transparent), reliable and robust voice, video and data communication services and capabilities. The current capability meets the established requirements but we provide this system (end-to-end, sender-to-receiver) currently leverages private and commercial, ad hoc and stove-piped terrestrial (or ground-based systems) and satellite network infrastructures to deliver its current services. However, information superiority and real-time access to an organization or enterprise's knowledge base (shareholders, stakeholders, and customers) to support a timely decision process requires delivering actionable information in a timely manner to any decision maker in the enterprise.

Some specific areas where there are potential areas for identifying incremental innovation improvements to an airborne communication system are:

■ Enhanced communications quality, service, and security (voice, video, and data)
■ Enhanced situational awareness through real-time access
■ Improved infrastructure access and performance (increased bandwidth and data transfer rates or managing bandwidth effectively)
■ Global seamless, autonomous, and reliable communications operations throughout all phases of flight
■ Communications equipment space, weight, and power (SWaP) requirements
■ Agile communications capabilities (ability to upgrade, augment, or replace communication components without degrading performance or lowering the baseline standards for the same)

Please keep in mind, these are only a few examples of potential target areas for incremental improvements in this scenario and we encourage you to identify others as you work through the exercises in this chapter. Unlike the scenario presented in Chapter 6, which provided metrics for performance, this discussion will lean more toward capability improvements in a narrative fashion. Baseline capabilities will be provided in the discussion and random improvement objectives offered through each step as tools are introduced or referred to from previous chapters. Further, employing the RNOVATE process, each step has a complementary process map for the reader's consideration as they seek to improve performance that already exceeds expectations. Finally, three additional subjects relative to this scenario we feel are important to mention are technological convergence, incremental innovation process, and organizational culture.

Technological Convergence

Telecommunications and network architecture are the tapestry of technologies (hardware and software) weaved into a convergent technological mesh built around a set of task or capability requirements. In our scenario, the voice, video, and data capabilities required to support airborne communications leverage terrestrial and satellite-based networks, which are required to work together to get these services from sender to receiver. Although the hardware and software systems supporting these capabilities may employ different approaches in achieving how they support the network, they do not all provide the same quality, efficiency, or reliability levels and are typically in an evolutionary state that follows the path of evolutionary convergence.

Incremental Innovation Process (Revisited)

As a precursor to the first step in the RNOVATE, recognizing the (innovation) opportunity, we offer a short introduction to the incremental innovation process map (Figure 8.1). This process was introduced in our prior work, *A Guide to Innovation Processes and Solution in Government* (McLaughlin and Kennedy, 2015), and we encourage the reader to review and have this text available as they work through the chapter and associated exercises.

It is expected that each organization will have its' own unique innovation identity or culture. Subsequently, they develop their own innovation DNA or fingerprint that is engrained across the organization typically through strong leadership buy-in and an established and distinct set of innovation processes and solutions.

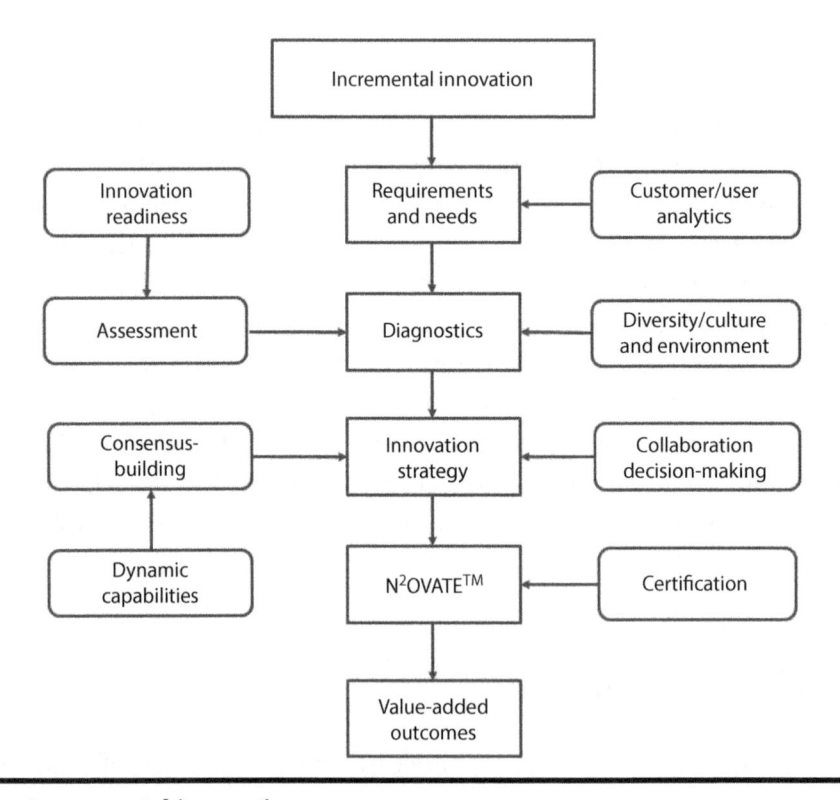

Figure 8.1 Incremental innovation process.

Successful organizations concentrate on evolving tailorable innovation processes and solutions that assist the organization in fostering a corp of human resources that consistently generate new innovation opportunities. Conversely, there are also a significant number of companies and organizations that simply do not have any organized or documented innovation processes or guidance in place to identify innovation opportunities for identifying opportunities. These organizations struggle with any type of innovation and often lack the capability to capitalize on value-added innovation opportunities for their processes, products, or services.

Organizational Culture

We have mentioned organizational innovation culture throughout this workbook and in several cases, the text that this workbook supports. Accelerating performance requires a different culture that is associated with improving performance. To determine whether the organization meets the cultural readiness criteria, we suggest an exercise that assesses what kind of climate and culture your organization is currently operating in. We identify three major types of organizational cultures: innovative (entrepreneurial, creative, risk taking), bureaucratic (focus on rules, regulation, and efficiency), and supportive (employee–customer centric; Berson et al., 2007). Identifying which of the three organizational types (criteria) your organization best aligns with can help provide a basis to judge and determine the influence of an organization's culture on its shareholders, stakeholders, and customers. To assess an organization's culture, we provide the organizational culture assessment matrix (Table 8.1).

Table 8.1   Organizational Culture Assessment Matrix

Major Characteristic	Subcomponent	Dominance	Significance	History
Innovative	Entrepreneurial			
Innovative	Creative			
Innovative	Risk taking			
Bureaucratic	Playing by the rules			
Bureaucratic	Regulatory			
Bureaucratic	Efficiency focused			
Supportive	Employee focused			
Supportive	Customer/user focused			
Supportive	Cooperative			

In completing the organizational culture assessment matrix, there are three measurement criteria that will help evaluate the general state of the organization:

1. Dominance—how frequently does the organization reflect this behavior?
2. Significance—how important (prevalent) is the organizational attribute?
3. History—how long has this attribute been part of the organizational DNA?

In evaluating *dominance*, use a three-point Likert scale (as defined below):

- 1—Minimal
- 2—Occasional
- 3—Frequent

In evaluating *significance*, use a three-point Likert scale (as defined below):

- 1—Not important
- 2—Marginal importance
- 3—Very important

In evaluating *history*, use a three-point Likert scale (as defined below):

- 1—Long history of practice (over 5 years)
- 2—Moderate history of practice (2–5 years)
- 3—Short history of practice (0–2 years)

To get a balanced score, try for a sample of 30 or more individuals (in various positions throughout your organization). Average the scores and look for patterns in position title, age, education, and years' experience. Compare with like organizations in the same sector. For accelerated performance, the culture must be innovative (creative entrepreneurial and risk taking).

> **EXERCISE 8.1: ORGANIZATION CULTURE ASSESSMENT**
>
> Using the matrix in Table 8.1, complete a quick assessment of your organization's innovation culture. Prepare to discuss your findings in a group setting.

Largely, knowing your organization's culture and affinity toward knowledge and information sharing is an important precursor on possible approaches to identifying or recognizing the innovation opportunities that "push the envelope" of performance and value improvement. This section will not cover innovation cultures in-depth, it is simply to introduce the reality that organizational culture has a significant influence on how the organization reacts to, supports, and fosters innovation opportunities in general. In simple terms, if your culture is closed-ended (one entry point and one exit point for innovative ideas), you will likely trend toward looking internally to your organization's own assets for identifying potential innovation ideas and opportunities.

Conversely, if your organization freely shares intellectual property and business intelligence through agreements such as joint ventures or alliances, you are more likely working in what Henry Chesbrough refers to as a, "culture of open innovation." In summary, there are multiple schools of thought on innovation, but central to all is the notion that organizational culture plays a big role in how the organization identifies, develops, responds, and approaches an innovation opportunity. If the organization's work force embraces change and views change (innovation) as a nonthreatening essential cultural norm, the innovation opportunity typically delivers improved value to a process, service, or product. The first step in improving a process, product, or service that is already meeting or exceeding standards is to recognize the opportunity.

Step 1: Recognize the Opportunity

The first step in improving on existing performance is recognizing that there is always room for improving the status quo (Figure 8.2). Seminal to this step is acknowledging that identifying innovation opportunities that lead to enhancing current performance of products, services, or processes is understanding the type of innovation environment you are operating within your organization.

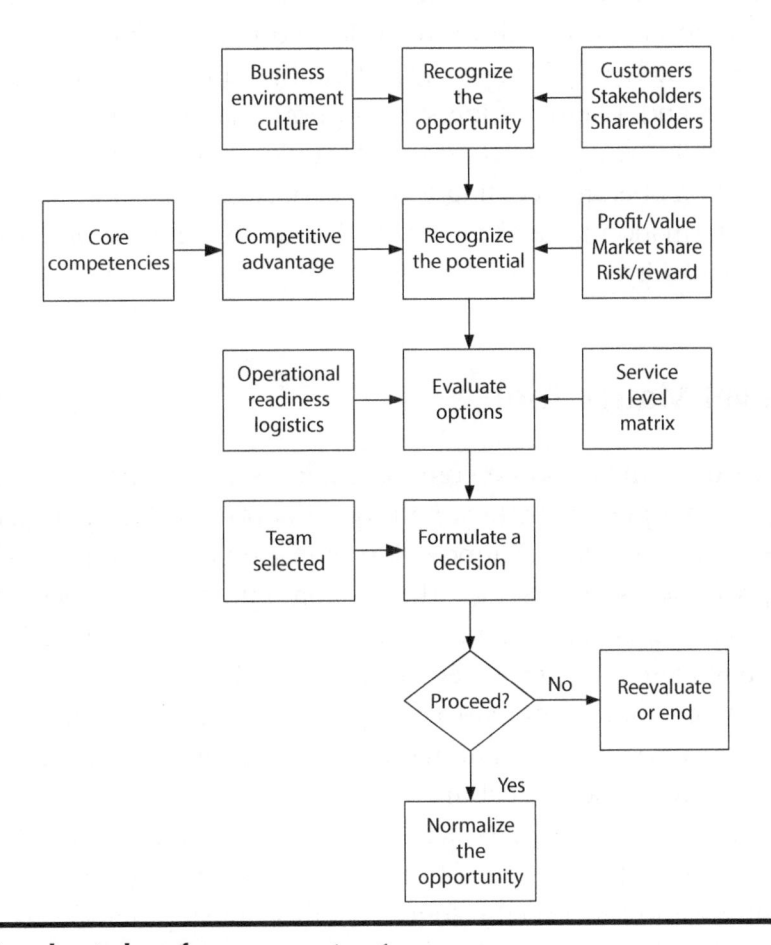

Figure 8.2   Accelerated performance—step 1.

When you understand your culture and climate, you will then need to clearly define and prioritize your core competencies (what your organization is good at and what makes your business successful) at the strategic (organizational), operational (system), and tactical (process) level. Next is determining the value and benefit potential and can this innovation opportunity be profitable? Further, is it possible to sustain a competitive advantage before the competition offers a different solution? In the early stages of this step, the team and management do their best to define these key attributes (KAs) and determine whether accelerated performance is worth the additional investment in resources (cost, staffing, and time). The word "recognize" is used more to mean acknowledgment, as at this stage, a distinctive benefit was identified previously. This is the time to reevaluate the benefit and determine its worth and sustainability.

Core competencies have several key elements that assist leadership at all levels. One of these elements strategically aligns resources toward a set of common goals and objectives. Core competencies also help provide a means of prioritizing the most important functions (processes, services, and processes) where innovation opportunities might prove to carry the best value added when adopted and implemented. Some of those key elements are key performance parameters (KPPs), key performance indicators (KPIs), critical success factors (CSFs), and KAs.

When reexamining the benefit (value added) and/or risk/reward, it is useful to evaluate options, before choosing a desired path or direction. Accelerated performance will likely require new operational parameters, training, reallocation of resources, and a litany of logistics support changes. In fact, too many modifications would be a negative, given the ratio of cost-to-benefit. Therefore, evaluate the options before deciding to proceed. A cursory analysis should provide enough information to determine whether to abandon or proceed with your innovation opportunity.

Service Level Matrix Tool

Shifting our focus to the airborne communication systems scenario for this chapter, there are many options for tracking requirements and factors essential in making a decision to pursue an innovation opportunity. In support of our scenario for improvements to existing airborne communication services that meet or exceed current expectations on the small tube aircraft, a service level matrix (SLM; Figure 8.3) example is provided. The SLM tool captures key service level requirements for customers (executives, supporting staff, and employees), level and type of service required, requirements and performance parameters (percentage of usage, reliability/availability rates, quality of service, and quantity of service). It is common to see KPPs, KPIs, KAs, and other CSFs find their way into service level matrices. These types of matrices can support your team's functional needs assessment and functional solutions analysis in step 3 and can also be updated and tailored to meet the innovation team's needs in selecting the right

Service Level Matrix						
Service Levels	Communication Descriptions (Day-to-Day Services)	Service Type	Percentage of Usage	Reliability/ Availability	Quality of Service	Quantity of Service

Figure 8.3   Service level matrix example—descriptions and service requirements.

tools for measuring, tracking, and reporting in step 6, Track to Improvement/ Performance.

EXERCISE 8.2: SERVICE LEVEL MATRIX

Using the example as a guide, build an SLM to support an innovation opportunity proposal or project submission within your organization. Share your results with your supervision, peers, and employees (where applicable). What are their thoughts on suggested changes to your initial matrix?

Shifting our focus to the airborne communication systems scenario for this chapter, some primary considerations for innovation team members could entail:

■ Knowledge of the equipment (i.e., airborne communications, satellite and telecommunications, terrestrial, and ground-based communications)
■ Standard operating procedures (i.e., communications operators, aeronautical engineering, and maintenance)
■ Training
■ Qualifications for running the airborne communications equipment, operations, and maintenance concepts
■ Preventive maintenance and recurring cleaning requirements
■ Production scheduling or orders
■ Daily performance and data collection requirements

Service Level Matrix						
Service Levels	**Communication Descriptions (Day-to-Day Services)**	**Service Type**	**Percentage of Usage**	**Reliability/ Availability**	**Quality of Service**	**Quantity of Service**
Executive-Level (C-Suite)	Most critical with the maximum acceptable levels of communications capacity and quality of service. Highest levels of reliability and availability.	Voice	>99%	0.99	High	High
		Data	>99%	0.99	High	High
		Video	>99%	0.99	High	High
Staff Level	Critical with the moderate to high levels of communications capacity and quality of service expected. Highest levels of reliability and availability.	Voice	>99%	0.95	High	Medium
		Data	>99%	0.95	High	Medium
		Video	<25%	0.95	Medium	Medium
Employee	Basic telecommunications (voice and email services) and video or streaming capability. High levels of reliability and availability are desired but not required for all employees who may not require access to any of these capabilities to accomplish their assigned tasks.	Voice	>25%	0.95	Medium	Medium
		Data	<20%	0.50	Medium	Medium
		Video	<10%	0.25	Low	Low

Figure 8.4   Service level matrix example—descriptions and service requirements.

After identifying team membership and assigning initial responsibilities, begin the process of developing the requirements (goals and objectives) and securing senior leadership (management) support. Schedule meetings and time requirements you will require from each member on the team. In our airborne communications scenario, reflect back on the SLM (Figure 8.4). Your goal and objective is to improve overall voice, video, and data capability (reliability and performance) beyond the published expectations captured in this matrix. An accompanying objective is to improve the SWaP profile or requirements if possible. Further, nominating the right complement of team members can be one of the most complicated steps a team leader will face in this process. Senior leadership buy-in, support, and cooperation are essential.

Finally, making a decision to move forward is the last deliverable for this step. The evidence should suggest the best course of action. You will know when this occurs when the amount and intensity of internal discussion significantly reduces over time. As management and the team acquiesce, the objective will become clearer and better defined. Therefore, the decision is either to proceed or halt discussion on the topic. This, then, is a major milestone as a rejection shuts down the project.

Other tools mentioned in previous chapters important to consider are the innovation team project charter (Figure 8.3) and the RACI or RASCI (responsibility, accountability, support network, consultant network, and information requirements) model (Figure 8.2). Combined, they are synergizing tools that assist the innovation team in maintaining focus on the objectives and goals of the project. Most specifically:

■ Who will own the activities, problems, or goals associated with the innovation project (responsibility)?

■ Who is the decision maker or approval authority for the work at each level building up to the final implementation of the innovation (accountability)?

■ Who can provide the necessary support throughout the stages of the project and ultimately the success of the innovation implementation (required support)?

■ Who has the knowledge and information necessary to support your project throughout the steps toward implementation (consultant support)?

■ Who in the chain of command or leadership hierarchy is notified at what stages or milestones as the project moves through the process steps (information requirements)?

Before moving onto the next step (step 2), we feel it is important to reiterate to the reader there are additional tools that can help an organization identify innovation opportunities to complement those offered throughout this workbook. Hence, we will assume the proposal received approval to move to the next step.

Step 2: Normalizing the Opportunity

In this step (Figure 8.5), the team will develop a method for testing whether the accelerated performance is sustainable and identify the expectations regarding performance. Further, key expectations (both present and future) are critical to defining the achievable limits.

Table 8.2 lists the requirement and type (customer, SOP), present day (reality), and future performance (expectations), and the final column lists the decision reached on whether the expectations, as expressed, are accepted or denied. Of course, the expectations are just presumptions until the next stage is completed. During this stage, we would expect both negotiation and compromise to be critical elements of the final (future) expectations. We must caution that presuming (or hoping) to meet an expectation with some sort of prior validation is often a waste of time. Presume that the future expectation is possible, but not sustainable. This, then, sets the stage for the testing.

EXERCISE 8.3: EXPECTATIONS EVALUATION TOOL

Develop a set of expectations for a product, process, or service that would benefit from accelerated performance. Consider the present expectation and develop future expectations. Discuss among the team if the future expectation could be a reality.

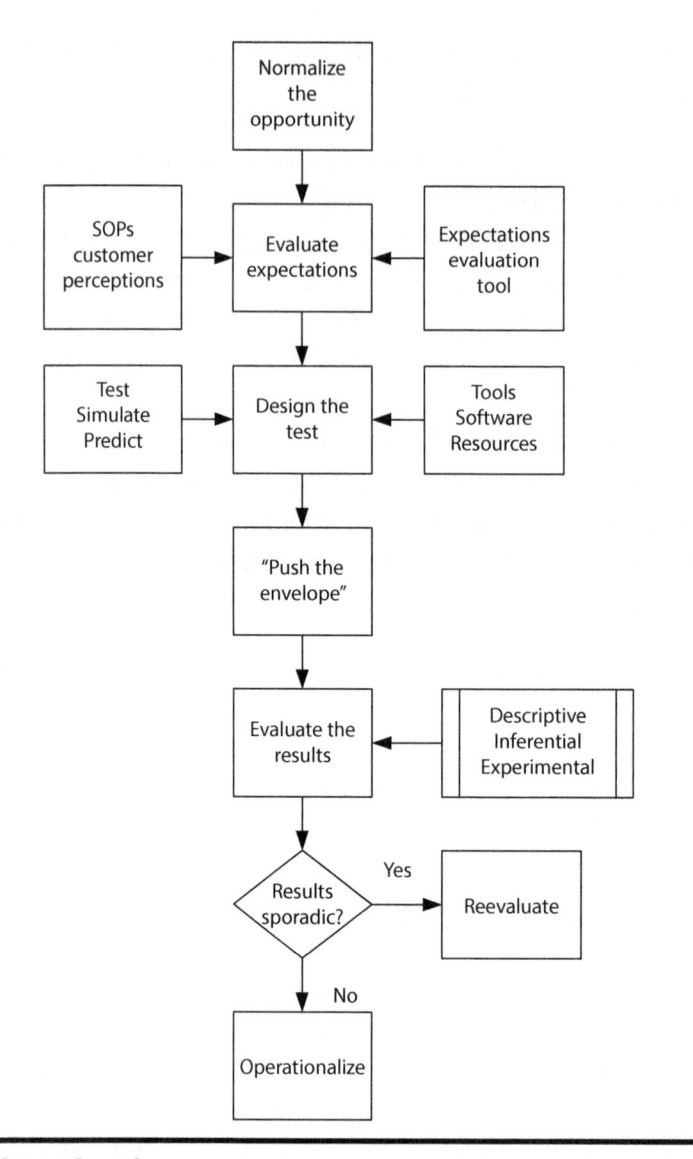

Figure 8.5   Accelerated performance—step 2.

Table 8.2   Expectations Evaluation Tool

Requirement	Type	Present (Reality)	Future (Expectation)	Decision
Connectivity	Customer	70%–75% Coverage	95%–100% Coverage	Approved
Download speed	SOP	5 Mb/s	50 Mb/s	Approved
No. of downtime events	Customer	10 downtime events per million miles flown	<1 downtime event per million miles flown	Denied

Testing whether the accelerated performance level is possible and then determining if it is sustainable requires designing a test plan. Begin with the information contained in the IOP document regarding, KPPs, KPIs, KAs, and CSFs or use these factors to help develop and refine the future expectations described in step 1. These IOP factors will help develop the test parameters used to accelerate and sustain performance. Figure 8.6 details a typical test plan.

Testing Protocol

Test conducted by: _____   Date: Click here to enter a date.

Requestor information (name, e-mail, telephone)	Key Variable Information:
	Key Process Variables:
	Key Performance Indicator:
	Key Performance Parameters:
Supervisor (e-mail and telephone)	Critical Success Factors:

A short description of the objective (what is to be accomplished)

Test design strategy, including what data will be collected:

Identify variables, SOPs, quality procedures that would be impacted:

Describe the results. How will these results aid in sustaining the new level of performance?

Approvals:	Estimated date that the research will commence and complete:
Manager: Name:_____	
Innovation specialist: Name:_____	Reason for delay:
Area Supervisor: Name:_____	

Figure 8.6   Test plan.

Test plans can be as simple as designing a test run or as complex as designing an experiment or simulation. Various methods of testing are possible.

■ Direct testing of the product, service, or process (varying variables, collecting data, plotting performance, recommend control charting)
■ Experimental design involves very small samples and a minimum of two variables to modify, while observing performance. This method permits an estimate of variation (controllable) and prediction
■ Simulations that involve constructing a model of variables tested at various settings while observing performance. Note: Experimental designs function well within the simulation environment

---

EXERCISE 8.4: TEST PLAN

Complete a test plan for a fictitious process, have each team member prepare a preliminary plan and then compare results. Discuss why the similarities and differences exist.

Testing is critical for "pushing the envelope" maintaining these levels of accelerated performance. Once the test is complete, evaluate the results using a descriptive, inferential (testing hypotheses), or experimental approach. If the results are sporadic, then reevaluate. If not, then move to operationalizing the process.

Step 3: Operationalization

In this step, we incorporate the learnings from step 2 into a new set of requirements, SOPs, and quality standards. The purpose of this step is to develop new operational procedures for maintaining a new level of performance. Figure 8.7 is the flowchart for this next step. The step begins with the test results from step 2 and builds these into a new set of standards that will facilitate accelerated performance. Using the empirical evidence from step 2 provides a level of assurance that the process will adjust to the new standard of performance.

The test data alone are not enough to make a final decision. Operationalize the decision within the capability of the organization to sustain and support the innovation. Changing the performance characteristics requires a new set of standards whether these are process oriented, customer oriented, or quality oriented. This step involves updating manuals, additional training, and new controls to assure consistency. Also, consider the resources needed and how suppliers will meet the requirements for a significantly changed process. Accelerated performance is truly innovative in that it meets an unsatisfied need (requirement) in a way attractive to the user or customer.

To develop these new standards, modify the existing information based on the new targets and goals achieved. Include new quality procedures and controls

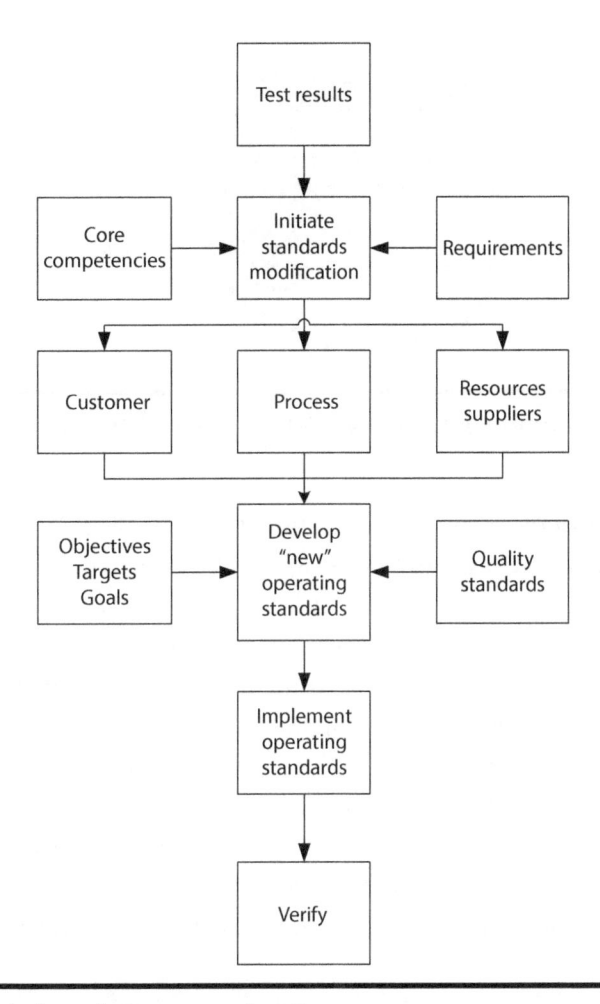

Figure 8.7   Accelerated performance—step 3.

based on the performance desired. Consider alternatives as a way of coping with changing conditions. Test and evaluate the new standards before implementing. Be careful not to introduce additional uncertainty or inconsistency to the process. Monitor the process carefully at start up and for at least 1 month after initiation. If the process remains consistent, then consider the standards as compliant. Use the month period to verify and validate the standard, using the stages in step 4.

EXERCISE 8.5: STANDARDS

Design a test plan for implementing a new set of standards for an accelerated performance innovation. Consider the present state and discuss what needs to change to meet the new performance guidelines. Describe how targets and goals influence the standards.

Step 4: Validate

The step 4 steps in the RNOVATE process, validate, adapt, track improvement/ performance, and evaluate and review, are very similar to the last four steps in

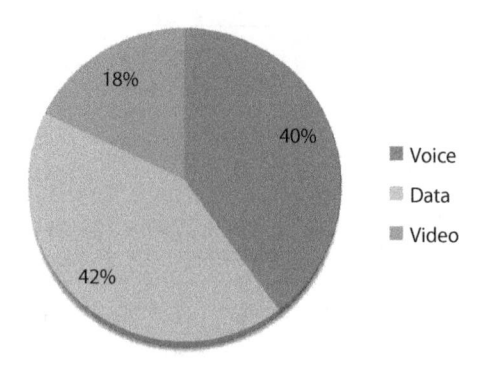

Figure 8.8   Executive airborne communication usage pie chart (voice, video, and data).

the improvement process described in the previous chapter. In this section, we address the validation step (Figure 8.8) and it begins with analyzing the data the innovation team has collected to validate the new process. When performing analysis on the data your team has and will collect during the incremental innovation opportunity processes, we maintain the innovation team should retain the focus of keeping things simple statistically (KISS Principle: keep it simple statistically). Although data analysis may use inferential statistical tools, simple descriptive analysis often serves a similar purpose. An example of this visible representations for tracking actual perfomance data in support of the validation and data analysis effort provided in Figures 8.9 and 8.10 are provided to reflect examples used in support of our airborne communications sceanrio.

EXERCISE 8.6: BUILD A USAGE PIE CHART

Consider a project or innovation opportunity proposal you are working on within your organization. Using the example in Figure 8.9, build your own basic usage pie chart for one KPP or KPI identified in Section II, Operational System Requirements Statement, of the innovation opportunity profile (IOP) you built in the previous exercises.

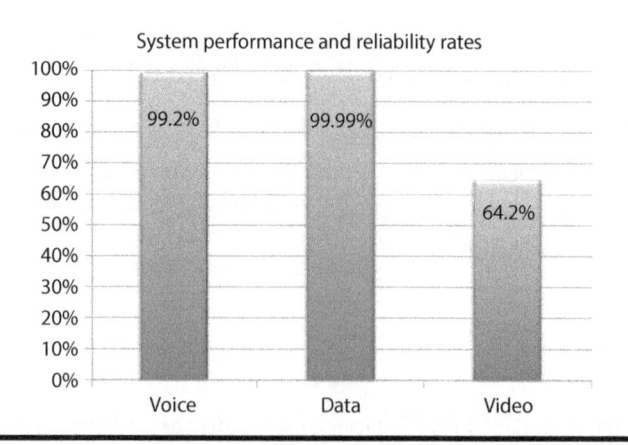

Figure 8.9   Airborne communication system perfomance and reliability rates bar graph.

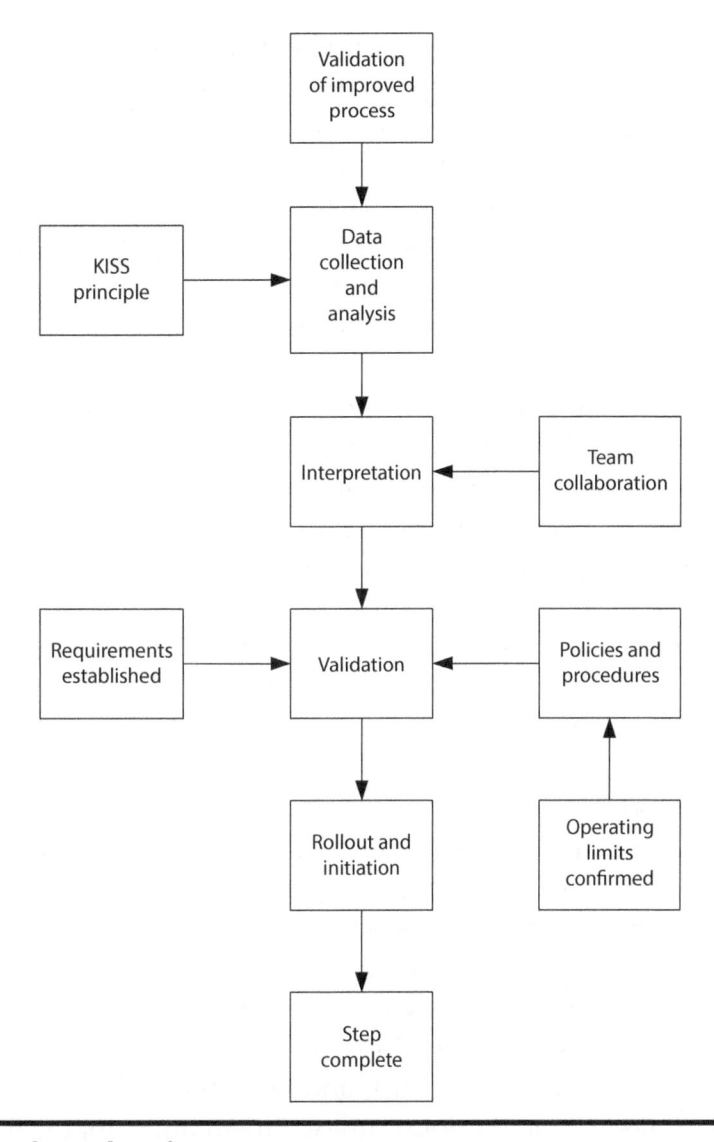

Figure 8.10 Accelerated performance—step 4.

EXERCISE 8.7: BUILD A BASIC PERFORMANCE AND RELIABILITY RATE BAR CHART

Consider a project or innovation opportunity proposal you are working on within your organization. Using the example in Figure 8.10, build your own basic performance and reliability bar chart for one KPP or KPI identified in Section II, Operational System Requirements Statement, of the IOP you built in the previous exercises.

The headings and content of charts and graphs supporting your data analysis efforts will obviously change based on the product, process, or service innovation opportunity. We encourage you to explore those mentioned in previous chapters of this workbook as they can be very useful tools for readily providing visual summations for decision makers. In improving performance through incremental innovation opportunities, the significant objective is providing the right information at the right time to make timely decisions. Further, they can also serve as status checks for the entire team and condense difficult messages and concepts you are trying to share with others. As previously provided in this chapter, there are a host of other automated tools widely available in today's business community and we recommend you leverage these capabilities to augment our process and to help interpret the data your team has collected.

In Figure 8.11, validate and verify key operational parameters and indicators (KPPs, KPIs, KA, and CSFs) identified in your IOP developed in Chapter 4, Operalization, are required. Using established requirements to verify the operational parameters your team has identified or have been provided, help expand and mature the proposal and prepare your organization and leadership for inititation of your proposed innovation solution. By developing policies and procedures from your validated operating limits, you want to ensure you make a concerted effort to inform, educate, and secure buy-in from your shareholders, stakeholders, and also your customers if the situation warrants their paritcipation.

The validation and data analysis step is often neglected as innovation teams race to meet deadlines or implement improvement-centric innovation opportunities. Never overlook the need to adapt or align the organization's human element (employees) to the incremental innovation improvement. Effective communication is vital function for those key to implementing improvement opportunities when the product process or service already meets or exceeds standards and expectations. Ensure you keep shareholders, stakeholders, and customers involved (those outlined in Sections I, III, VI, VIII, and IX of the IOP) even if they are not directly related to the innovation opportunity. Buy-in and support from champions, support staff, and other key players is paramount as you prepare to roll out your innovation opportunity for adoption. In our aircraft communication capability performance improvement example, key players this effort expands the pool of key players you will need to inform, educate (train), and gain support and buy-in from include, but are not limited to:

- Executive and support staff travelers
- Flight (aircrew) and ground crew operation members
- Flight operations and airfield management
- Aircraft and IT maintenance (in-house or the contractor representative if your equipment is maintained under warranty or contract support)
- Quality assurance and safety managers
- Customer service and certification/waiver authorities (FCC and FAA)
- Supporting organizational business units, groups, and personnel
- Any on-site contractor support and key suppliers (partners) involved with the machine, process, or service your project focuses on

Success Methods and Performance Analysis
SMPA

Process Step	Key Process Input	Potential Success Modes	Potential Performance	P r o b	Potential Causes	M E A S	Current Actions or Controls	O c c u	S P N	Actions Recommended	Resp.	Actions Taken	P R B	N E P	S U S	S P N
Process Step	What is the component, part, or element?	In what ways can the component, part, or element improve?	What is the effect on performance?	Impact Probability - Rate the chance of continued improvement	What could cause the component, part, or element to effect performance negatively?	How frequently would a negative effect occur?	What actions (controls) are needed for this improvement to be sustained?	How well can the improvement sustain increased performance?	Success Priority Number	What are the actions required for maintaining improved performance?	Who is responsible for the recommended actions?	What are the completed actions taken? Be sure to include completion month/year.				
	Routing	Faster	Arrival Time	6	Weather	9	Improved Forecasts	5	270							0
	Routing	Faster	Departure Time	8	Weather	9	Improved Forecasts	5	360							0
	Routing	Less Fuel	Less Cost	8	Traffic	8	Controller	7	448							0
	Routing	Less Fuel	More Profit	7	Traffic	8	Controller	7	392							0
	Routing	Accurate	Less Delays	8	Weather	9	Operation Center	8	576							0
	Routing	Accurate	Fewer Disruptions	5	Problems	6	Terminal and Airline Practices	7	210							0
	Routing	Accurate	Less Stress	9	Disruption	6	Crew Training	5	270							0
	Routing	Direct	Absorbs Delays	9	Terminal Delays	6	Terminal and Airline Practices	8	432							0

Process or Product Name: Routing Issues — Responsible: — Prepared by: — SMPA Date (Orig) ___ (Rev) ___ — Page ___ of ___

Figure 8.11 SMPA template example (routing issues).

> ## EXERCISE 8.8: KEY PLAYER LIST
>
> Using the key organization business unit, group, and personnel list provided above, build a quick key player list for a project or proposal you are working or might propose. Consider the entries made in the innovation opportunity form. In what sections are your key players identified?

You may recall in the operationalization step, your team identified and prepared the new or modified requirements prior to full rollout and implementation of the product, service, or process. If the validation and data analysis step is skipped or diluted, the risk of failure increases due to unplanned or untested conditions. The less you know about a process the greater the chance of errors, mistakes, and miscalculations. Further, consider aligning the employees to the new realities your incremental improvement will bring as a CSF and cruical for success. As innovations become more commonplace, the organizational culture and employee attitudes toward innovation will become better prepared to adapt to new outcomes. Alignment and finalization of the innovation opportunity's benefit and value will lead to new baseline perfomance standards and expectations.

The SMPA tool is a method to define successful performance as a function of those elements that improve performance over the life of the product, process, service, or technology. Two elements that directly affect aircraft communication systems performance are routing problems and software. This holds true in our aircraft communications scenario. The example demonstrates how to improve routing issues by examining elements that directly influence this key performance measurement. This tool is an excellent brainstorming tool used in a face-to-face environment or completed virtually. This tool can assist in determining the best measures (empirical data) to control the improvement in performance. SMPA also involves employees in the problem-solving process. Clients find this tool useful for planning and operational purposes.

Step 5: Adapt and Align

Adapting and aligning your organization with the incremental improvement opportunity is of tantamount importance (see Figure 8.12). The processes in this step are very similar to those identified in the N²OVATE™ process, so we recommend reviewing the discussion in Chapter 7, Implementing a Successful Improvement Project—Performance Below Expectations, to complement this discussion. In adapting and aligning the organization, the innovation team must clarify and identify the changes or modifications as well as articulate the new set of benchmarks, expectations, and/or standards. New expectations and standards should be shared through training, published or documented procedure and guidelines, policy change notices, and face-to-face meetings at the group or individual level. Gaining concesus on perfomance strategy from leadership

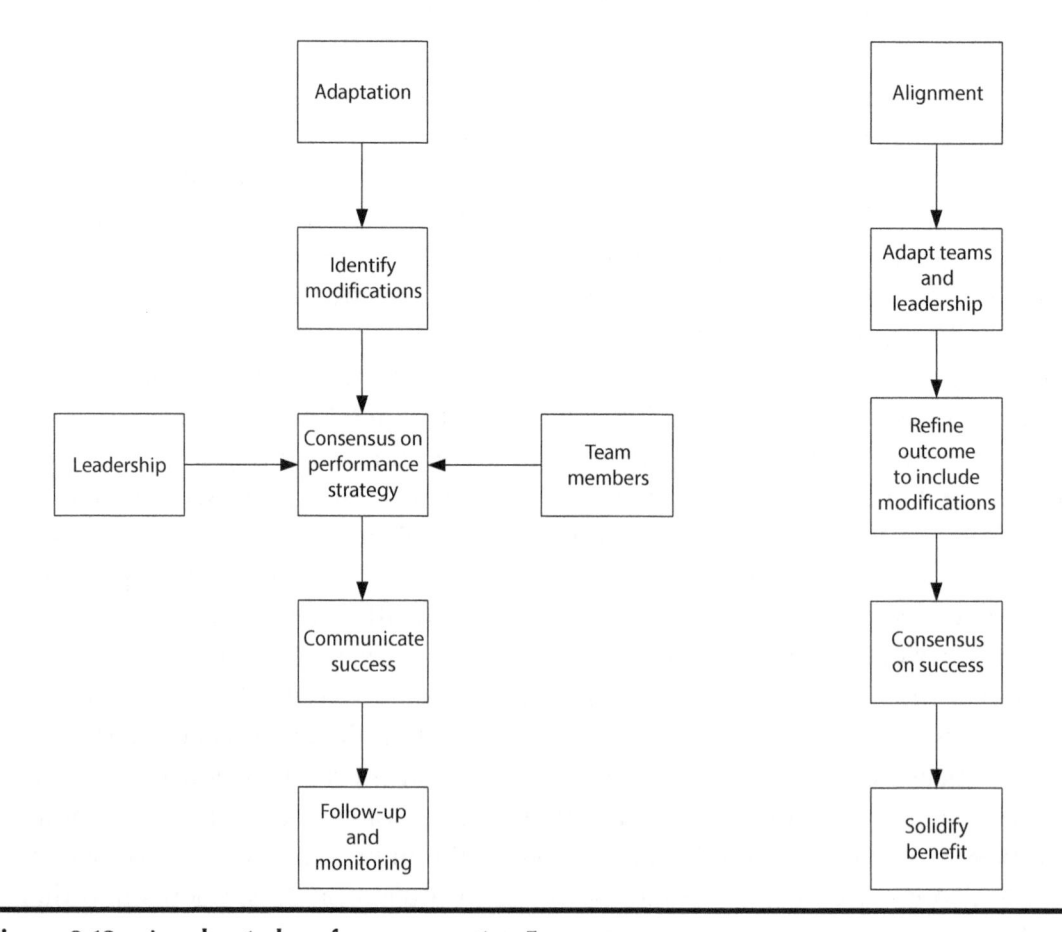

Figure 8.12   Accelerated performance—step 5.

and team members is also essential as it can result in the perpetuation of new knowledge and ideas on how to better improve the recommended changes (innovation opportunity) you are seeking to gain from the innovation opportunity. Consensus building reinforces an incremental innovation and change mentality which enriches the organization's acclimation and attitudes toward innovation opportunities which are essential for enterprise-wide adoption and success.

Some of the tools the reader may find useful in this section are applicable to our aircraft communications scenario. As these tools have been presented in other chapters throughout this workbook, they are mentioned below and their potential use are provided for the reader's reference and convenience.

■ Storyboards (track, share, and publicize the innovation improvement opportunity throughout the organization)
■ Graphs, charts, and worksheets (track and monitor usage rates, performance, accounting, and financial metrics)
■ Feedback forms and processes (provide avenue from shareholders, stakeholders, and customers to gain valuable insight and status on how the innovation improvement opportunity is performing; and ideas and suggestions on potential improvements, etc.)

EXERCISE 8.10: ADAPTING AND ALIGNMENT TOOLS

Considering the tools mentioned above and throughout the workbook, pick one tool and apply a set of adapt, and alignment goals for your organization's assets to achieve a positive outcome for a project or proposal you are working on or might propose. Are there any additional tools not identified that you feel could help you accomplish your goals and objectives in this area? Name one tool not listed in each area (adapt and align) and provide a short discussion on how they would be used and what information they would provide to help you achieve a positive outcome for your project or proposal?

Some of the key objectives and questions the innovation team should seek to answer in this step are:

■ What is the initial gauge on efficiencies, effectiveness, or cost saving improvements that bring benefit and value?
■ Does the performance benefit or value-added link directly to associated process measures?
■ Have you achieved the appropriate level of buy-in from leadership and the workforce (shareholders, stakeholders, and customers)?

- Do leaders and employees understand their new roles and responsibilities?
- Have the appropriate leaders and personnel affected by the innovation improvement opportunity been trained?
- Do leaders and employees understand the new requirements, expectations, and standards?
- Does the team have a well-known performance feedback and monitoring process in-place for capturing performance changes?
- Does the innovation team have a well-defined and understood feedback mechanism in-place for fielding comments and/or suggested changes generated by the new process from leadership and the workforce (shareholders, stakeholders, and customers)?

As a final comment for this step, we reiterate that gaining consensus throughout the organization is paramount in instituting sustained incremental innovation improvements. This typically starts with leadership buy-in and support. Organizational leaders have a seminal and critical role in supporting your team as innovation evangelists continue to reinforce the new or additional responsibilities through open and transparent communication, education, and confirmation. Do not forget to inlcude your shareholders, stakeholders, and customers—such as suppliers, embedded contractors, and users, who are affected by the improvement.

Revisiting key take aways from this step, aligning the employees to the new realities is cruical for success. As incremental innovation opportunities become more commonplace, it will become easier for an organization to continuously set new benchmarks and standards that continuously elevate the performance and outcomes even when they currently meet or exceed expectations and established standards. The next step in establishing an organization focused on generating a sustainable, value-added incremental innovation culture is tracking and tying the effort to performance.

EXERCISE 8.11: KEY OBJECTIVES AND QUESTIONS

Using the list of potential key objectives and/or questions mentioned in this section, identify three that you feel are most important in adapting and aligning your organization's assets to achieve a positive outcome for a project or proposal you are working or might propose. Discuss why you chose these questions. Are there any additional questions not listed in this section you feel are important considerations in achieving the objectives of this step? If so, what are they and why do you feel they are important to a positive outcome for your project or proposal?

Step 6: Track to Improvement/Performance

If the project continues to generate benefits identified in the initial phase of step 6 (Figure 8.13), then continue to pursue a successful outcome and focus on setting the stage for evaluating and reviewing your innovation implementation. In the first phase your innovation team will focus on linking your incremental innovation opportunity to measurable, validated, and verified value. Measures unique to innovation efforts are new (internal and external), improved (internal and external) and change (internal and external). Since this discussion focuses on improving performance that already meets or exceeds standards and expectations, your team will concentrate on measuring the elements of efficiency and effectiveness, productivity, risk and reward, user acceptance, satisfaction, and ultimately success.

Tools for tracking improvement and performance should all you track performance, detect performance, and quality of service issues, and should help you address or fix issues and verify the results in a timely manner (Figure 8.13). Areas to track in our example of aircraft communications capability could be:

- Efficiency and effectiveness—Service and system level performance for hardware and software (ground and airborne environments); fault detection and diagnostic tools
- Productivity—Voice, video, and data transmission, capacity and utilization rates
- Risk and reward—Return on investment or cost versus improvement value and benefits
- User acceptance—Traveler surveys and questionnaires
- Satisfaction—Customer feedback, service quality levels, and reliability reporting systems
- Success—Software and hardware reliability, maintainability, sustainability, and availability; cost and accounting changes of external service providers and services

EXERCISE 8.12: ESTABLISHING CONTROLS EXERCISE

Using the discussion and process map provided in Figure 8.14, walk through each step and identify and list two to three important measurements and/ or controls that you feel are tantamount to achieving an effective monitoring process.

Once your team has reviewed the performance measures and methodologies, determine whether they are effectively measuring the events you

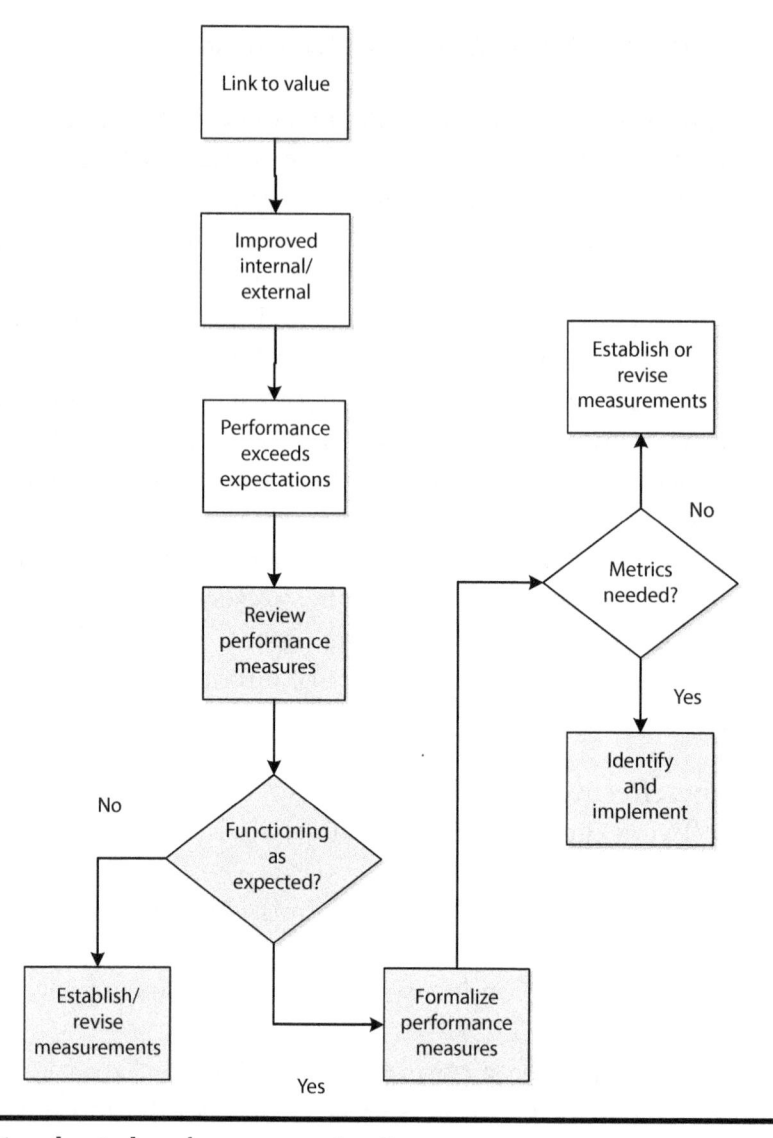

Figure 8.13 Accelerated performance—step 6.

desire and providing useful data points to assess benefit and performance. If your team concurs the measurements are achieving the level of fidelity (parameters) you have established (documented) in your IOP, then formalize the performance measurements and decide what metrics you want to collect, analyze, and publish as benchmarks for full adoption and organization-wide implementation. If the measurements do not provide the level of fidelity that meet your established requirements, revise, and establish new measurements.

This is a short list on potential measurements; they do represent the common elements that are important to aircraft communications performance. In completing this step in the process, your final step before establishing evaluation and review controls is to include and fully aligning your measures to financial and accounting parameters associated with the incremental IOP.

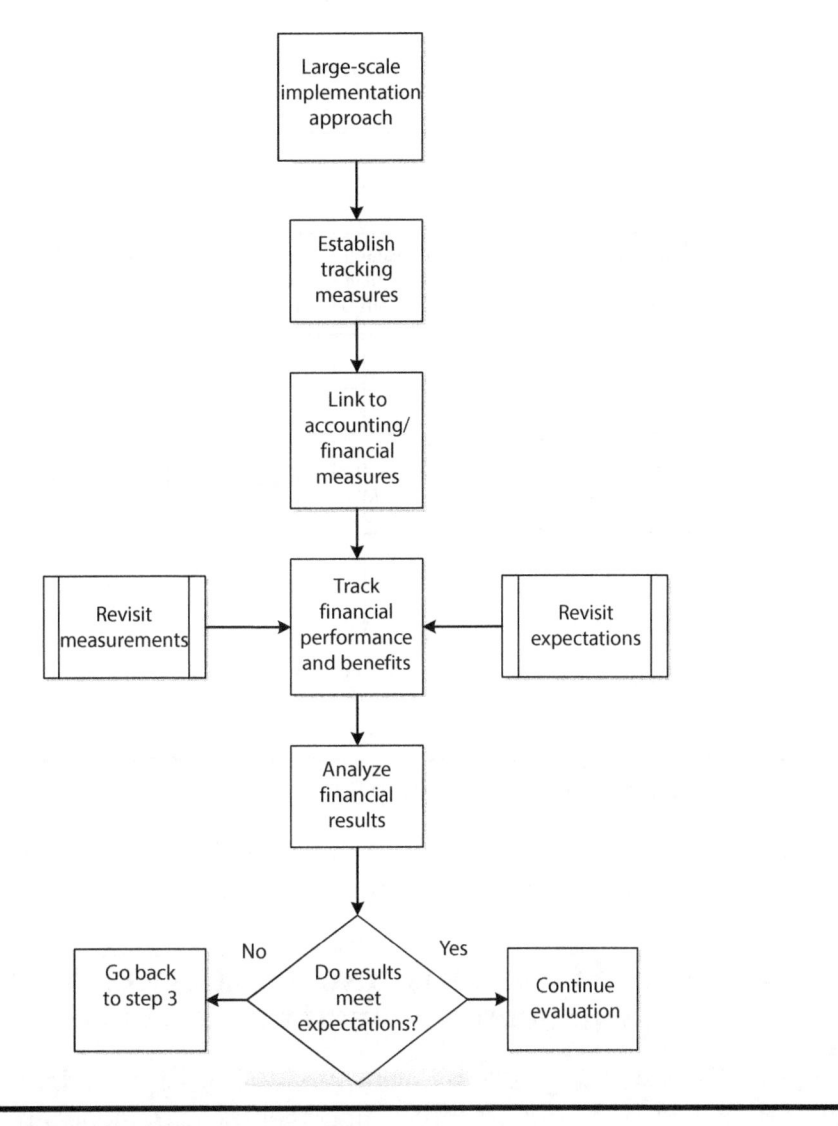

Figure 8.14 Accelerated performance—step 6.

Step 7: Evaluate and Review

Although the final step (Figure 8.15) in the RNOVATE process appears simple and straightforward, it actually requires an innate amount of discipline and rigor. In essence, this step ensures your prior efforts culminate in the sustained value, benefits, and performance of the new process, product, or service. Further, at this point, the discussion and RNOVATE process flow are complete.

The phases in this final step are full implementation of the new process or launch of the new product or service in conjunction with the formalization and establishment of the recurring system of evaluation controls and periodic reviews. The evaluation controls and periodic reviews should measure the metrics necessary actively and passively monitor variance. Tools such as failure mode and effects analysis or cause and effect matrix assess variance if it falls out of range of the established upper control limits and lower control limits established

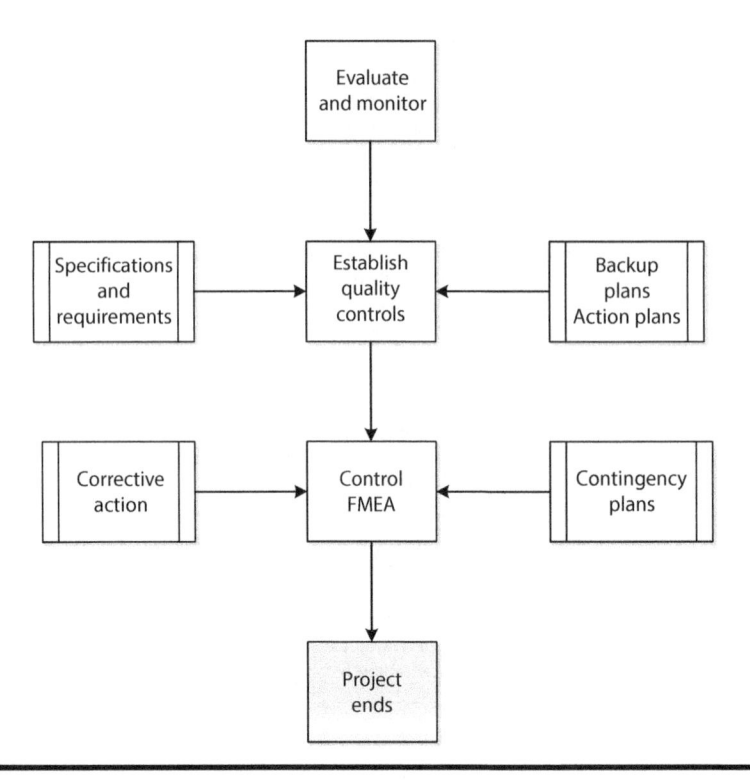

Figure 8.15 Accelerated performance—step 7.

in your test plans to monitor performance identified in Section VII of your IOP discussed in Step 3, Operationalize, of the RNOVATE process.

> **EXERCISE 8.13: ESTABLISHING EVALUATION CONTROLS AND PERIODIC REVIEWS EXERCISE**
>
> Using the discussion and process map provided in Figure 8.15, walk through each step and identify and list three important measurements and/or controls that you feel are tantamount to achieving and effective monitoring process. Consider their use in a project or proposal you are working at present. If you are working in a group course room, be prepared to discuss your thoughts on the three tools you selected (i.e., why they are important to evaluating outcomes and reviewing the results).

As with every process, there are far too many unknowns to have a "one size fits all." Each process is unique, yet fundamental issues remain constant. This process deals with these issues that leaders and executives must manage. Failure to do so increases risk, waste, and the failure.

Summary

In this chapter, our goal was to provide you with additional tools to complement the RNOVATE performance acceleration process focusing on improving performance, value, and benefits when a process, product, or service already exceeds standards and/or expectations. Remaining in the realm of incremental innovation focused on continuously improving processes, services, or products, we assume that readers will have varying levels of understanding and use of well-known Six Sigma tools that support CPI efforts. To add to those tools, we have presented several innovation opportunity tools, most notably the innovation opportunity proposal (short form) and the IOP (long form—request from the authors). By design, these two forms support the innovation philosophy by capturing the central information and data elements leaders and decision makers require to make a strategic determination on pursuing or not pursuing an innovation opportunity. Finally, although many projects and programs are focused on incremental innovation improvement over the short term, these tools will assist organizations in establishing a sustained and repeatable approach to their innovation opportunities if implemented with consistency and discipline.

DISCUSSION QUESTIONS

1. Following each letter of the RNOVATE acronym below, provide the name for each step the letter represents. For the each step in the process, define the key process elements (or sub-steps) in the blanks provided following each letter.
   a. **R**: _____
   b. **N**: _____
   c. **O**: _____
   d. **V**: _____
   e. **A**: _____
   f. **T**: _____
   g. **E**: _____
2. Name two (2) innovation opportunity tools from this chapter's discussion. Explain their use and discuss the three (3) key elements in each tool. How are the elements you chose important to the innovation opportunity performance acceleration process?
3. What is the importance of the recognizing and confirming the innovation opportunity?

ASSIGNMENTS

1. Identify a process, product, or service that has the potential to accelerate its performance. Explain why this is critical for sustained innovation success.
2. Using the information you gathered during the exercises, complete the IOP executive summary section and submit your final product to another class member for review and feedback. Discuss the feedback in a short discussion and update your executive summary accordingly.

References

Berson, Y., Oreg, S., and Dvir, T. 2007. CEO values, organizational culture and firm outcomes. *Journal of Organizational Behavior*, 29(5), 615–633, July 2008. doi: 10.1002/job.499.

McLaughlin, G. and Kennedy, W.R. 2015. *A Guide to Innovation Processes and Solutions for Government*. Productivity Press, Boca Raton, FL. ISBN: 978-1-4987-2157-8.

Chapter 9

Innovative Change: The Art of Replacement

Introduction

The idea that change is innovative may be hard for some to accept. Change is often experienced as an "out with the old, in with the new" radical approach. Yet, at times, change is the only alternative as nothing but a complete revision is required. As with all innovation, there must be a need and a significant decrease in performance to spur action. This chapter is a refinement of Chapter 10 in our book entitled, *A Guide to Innovation Processes and Solutions for Government* (McLaughlin and Kennedy, 2015). Given the diversity of meanings associated with change as it relates to an innovation opportunity, we have refined the focus to be that associated with "replacement." If a product, process, or service required a small or incremental change, we suggest you consider using the improvement strategies to implement the modification versus replacing what is already in place. However, if after deliberation, your management desires or needs a complete change, we recommend using the methodology presented in this chapter.

Replacement seems simple. We replace items every day without problems or concerns, yet when dealing from an organizational perspective, replacement can lead to a waterfall effect and a wide variety of outcomes the innovation team must consider. Thus, a positive outcome would be innovative if it met the prevailing need. However, the opposite is true as well as a negative outcome can cause serious disruptions and often leads to dissolution. We would expect that similar outcomes exist for the replacement course of action. Further, defining replacement is critical to understanding its true value. Replacement involves any if not all of the following activities (processes):

1. A complete overhaul of an existing process
2. Replacement of an existing process

3. Offshoring/outsourcing of a process
4. An existing process with new outcomes

Replacement certainly covers a variety of change states. We contend that replacement is also inappropriate for partial changes, changes in personnel only, or changes due to technology advancements. The key is process change (Figure 9.1).

Replacement provides a strategy that enables a fresh start. As with any change, there needs to be a clear set of unambiguous communications, a clear objective, and a desire for alignment with the organizations key business strategy, objectives, and/or core competencies. The seven-step process offered in this chapter provides a mechanism (methodology) to replace a process, product, or service with maximum benefit and minimal disruption.

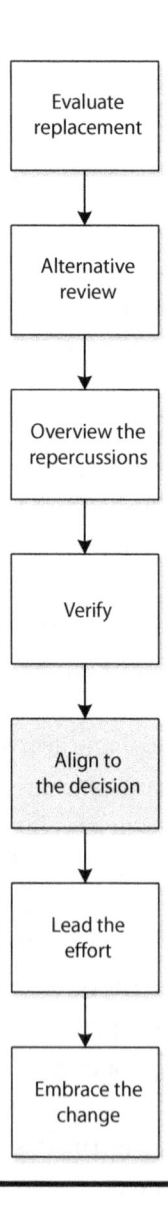

Figure 9.1 Replacement cycle.

To ensure sustained innovation success, companies and organizations need a long-term plan that is consistent over time and resistant to frequent modifications and changes. The objectives must be measurable, and the plan logical in order to succeed. The organization must commit to a long-term strategy combined with the desire to ensure that the innovation effort succeeds.

Step 1: Identifying Replacement Value

The next logical step after assessment and diagnostics is the development of an innovation management strategy. In simpler terms, innovation must be a corporate (executive) strategy, accepted, and promoted by management, who operationalize it on a daily basis. The central purpose of step 1 (Figure 9.2) is to review the potential change by asking the "why change" question and ultimately

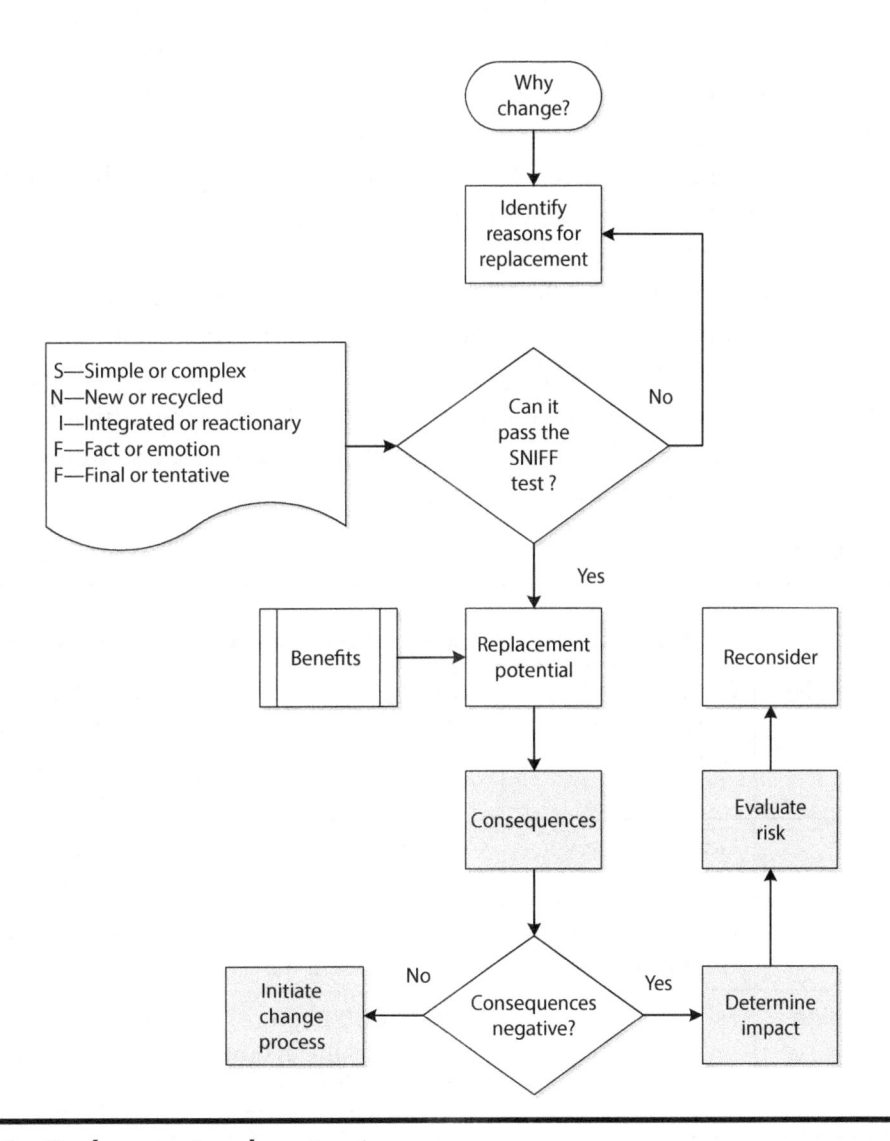

Figure 9.2 Replacement cycle—step 1.

determining if the replacement value warrants the time and resources the organization will invest. The first tool to consider is the SNIFF test.

S: *Simple/Complex:* Evaluate the difficulty in implementing the change
N: *New idea/Recycled:* Is this a new or a recycled approach?
I: *Integrated or Chaotic:* How well will the organization incorporate the change?
F: *Fact or Opinion:* Reasons for the change based on fact (data) or emotion?
F: *Final or Tentative:* Is this permanent or temporary?

Consider, as an example, a restaurant that wants to replace their existing food ordering processing (which relies on servers) to hand write orders with a new electronic system. Orders are entered into the peripheral device (handheld tablet or register keyboard) and moved to the kitchen for processing, eliminating the need to hand carry orders. The electronic device automatically calculates the price and signals the server when the order is ready. The value proposition (outcomes) is savings in time and cost. Before purchasing this system, use the SNIFF test to determine whether there is potential value added to the current mode of operation.

To complete the SNIFF test table, first list each element of the SNIFF acronym as provided in Table 9.1. Next, assess each component for use and applicability. Examine each outcome influence of the assessment and state the influence on the objectives. Finally, list the longer-term consequences.

This tool provides a simple but integrated approach to assess change before making a final decision to proceed to the next step. This tool is flexible and agile, so feel free to add different or additional elements that apply to your innovation opportunity. Worthy of note, the administrative component typically occurs at the executive (director) and above level within the organization; and the operational component functions as a project management strategy dedicated to achieving sustained innovation success.

Table 9.1 SNIFF Test

SNIFF Component	Assessment	Outcome Influence	Consequences
Simple/complex	Complex early, simple after initial use	Cost: High Time: Low	More server time spent with patrons No handwriting problems
New idea/ recycled	New idea (server)	Cost: Low (to offer ideas) Time: High (training)	More cooperation, less friction
Integrated or chaotic	Chaotic 1–2 weeks highly integrated	Cost: Low Time: Loss at first	Few, if any negatives
Fact or opinion	Fact	Cost: (Profit) higher customer satisfaction Time: Less time	More use of technology
Final or tentative	Final		

After completing the initial SNIFF test, if the consequences are negative, then determine the impact, evaluate the risk, and reconsider the general intent of the project. In sum, accomplishing the SNIFF test is an instrumental component in accomplishing this step.

> **EXERCISE 9.1: REPLACEMENT CONSIDERATION**
>
> Consider a replacement that occurred at work (either recent or in the past). Apply the SNIFF test and create a table such as Table 9.1. What did you learn from the exercise?

Step 2: Review of Alternatives

The next step in the replacement process is a review of alternatives (Figure 9.3 and Table 9.2). Assuming that the most obvious or recommended choice is always the best choice; we recommend an evaluation of alternatives. As with any alternative, there is a positive (benefit) and a negative (consequence). Identifying an alternative generally initiates a consequence.

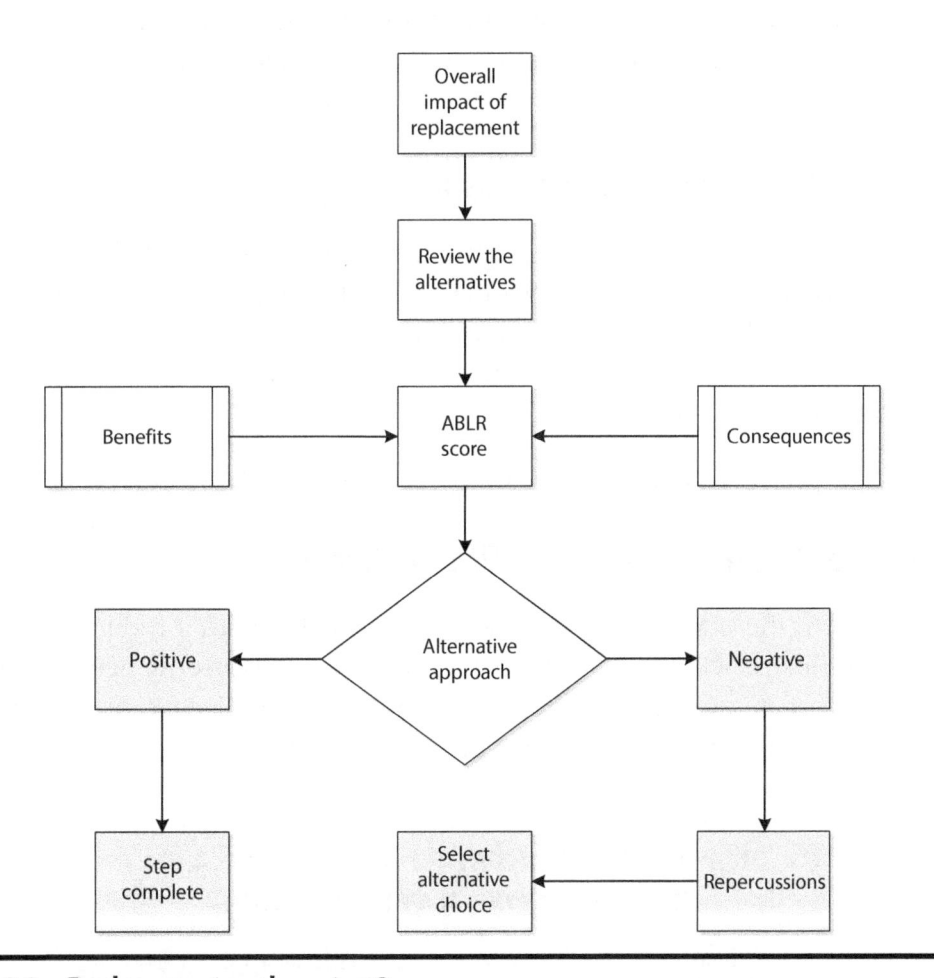

Figure 9.3   Replacement cycle—step 2.

Table 9.2 Alternative Benefit Loss Ratio

Alternative	Benefit	Score	Loss	Score	Ratio

We recommend the innovation team examine a number of alternatives with the objective of identifying the benefits and losses, while examining and determining the overall impact (influence) of each alternative. If an alternative has fewer losses and has much more benefit, it may be the best choice. To reiterate an earlier point, an individual plays a seminal role in identifying the alternatives, benefits, losses, and repercussions. The author's experiences have been that when management wants to innovate and has established a position on a particular benefit, potential loses are often overlooked and never considered. Table 9.2 helps the innovation team and organization keep their focus on potential losses.

Scoring the Alternative Benefit Loss Ratio

Benefit score: 1–5: 1—no benefit; 2—minimal benefit; 3—some benefit to the outcome; 4—benefits the outcome; 5—maximum benefit to the outcome.

Loss score: 1–5: 1—no loss to the outcome; 2—minimal loss affects the outcome; 3—some loss affects the outcome; 4—losses affect the outcome; 5—major loss affecting the outcome.

$$\text{Ratio} = \text{Benefit score (B score)}/\text{Loss score (L score)}$$

Interpreting the Alternative Benefit Loss Ratio

If the ratio is >1, the effect is positive (adequate benefits with a reduced threat of losses). If the ratio is <1, reconsider the alternative as its consequences affect the outcome in a negative manner. Values close to zero are indicative of a situation where benefits and consequences have an equal effect.

EXERCISE 9.2: CONSTRUCT AN ALTERNATIVE BENEFIT LOSS RATIO TABLE

What learnings did you or your innovation team find interesting?

Step 3: Evaluate Repercussions

In the next step (Step 3; Figure 9.4), the innovation team reviews the alternatives and evaluates the benefits and consequences of potential alternatives. The alternative approach involves the dynamics of implementation. Selecting the alternative requires further analysis (and a decision) that may reveal positive and/ or negative aspects. Implementation will have either a negative or a positive effect on the outcome. Negative effects require an examination of repercussions. Positive effects permit the implementation to proceed immediately.

Consider an example where a large organization wants to outsource their procurement department. The organization conducted research and determined that an Asian country would be the most cost-effective location to conduct procurement affairs. The research results showed an established benefit, which subsequently drove the implementation. However, the research effort never considered the risk involved in moving an entire department to a foreign country or whether a better alternative existed. The organization took action and moved the department to Asia only to discover the new personnel in Asia received inadequate training and lacked the required experience to effectively run a procurement process. In fact, rather than saving money, the cost of the department doubled. No one considered the consequences that can occur in moving a complete department from one country (or culture) to another. Finally, the organization

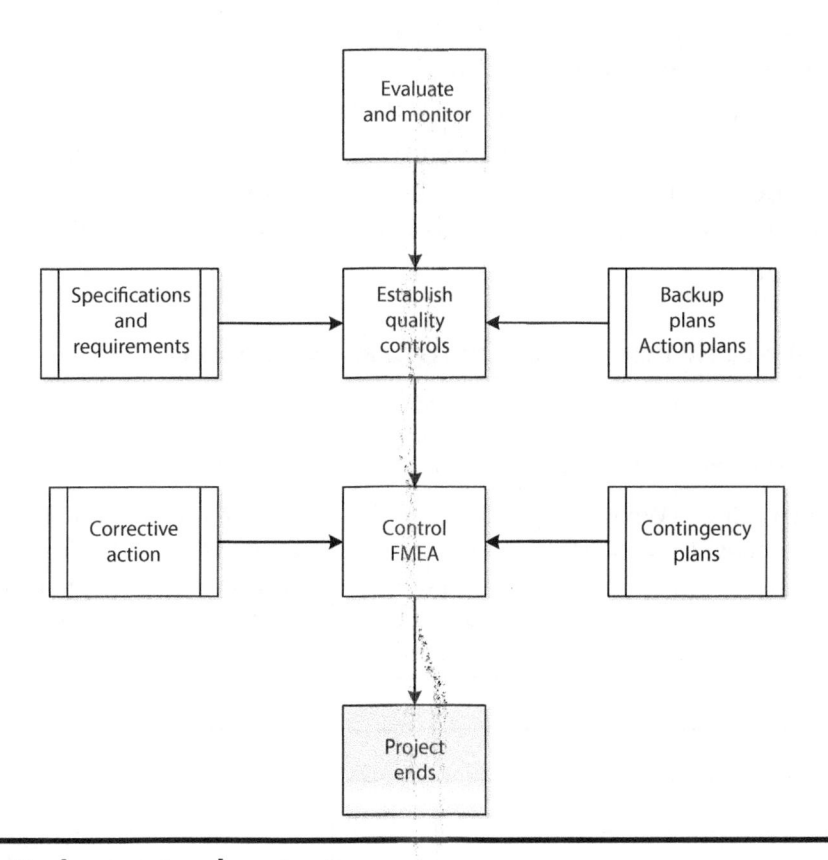

Figure 9.4 Replacement cycle—step 3.

had to reverse course on their decision and moved the procurement business back in-house to its original location. This is a perfect example of what can happen when an organization fails to consider both consequences and repercussions when fully researching potential alternatives.

Alternative Repercussion Effects Analysis Worksheet Tool

Completing the alternative repercussion effects analysis (AREA) worksheet begins with identifying all alternatives and repercussions (Table 9.3). The innovation team's focus should be on determining the effect of the alternatives on the outcome and the reasons and cause for the repercussions. The repercussion (what can go wrong) can be a limiting factor (LIMFAC) or a failure point associated with the alternative. Once the worksheet is complete, transfer the information the innovation team has collected to the AREA template (Figure 9.3). The next step involves a risk assessment of each alternative (Figure 9.5).

When completing an AREA risk assessment, there are generally three measures of risk: severity (SEV), occurrence (OCC), and detectability (DET). To evaluate the effect of risk (Figure 9.6), use a scale from 1 to 10. SEV measures the effect of the repercussion on the outcome. OCC measures the frequency of the repercussion (the failure), and DET measures its overall effect. A final assessment is the risk priority number, which evaluates the overall viability of the alternative. When replacing a process, product, or service, evaluate potential alternatives as a method of making the best decisions and right choices. Figure 9.5 demonstrates the use of the AREA tool. For this example, a healthcare innovation team was trying to determine what the best alternative to collecting patient satisfaction data is. The AREA tool suggests less problems with Focus Groups as compared to the use of Interviews for collecting patient satisfaction data.

Table 9.3 Alternative Repercussion Effects Analysis Worksheet

Process Step or Item	Alternative	Repercussion	Potential Failure Effects	Potential Causes	Current Controls
What is the actual item?	What is the alternative?	What can go wrong?	How do the repercussions affect the outcome?	What are the causes or reasons for the repercussions?	What are the existing controls and procedures that minimize the repercussion?

Alternative and Repercussion Effects Analysis
(AREA)

Process or Product Name:		**Patiet Satisfaction Data Collection**			Prepared by:		Page ___ of ___	
Responsible:					AREA Date (Orig) _____ (Rev) _____			

Process Step	Alternative	Potential Failure Modes	Potential Failure Effects Repercussions	S E V	Potential Causes	O C C	Current Controls	D E T	R P N	Actions Recommended	Resp.	Actions Taken	S E V	O C C	D E T	R P N
Identify the step, element, or item	What are the Alternatives ?	What can go wrong?	How does the Repercussion affect the outcome?	How severe is the failure effect to the project outcome?	What are the causes or reasons for this Repercussion ?	How often does a failure occur?	What are the existing controls and procedures that minimize the effect of the repercussions?	How well can you detect the failure?		What are the actions for reducing the occurrence, or improving detection?	Who is Responsible for the recommended action?	What are the actions taken with the recalculated RPN? Be sure to include completion month/year				
Patient Satisfaction data collection Survey	Focus Groups	Incorrect mix of Respondents	Bias due to poor mix of people	8	Poor sampling	5	Sampling approved by content expert	5	200							0
	Focus Groups	Incorrect mix of Respondents	Distorted Information	7	Lacks test before use	7	Questions approved before Use	5	245							0
	Focus Groups	No Diversity of Opinion	Group Think	5	Moderator inexperience	7	Better training	7	245							0
	Interviews	Too few people	One-sided information	9	poor sampling or recruitment	8	Sampling approved by content expert	5	360							0
	Interviews	Inappropriate questions	Inconsequential information	9	Lacks validity testing	6	Questions approved before Use	5	270							0
	Interviews	Leading the respondent	Getting the answers someone wants	5	Interviewer bias or inexperience	7	Better training	7	245							0
									0							0

SEV—Severity; OCC—Occurrence; DET—Detectability; RPN—Risk Priority Number

Figure 9.5   Alternative repercussion effects analysis template.

Score	Severity	Score	Occurrence
10	The repercussion always or nearly always impacts the outcome	10	A repercussion always occurs
9	The repercussion impacts the outcome more than 85% of the time	9	A repercussion nearly always occurs
8	The repercussion impacts the outcome more than 75% of the time	8	A repercussion occurs frequently
7	The repercussion impacts the outcome more than 60% of the time	7	A repercussion occurs often
6	The repercussion impacts the outcome slightly more than 50% of the time	6	A repercussion occurs slightly more than 50% of the time
5	The repercussion impacts the outcome about 50% of the time	5	A repercussion occurs about 50% of the time
4	The repercussion impacts the outcome less than 50% of the time	4	A repercussion occurs less than 50% of the time
3	The repercussion has a small impact on the outcome	3	A repercussion rarely occurs
2	The repercussion has little impact on the outcome	2	A repercussion very rarely occurs
1	The repercussion has no impact on the outcome	1	A repercussion never occurs

Score	Detectability	
10	Never detects the cause of the repercussion	
9	Very rarely detects the cause of the repercussion	
8	Rarely detects the cause of the repercussion	
7	Detects the cause of the repercussion about 1/3 of the time	Note: Failure Mode = (What can go wrong) Repercussion (Failure Effect)= How is the Outcome effected?
6	Detects the cause of the repercussion less than 50% of the time	
5	Detects the cause of the repercussion about 50% of the time	
4	Detects the cause of the repercussion slightly more than 50% of the time	
3	Frequently detects the cause of the repercussion	
2	Nearly always detects the cause of the repercussion	
1	Always detects the cause of the repercussion	

Figure 9.6   AREA template risk codes.

> ### EXERCISE 9.3: ALTERNATIVE CONSIDERATION
>
> Consider an alternative to an existing process. Run this one alternative through the AREA template, focusing on the repercussions (the failure points) and its impact on the outcome.

The purpose of this tool is to highlight alternatives and possible repercussions. The innovation team will begin the process by choosing the consequence of a particular action. Next, identify possible alternatives and repercussions. Follow by identifying the impact (influence) on the consequence. Next look for reasons and root causes. Finally, determine what controls are in place to prevent the repercussions from influencing the consequence (outcome) and what controls may need to be in-place that currently are missing. Understanding what affects the consequences will have can assist the innovation team in choosing and recommending or not recommending a viable (best) alternative.

Step 4: Evaluate Repercussions

After reaching a preliminary decision, the process of developing and testing the alternatives can begin (Figure 9.7). The elements are in place to formulate the change. Create a value stream or process map, identifying value-added and nonvalue-added steps. Be cognizant that alternatives can provide a solution for nonvalue-added steps. Also consider the presence of waste (scrap or a repeated process), inefficiency, and delays.

Identify activities (who, what, when, and how). Conceptualize the process before trying to implement and then be faced with fixing the oversights later. Finally, be sure to include (or develop, if needed) the requirements (operating limits, specifications) for the alternative(s). Once completed, finalize the decision.

With the alternative finalized, it is time to examine and evaluate the new process. Previous chapters have discussed methods to validate processes. An additional evaluation is the IMPACT statement test (Table 9.4). The IMPACT statement test was designed to examine various characteristics of the process. In fact, using this test at the beginning and ending of the process may give an additional perspective. We suggest this tool at this point, as there may be little data available to evaluate the process. In addition, use this tool in a team setting to explore and address differing opinions.

To use the tool, define the six "IMPACT" terms for a particular project. Determine the present state and future state providing reasons why performance, for example, is less than expected. This is a good tool for alignment purposes as well. Precision is not the key, rather getting stakeholders aligned and adapted to the new reality (the replacement). Do not confuse the simplicity of the tool with its intended purpose. At this point, agreement and consensus are the acceptable outcomes.

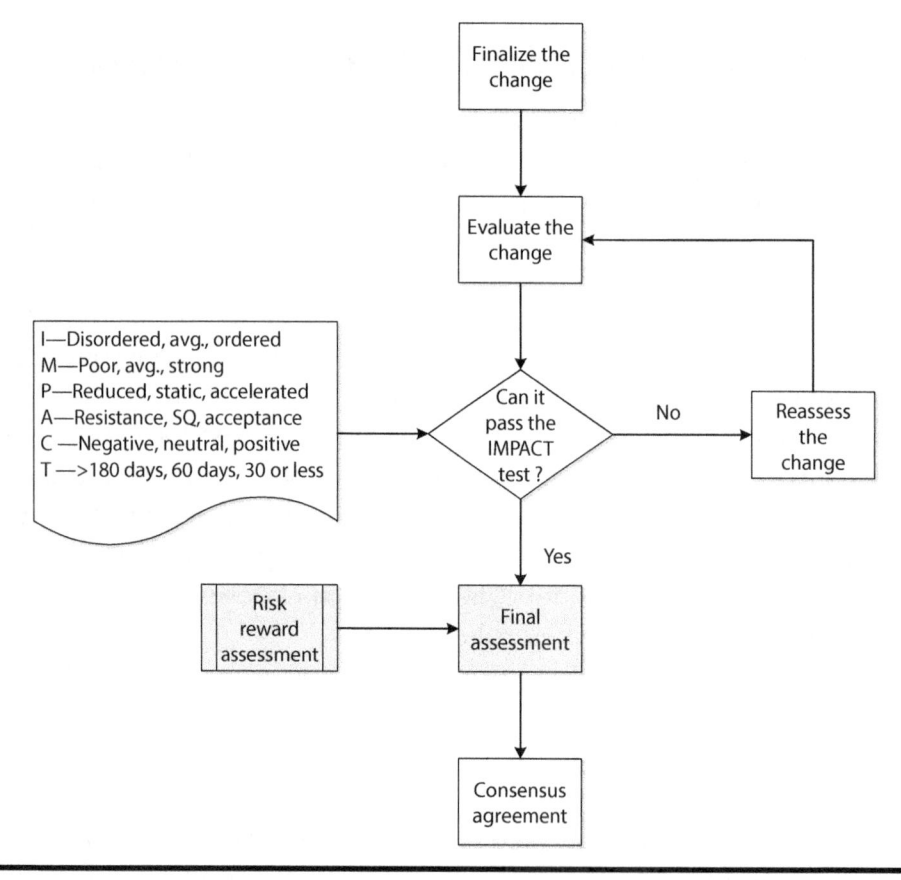

Figure 9.7   Replacement cycle—step 4.

Table 9.4   IMPACT Statement Test

IMPACT	Response 1 Less than Expected	Response 1 Expected or Typical	Response 1 Greater than Expected	Reasons for the Choice
Integration	Disordered	Average	Ordered	
Managed change	Poor	Average	Strong	
Performance	Reduced	Static	Accelerated	
Acceptance	Resistance	Status-Quo	Acceptance	
Communications	Negative	Neutral	Positive	
Timeliness	Greater than 180 days	30–60 days	Less than 30 days	

Instructions:	Choose an innovative outcome that you expect to occur. Determine the effect of the innovation using the IMPACT criteria. Choose one of three responses, based on what you expect to occur, and then give a reason for that choice (optional).

Integration—Expected results of incorporating the innovation
Managed change—How well the innovation is managed/supported
Performance—Expected output versus present standards
Acceptance—How well (users) embrace the innovation
Communications—How well information is received and understood regarding the innovation
Timeliness—When the improvement from the innovation expects to begin

EXERCISE 9.4: IMPACT TEST

Use the IMPACT test to evaluate an alternative. Try adding different (more specialized to the problem) criteria. Discuss how the criteria interact and how a failure in one criterion will influence the outcome. What can be done to ensure a positive introduction of an alternative?

Step 5: Alignment

Once the decision is made and the choice validated, it is time for alignment to begin. The alignment step (Figure 9.8) consists of aligning all personnel and stakeholders to the new reality. As with change there will be resistance, the process management uses to implement the replacement is either a positive, a neutral, or a negative experience. The entire field of change management addresses these strategies and this book is not the venue to debate the best approach. Rather, the discussion is on innovative change—change that yields positive results.

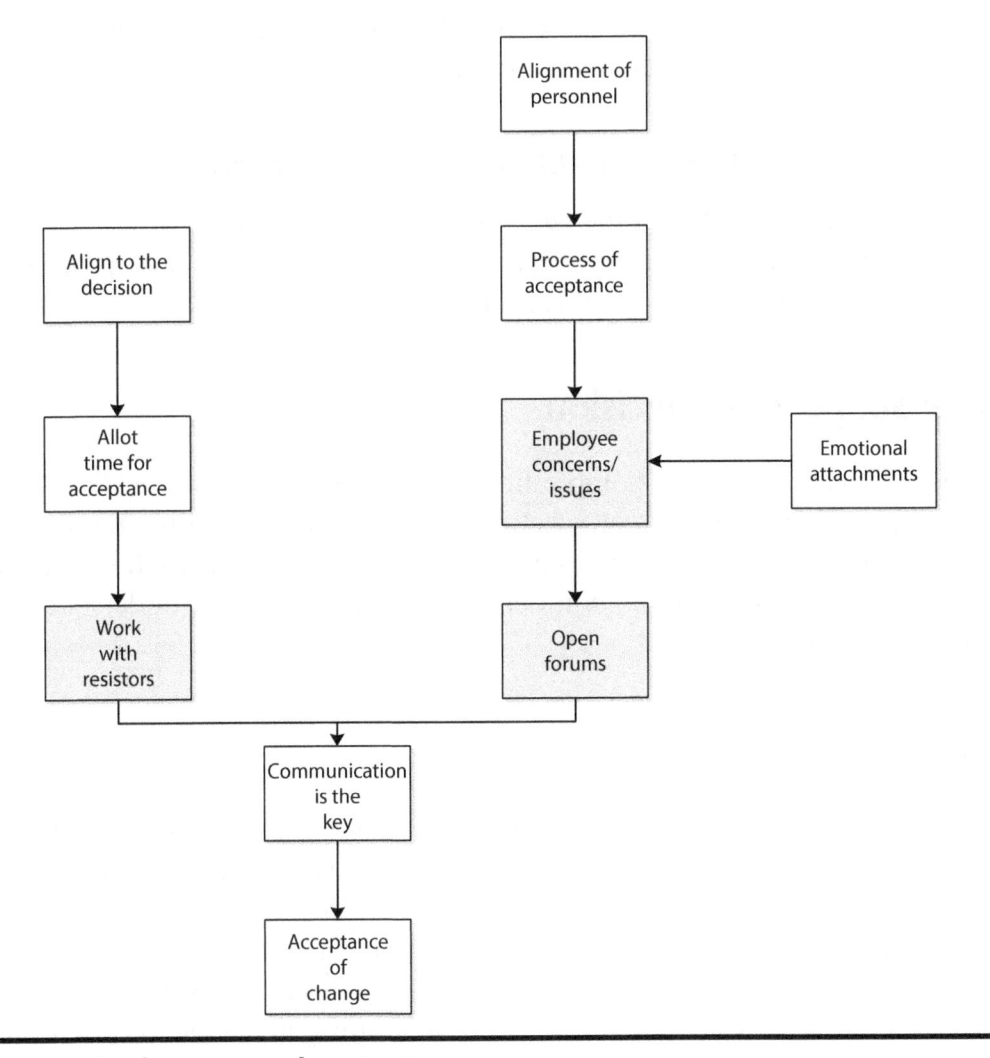

Figure 9.8   Replacement cycle—step 5.

Alignment involves both people and process. Change requires time, patience, and an open forum (communications) to flourish. Management must work with people who resist as they offer a unique perspective that should always be considered. People who resist must bring evidence (data and information) to the table, not a set of feelings and emotions. Allow time for people (stakeholders) to adjust as change, especially that perceived as negative, can be a life-altering event for those who are new to or do not adapt to change easily. Communicate honestly and do not be afraid to admit mistakes. Conduct open and unbiased forums, provide opportunities, and keep the lines of communication open at all times. Try to gather the people to discuss the change, objectives, and values.

Consider the acceptance of change survey (Table 2.11) to evaluate acceptability of a particular change. The survey gives a quick overview of employees perceptions about a particular change (be sure to indicate the change element before distributing the survey). If resistance is high, consider an alternative.

The acceptance of change instrument meets validation and reliability criterion and has performed well in both scholarly (peer reviewed) and practitioner applications. Further work may center on expanding the number of questions or in introducing one or more additional components (dimensions).

> **EXERCISE 9.5: ACCEPTANCE OF CHANGE**
>
> Distribute the acceptance of change survey to employees. Ask them to consider a previous change they encountered or one presently underway in their companies or organizations. Compare and contrast the answers.

Step 6: Support the Decision

The leader should always solicit input from stakeholders in whatever decision involves change especially that associated with replacement. Allow time for acceptance and support to return (Figure 9.9). Change is similar to the grief process in that at first it is a shock, then denial, and after sometime understanding and finally acceptance.

Leadership

The last two steps are those assigned to management. Leadership (Figure 9.9) is critical for replacing a process and ensuring success. Leaders provide a vital role and channel that includes open, two-way communications, required for success. Leaders are charged with providing the organization's roadmap for success. Employees will follow leadership when the benefit is clear (positive) and objective achievable. Even when circumstances require a negative outcome, if communicated and executed well, employees will adjust and acquiesce over time.

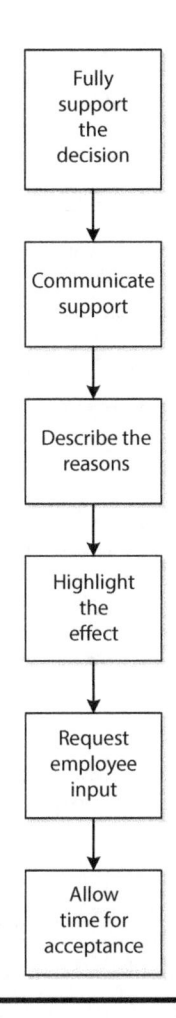

Figure 9.9   Replacement cycle—step 6.

Leading an effort inspires those that support the effort. Leadership provides stability, vision, and purpose. Employees that see (and experience) strong support will trust the leader's decision. Leaders that explain the reasons for change, detail the process, and describe the expected outcomes will be able to successfully initiate change within the organization. Those that assume that change is not the concern of stakeholders will find less acceptance and more resistance. Change, although shunned by some, is a natural process that provides new avenues of business and commerce. Figure 9.9 details the process of leading the change.

Step 7: Implement

Finally, embrace the change and the change will become permanent (Figure 9.10). This is the rollout phase. Accept feedback from those whom the process "touches" as they have a unique insight. Ask experienced people to validate the decision—let them provide the "best" reasons for the replacement. In

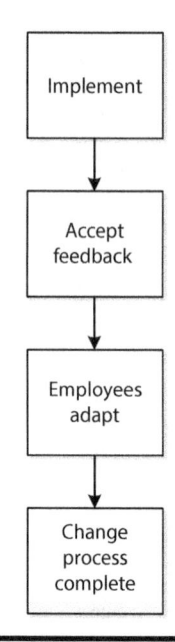

Figure 9.10 Replacement cycle—step 7.

addition, let employees adapt to the replacement, accept the decision, and share in the benefit (McLaughlin and Kennedy, 2015, p. 222–223).

EXERCISE 9.6: ROADMAP

Develop a leadership roadmap for change. Include items such as communication effectiveness, employee input, sufficient reasons for the change, and an expected outcome (what can stakeholders expect).

Summary

This chapter has developed a process for implementing an innovation project when management decided to replace the existing system with a suitable alternative. The process focuses on selecting the best alternative that addresses a desired outcome. To be innovative, the alternative must provide a level of performance that exceeds expectations as well as meet a unique need. This innovative posture presents the company or organization with a distinct competitive advantage.

Alternatives bring both benefits and repercussions. Alternatives permit the opportunity to explore options, new methods, and refine objectives. After finalizing the decision, management must lead the effort, define the benefits, and consider the fate of employees impacted by the decision. These actions will influence the organization well into the future. Work to align stakeholders (both external and internal), provide open communications and feedback. Give employees time to adjust and accept the decision; recognize and highlight the benefits.

DISCUSSION QUESTIONS

1. Describe the circumstances that would lead an organization to require a process or product replacement.
2. Why is replacement a more common practice for a service business?
3. How would you align group of employees, who work for you, to accept and support an upcoming replacement?

ASSIGNMENTS

1. Create five to seven elements of a communication plan to announce change to employees.
2. Consider something you would like to change in your organization. Develop a plan to choose alternatives. What criteria would you use to assess the alternative?
3. Complete an AREA chart (template) by considering a possible change that will directly impact you or your department.

Reference

McLaughlin, G. and Kennedy, W.R. 2015. *A Guide to Innovation Processes and Solutions for Government*. Productivity Press, Boca Raton, FL. ISBN: 978-1-4987-2157-8.

Index